Handshake Circuits

Cambridge International Series on Parallel Computation: 5

HANDSHAKE CIRCUITS

An asynchronous architecture for VLSI programming

Kees van Berkel
Philips Research Laboratories
Eindhoven

CAMBRIDGE
UNIVERSITY PRESS

PUBLISHED BY THE PRESS SYNDICATE OF THE UNIVERSITY OF CAMBRIDGE
The Pitt Building, Trumpington Street, Cambridge, United Kingdom

CAMBRIDGE UNIVERSITY PRESS
The Edinburgh Building, Cambridge CB2 2RU, UK
40 West 20th Street, New York NY 10011–4211, USA
477 Williamstown Road, Port Melbourne, VIC 3207, Australia
Ruiz de Alarcón 13, 28014 Madrid, Spain
Dock House, The Waterfront, Cape Town 8001, South Africa

http://www.cambridge.org

First published 1993
First paperback edition 2004

A catalogue record for this book is available from the British Library

ISBN 0 521 45254 6 hardback
ISBN 0 521 61715 4 paperback

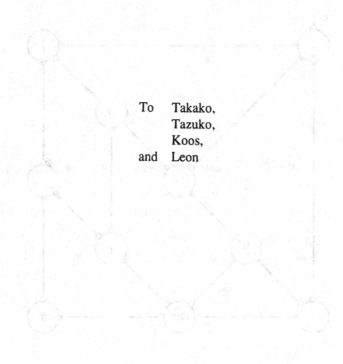

To   Takako,
       Tazuko,
       Koos,
and   Leon

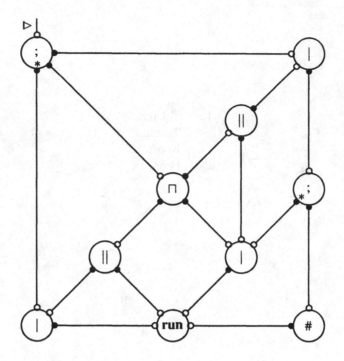

A fantasy handshake circuit shaped according to the ancient Chinese Tangram puzzle

Contents

Foreword   ix

Preface   xi

0 Introduction   **1**
   0.0 VLSI systems   2
   0.1 VLSI circuits   4

1 Introduction to Tangram and handshake circuits   **11**
   1.0 Some simple Tangram programs 14
   1.1 Some simple handshake circuits 16
   1.2 Cost performance trade-offs 20

2 Examples of VLSI programs   **27**
   2.0 FIR filter   27
   2.1 Median filter 29
   2.2 Block sorter   31
   2.3 Greatest common divisor 33
   2.4 Modulo-N counters 35
   2.5 Stacks   39
   2.6 Nacking arbiter 42
   2.7 Discussion   43

3 Handshake processes   **45**
   3.0 Introduction   45
   3.1 Notational conventions   46
   3.2 Handshake structures   49
   3.3 Handshake processes   53
   3.4 The complete partial order $(\prod \cdot A, \sqsubseteq)$ 65
   3.5 Nondeterminism   71

4 Handshake circuits   **73**
   4.0 Introduction   73
   4.1 Parallel composition   74
   4.2 Handshake circuits   85

5 Sequential handshake processes   **89**
   5.0 Introduction   89
   5.1 Sequential handshake processes   89

5.2	Handshake process calculus	93
5.3	Examples	103
5.4	Directed communications	104

6 Tangram   **111**

6.0	Introduction	111
6.1	Tangram	111
6.2	Tangram semantics	117
6.3	Core Tangram	118

7 Tangram $\rightarrow$ handshake circuits   **123**

7.0	Introduction	123
7.1	The compilation function	125
7.2	The compilation theorem	139

8 Handshake circuits $\rightarrow$ VLSI circuits   **147**

8.0	Introduction	147
8.1	Peephole optimization	148
8.2	Non-receptive handshake components	150
8.3	Handshake refinement	152
8.4	Message encoding	158
8.5	Handshake components $\rightarrow$ VLSI circuits	159
8.6	Initialization	164
8.7	Testing	168

9 In practice   **175**

9.0	VLSI programming and compilation	175
9.1	A compiled Tangram IC	184
9.2	Appraisal of asynchronous circuits	190

A Delay insensitivity   **195**

B Failure semantics   **201**

Bibliography   **209**

Glossary of symbols   **217**

Index   **222**

Foreword

Too often there is thought to be a dichotomy between science and engineering: science as a quest for knowledge and understanding, and engineering as the art of constructing useful objects. This book, based on the author's experience in leading a silicon compilation project at Philips Research, is exceptional in that it very convincingly demonstrates the effectiveness of combining the scientific method with sound engineering practices.

Aimed at bridging the gap between program construction and VLSI design, the research reported in this book extends over an unusually wide spectrum of disciplines, ranging from computer science and electrical engineering to logic and mathematics. In this exciting arena we encounter such topics as the power dissipation of an assignment statement, the mathematical theory of handshake circuits, the correctness proof of a compiler, and the problem of circuit initialization without reset wires, to mention just a few.

Such a multi-faceted study can be successful only if it is able to demonstrate a clear separation of concerns. In this respect, Kees van Berkel does an admirable job: his concept of handshake circuits provides an extremely elegant interface between algorithm design on the one hand and circuit implementations on the other. This separation between 'what' and 'how', which many researchers and practitioners find difficult to apply, turns out to be amazingly fruitful, as the readers of this book are encouraged to discover for themselves. In my opinion we are, with the publication of this book, witnessing a major step forward in the development of the discipline of VLSI programming.

Martin Rem

Preface

This book is about the design of asynchronous VLSI circuits based on a programming and compilation approach. It introduces *handshake circuits* as an intermediate architecture between the algorithmic programming language Tangram and VLSI circuits.

The work presented in this book grew out of the project "VLSI programming and compilation into asynchronous circuits" being conducted at Philips Research Laboratories Eindhoven, since 1986. Our original motivation was to increase the productivity of VLSI design by treating circuit design as a programming activity. We chose asynchronous circuits as target for automatic silicon compilation, because asynchronous circuits simplified the translation process and made it easier to take advantage from the abundantly available parallelism in VLSI. Later we discovered that the potential for low power consumption inherent in asynchronous circuits may turn out to be highly relevant to battery-powered products.

The core of this book is about handshake circuits. A handshake circuit is a network of handshake components connected by handshake channels, along which components interact exclusively by means of handshake signaling. It presents a theoretical model of handshake circuits, a compilation method, and a number of VLSI-implementation issues. This core is sandwiched between an informal introduction to VLSI programming and handshake circuits on the one side and a discussion on practical experiences including tooling and chip evaluations on the other side.

The book can be read at three levels:

A. Computer scientists and electrical engineers with a general interest in digital VLSI circuits will find a general introduction in Chapter 0, a self-contained overview in Chapters 1 and 2, and a discussion on design tools and some VLSI-programming experiences in Chapter 9. Some familiarity with traditional programming is assumed.

B. Graduate students in digital electronics, computer science, and computer engineering will get a more comprehensive understanding of VLSI programming and handshake circuits by also reading the chapter on Tangram (Sections 6.0 and 6.1) and the chapter on compilation (Sections 7.0 and 7.1). The compilation method is described in such way that it can be appreciated in full from the pictures and verbal texts, ignoring the formal definitions. The handshake components used in Chapter 7 are presented in Examples 3.23 and 5.37. Chapter 8 in particular Sections 0,1,4,5, and 7 then links handshake circuits to VLSI.

C. Researchers in asynchronous circuits, VLSI architectures, concurrency, and compiler construction are advised to read the chapters in their natural order.

This book is based on my PhD research. Compared with [vB92b] I have paid more attention to the central role the concept of *transparency* plays in our VLSI-programming approach. Transparency is the attribute of the compilation method that facilitates reasoning about circuit area, speed, and power consumption on the basis of the program text from which it is compiled. Also I have included more examples of Tangram programs and corresponding handshake circuits, as well as a detailed evaluation of Tangram-compiled silicon.

Overview

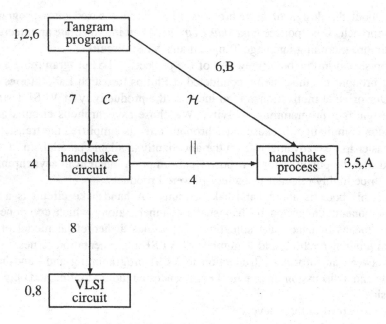

Overview of this book (numbers denote chapters).

A diagrammatic view of this book is presented above. Chapter 0 provides the motivation and the context for our work. It focuses on a CD decoder as an example of a VLSI system, and it introduces the VLSI medium in terms of wires and voltage transitions rather than, as is customary, in terms of transistors and voltage levels. By means of simple examples (buffers and shift registers) Tangram and handshake circuits are introduced informally in Chapter 1. Concerns for cost (circuit area) and performance (circuit speed and power) get special attention, since they make VLSI programming different from—and also more difficult and more exciting than—traditional computer programming. By means of a variety of telling examples, Chapter 2 extends Tangram and handshake circuits to handle expressions, guarded commands, broadcast, and choice.

The key notion in the theory of handshake circuits is that of a *handshake process* (Chapter 3). A handshake process is a mathematical object that describes the communication *behavior* of a handshake circuit. Handshake processes are compositional in that the behavior of a handshake circuit can be defined through parallel composition '||' of the behaviors of its constituent components (Chapter 4). In Appendix A the insensitivity of handshake circuits to wire delays is related to the theory reported in the literature. Chapter 5 develops a calculus for handshake processes, using a Tangram-based syntax. This calculus allows concise descriptions of behaviors of handshake circuits and components.

In Chapter 6 a precise definition of Tangram is given. For a subset of Tangram, which we call *Core Tangram*, a formal denotation '$\mathcal{H}$' is given in terms of handshake processes. This denotation is based on the calculus of Chapter 5. In Appendix B a link to the well-known failure semantics of CSP is established. Chapter 7 describes the translation of Tangram programs into handshake circuits by means of the mathematical function '$\mathcal{C}$'. For Core Tangram it is proven that the behaviors of the compiled handshake circuit and that of the original program are equivalent in a well-defined sense.

The realization of handshake circuits in VLSI is the subject of Chapter 8. Due to the variety of issues and the large number of choices involved we had to be selective in the subjects covered. Issues such as peephole optimization, handshake refinement, data encoding, decompositions into VLSI-operator networks, initialization and testing are discussed in varying degrees of depth and completeness. Chapter 9 discusses some practical experiences with VLSI programming and silicon compilation at Philips Research. It includes a report on compiled silicon and an appraisal of asynchronous circuits.

The book does not include a full definition of Tangram [1]. Neither does it provide a complete and detailed description of all compilation issues. Most notably, of the many possible gate-level circuit implementations we discuss just one form, and then only briefly. At this level I expect much development in the coming years.

Acknowledgements

The project "VLSI programming and silicon compilation" at Philips Research combines the research efforts of Ronan Burgess, Joep Kessels, Marly Roncken, Ronald Saeijs, Frits Schalij and myself. Together we defined the VLSI-programming language Tangram, constructed a silicon compiler, developed interesting demonstrations, and tested functional silicon. This book could only be written on the fertile ground of this inspiring and pleasant cooperation.

Special thanks go to Cees Niessen. Numerous illuminating, critical, stimulating, and sometimes curious discussions with him helped me in choosing directions and setting priorities. Jos van Beers is gratefully acknowledged for his support in testing the IC discussed in Chapter 9.

I am grateful to the management of Philips Research Laboratories, in particular to Theo Claasen and Eric van Utteren, for their support of the project, the provision of a very stimulating working environment, and for their encouraging me to write a PhD thesis.

I am indebted to Martin Rem who supervised the work on my PhD thesis, and stimulated me to write this book. Also, his active interest in the topic provided a constant source of inspiration and motivation. Martin Rem is a scientific advisor to the project at Philips Research Laboratories.

Numerous people have given me substantial and constructive criticism on all or parts of draft versions of the thesis preceding this book. For their help I would like to thank Jos Baeten, Ronan Burgess, Ton Kalker, Joep Kessels, Frans Kruseman Aretz, Ad Peeters, Marly Roncken,

---

[1]Copies of the Tangram manual are available [Sch93].

Frits Schalij, and Kees Vissers. This book could not have been built without TEX and LATEX, for which I thank Donald Knuth and Leslie Lamport.

Finally, the anonymous reviewer of Cambridge University Press is gratefully acknowledged for his many contributions, technical as well as presentational.

September, 1993   Kees van Berkel
Heeze, The Netherlands   berkel@prl.philips.nl

Chapter 0

Introduction

This book is about the design of digital VLSI circuits. Whereas LSI circuits perform basic functions such as multiplication, control, storage, and digital-to-analog conversion, VLSI circuits contain complex compositions of these basic functions. In many cases all data and signal processing in a professional or consumer system can be integrated on a few square centimeters of silicon. Examples of such "systems on silicon" can be found in:

- Compact Disc (CD) players,

- Compact Disc Interactive (CDI) players,

- Digital Compact Cassette (DCC) players,

- Digital Audio Broadcast (DAB) receivers,

- cellular radios and mobile telephones,

- High-Definition TeleVision (HDTV) sets,

- digital video recorders,

- display processors,

- car-navigation systems,

- image processors, and

- digital test and measurement systems.

These systems generally process analog as well as digital signals, but the digital circuits dominate the surface of an IC. The memory needed for storing intermediate results often covers a significant fraction of the silicon area.

Systems on silicon are tending to become more complex and are tending to increase in number. The increase in complexity follows from advances in VLSI technology, and the rapid growth of the number of transistors integrated on a single IC. The constant reduction of the costs of integration makes integration economically attractive for an increasing number of systems. Also, the rapid succession of generations of a single product increases the pressure

1

on design time. The ability to integrate systems on silicon effectively, efficiently, and quickly has thus become a key factor in the global competition in both consumer and professional electronic products. This recognition has led to a quest for design methods and tools that increase design productivity and reduce design times.

At Philips Research a number of approaches to this goal are being investigated [WD89, NvBRS88, LvMvdW+91]. One of these, namely "VLSI programming and compilation into asynchronous circuits", forms the background of the research reported in this book. The central idea is that of viewing VLSI design as a programming activity, and thereby capitalizing on the achievements in computing science with regard to complexity control [Sei80, Rem81, vdS85, Mar89].

VLSI programming assumes a VLSI-programming language that provides the programmer with a suitable abstraction from the VLSI technology and circuit techniques. This abstraction allows systems on silicon to be designed by system (e.g. digital audio) specialists without detailed involvement of IC specialists. Ideally, this avoids the costly, time-consuming, and error-prone transfer of design data from system specialists to VLSI-circuit specialists. The degree of abstraction is constrained by the required cost and performance of the resulting IC. A VLSI programming language is thus a compromise between programming convenience and silicon efficiency.

The automatic translation of VLSI programs into VLSI circuits is often called *silicon compilation*. This book proposes a compilation scheme that results in asynchronous circuits. This relatively uncommon circuit style has specific advantages with regard to system modularity and IC power consumption.

The central contribution of this book is that of *handshake circuits*. A handshake circuit is a network of handshake components connected by point-to-point channels along which components interact exclusively by means of handshake signaling. Handshake circuits are intended as an intermediary between VLSI programs and VLSI circuits. The role of an intermediary is generally that of separation of -- more or less orthogonal -- concerns. This introductory chapter continues by taking stock of these concerns.

First we shall have a closer look at a particular system on silicon: a Compact Disc Decoder IC. This example shows the variety in interfaces, protocols and data types involved in system design. The final section examines the VLSI medium by means of the mainstream VLSI technology CMOS. A computation will be viewed in terms of voltage transitions on wires. Differences between synchronous and asynchronous circuits are explained by discussing how to deal with the phenomenon called *interference* between transitions. Reasoning about circuit speed and power is in terms of individual transitions on wires.

0.0   VLSI systems

One of the key modules of the Compact Disc (CD) player is its chip set. Other key modules are: a laser-optical pick-up, a turntable, and a user interface consisting of a keyboard and a display. Typically, the chip set consists of a servo controller, a decoder, a digital filter, a digital-to-analog converter, a DRAM, and a microprocessor [Phi90]. There is a tendency towards single-chip solutions. The decoder has been selected to illustrate a number of issues relevant to VLSI programming.

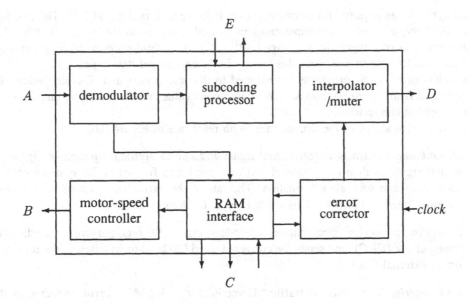

Figure 0.0: Simplified block diagram of the Compact Disc Decoder SAA7310.

The main function of the decoder is to convert the digital signal from an optical disc into a digital (stereo) audio signal. The block diagram of the decoder in Figure 0.0 has been adapted from [Phi90]. The interface of this decoder comprises:

- *clock*: crystal oscillator input (11.2896 megahertz),

- A: bit stream from the optical pick-up (*average* bit frequency: 4.32 megahertz),

- B: disc-motor control signal, pulse-width modulated (88.2 kilohertz, duty factor ranges from 1.6% -- 98.4%),

- C: interface to external DRAM of 16k × 4 bits (12 clock cycles for a single read or write access),

- D: bit serial output of stereo samples (2 × 16 bits) with an error flag per sample in parallel (rate: *clock*/4 ≈ 2.82 megahertz),

- E: subcode signal to external microprocessor (bit-serial, in bursts of 10 bits at 2.82 megahertz; one handshake per burst).

The above overview indicates a variety in data rates and clock frequencies. Most frequencies are derived from *clock* by division. The incoming bit stream A, however, contains an implicit clock that must be recovered through frequency and phase detection. This clock frequency varies with the rotation speed of the disc. A feed-back mechanism guarantees that *on average* the incoming data rate matches the outgoing data rate.

There is also a considerable variety of data types involved. The incoming data are a formatted stream of bits. Frames of 32 symbols of 8 bits are extracted internally. The arithmetic applied to these symbols, as required for error correction, is in the Galois field $GF(2^8)$. The interfacing to the RAM requires address computations in natural numbers in the range $[0..2^{16})$. Audio samples are pairs of integers in the range $[-2^{15}..2^{15})$. A general-purpose VLSI-programming language must be able to deal with this variety in data rates and data types.

The behavior of VLSI programs is restricted to discrete events and discrete values. Conversion to and from time-continuous and/or continuous values requires adapter circuits such as digital-to-analog converters.

The main submodules of the decoder are (with reference to Figure 0.0):

- *Demodulator*: extracts a clean digital signal *and* a clock signal from the disc signal. This digital signal is then demodulated and converted into frames of 32 symbols of 8 bits, error flags and subcode information. The rate of the extracted clock signal follows the rotation speed of the disc. This clock is local to Demodulator.

- *Subcoding processor*: accumulates subcode words of 96 bits, performs a cyclic redundancy check (CRC), and sends the corrected word (80 bits) to an external microprocessor on an external clock.

- *RAM interface*: controls the traffic "Demodulator $\rightarrow$ RAM $\rightarrow$ Error corrector $\rightarrow$ RAM $\rightarrow$ Error corrector". The external RAM is used for two distinct purposes: that of a first-in first-out queue (FIFO) to buffer the irregularly produced data from disc, and that of a store for de-interleaving the symbol stream.

- *Motor-speed controller*: controls the speed of the disc motor based on the degree of occupancy of the FIFO.

- *Error corrector*: corrects the code words according to Cross Interleaved Reed-Solomon Code (CIRC) with a maximum of 4 errors per frame of 32 symbols.

- *Interpolator/Muter*: converts symbols in stereo audio samples, interpolates single errors and mutes in the presence of two or more successive erroneous samples.

These submodules operate in parallel. It is therefore hard to describe the behavior of the decoder in a traditional imperative programming language (such as Pascal, C or Fortran). The behavior of each submodule, however, can be conveniently described in such a language extended with appropriate primitives for input and output. This expresses exactly the idea of Communicating Sequential Processes (CSP) as proposed by Hoare in [Hoa78], and forms the basis of the VLSI-programming language Tangram[0] developed at Philips Research.

0.1   VLSI circuits

A typical VLSI circuit is almost 1 cm^2 in size and consists of about 10^5 - 10^6 transistors, 10-100 meters of wiring, and about 100 bonding pads. During its operation, when connected

---

[0]Tangram is the name of an ancient Chinese puzzle [Elf76]. It consists of a few, simple forms (five triangles of three different sizes, one square and one parallelogram) with a simple composition rule (forms may not overlap), and allows the construction of a large variety of intricate and fascinating shapes. This view on design also shaped our VLSI-programming language Tangram.

to a power supply, more than 10^{11} events (voltage transitions) may occur each second, of which often less than one percent are observable at the bonding pads. An event consumes about a picojoule of energy; the power consumption of a chip is usually less than one watt.

These rounded numbers apply to digital VLSI circuits manufactured in CMOS, the dominant VLSI technology of today. For state-of-the-art chips most of the above numbers may be an order of magnitude higher. The yearly world production of integrated transistors is in the order of 10^{15}, or about a thousand transistors per world citizen per day[1]. The observations in the sequel of this section are made with CMOS technology in mind, assuming a 1 micron feature size.

Transitions

The voltage transitions observable at the bonding pads are the only evidence of a computation going on inside a VLSI chip, apart from indirect evidence such as power consumption. We shall therefore first concentrate on such events, in particular on their occurrences on wires.

Wires are metal conductors usually connecting two or more (distant) transistors. Electrically they can be regarded as capacitors to the IC substrate. Except for the very long wires, the metal area may be considered *equipotential*: differences in potential along the wire tend to equalize in a time period shorter than the switching time of a transistor[2]. For long wires and wires made of material with a high sheet resistance such as polysilicon this approximation is not valid. Then the transmission delays caused by wire resistance and the speed of light may no longer be neglected (cf. Chapter 5 in [H.B90]).

A wire may be charged ("pulled up") through a path of transistors connected to the power-supply rail. Such a pull-up path usually consists of pMOS transistors, a type of transistor that conducts when its gate potential is low, i.e. connected to an uncharged wire. Similarly, wires may be discharged ("pulled down") by a path of nMOS transistors connected to *ground*. An nMOS transistor conducts when its gate potential is high. Often such paths may be merged, i.e. individual transistors or combinations of transistors may be part of more than one path.

Generally, the situation in which a pull-up path and a pull-down path compete in charging and discharging a wire is avoided, or at least restricted to a very short duration. For longer durations this form of short-circuit dissipation may form a considerable power drain.

When a wire is neither pulled up nor pulled down (it "floats"), its potential may not be constant due to charge leakage. A circuit is *static* if it has the property that its wires never float. If the floating of wires is essential for the operation of a circuit, the circuit is called *dynamic*.

Interference

So far, it was tacitly assumed that voltage transitions are complete, i.e. they proceed all the way from the ground to the supply voltage or vice versa. But what if the (dis-)charging of a wire is interrupted?

---

[1] A similar type of estimate was presented during an invited lecture delivered by G. Moore at the Decennial Caltech Conference on VLSI, 1989.

[2] For equipotential wires the image of a voltage transition propagating along a wire is false; when applied with care, the metaphor (as for example applied in the foam-rubber wrapper principle [Udd84]) may be useful.

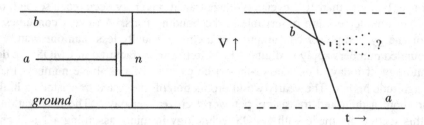

Figure 0.1: Interference occurs e.g. when wire a is discharged during the discharging of b.

Figure 0.1 illustrates a case of interference. When wire a has a high potential, the nMOS transistor n forms a conducting path between wire b and ground. Assume that b is being discharged through n when the potential on a drops to the ground level: the discharging of b is interrupted. Wire b is discharged partially and its potential is somewhere between the ground and the supply voltage. In such a situation, the transition on a is said to *interfere* with the transition on b. The transistors controlled by b may or may not have changed their state of conductance, and may or may not be involved in (dis-)charging other wires, etcetera. If b is subsequently recharged, the effect of this ''runt'' pulse on other wires critically depends on transistor sizes and thresholds, wire capacitances, and the time interval between the two events. The runt pulse may have caused a multitude of partial or complete transitions on other wires, or not. Similar complications occur when the discharging of b is interrupted by a short period of charging. Figure 0.2 gives examples of a proper transition (monotonic and complete), a runt pulse and a non-monotonic transition.

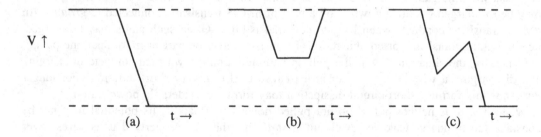

Figure 0.2: A proper transition (a), a runt pulse (b), and a non-monotonic transition (c).

There are two ways of dealing with interference:

- Accept the possibility of interference, but insist that at specific moments the mess has cleared, i.e. the circuit is in a quiescent state and all wires are stable at well-defined potentials. Synchronous timing disciplines are based on this principle: an externally supplied clock defines the moments at which the circuit *must* be quiescent.

- Avoid interference: guarantee that all transitions are monotonic and complete. Many *asynchronous* timing disciplines are based on this principle, *self-timed* and *delay-insensitive* being two of them.

The overwhelming majority of today's digital VLSI circuits are synchronous.

Proper transitions

Our interest in asynchronous circuits justifies some elaboration on the notion of *proper* transition. A nice and effective way to capture all requirements on proper transitions is by means of a phase diagram as proposed in [Bro89]. The evolution of the voltage of a wire in time is then recorded by a so-called trajectory in the space $(V, dV/dt)$. The values of V and dV/dt are bounded by a doughnut shape as in Figure 0.3. With this choice of axis orientations, changes in V result in counter-clockwise trajectories. Lower bounds on $(V, dV/dt)$ exclude runt pulses and non-monotonic transitions as illustrated in Figure 0.3.

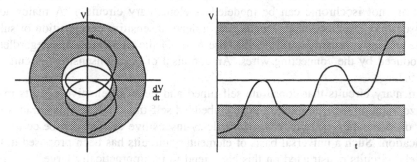

Figure 0.3: Phase and time diagram for a runt pulse followed by a non-monotonic transition.

The thickness of the doughnut determines amongst others the margins in the voltage to count as logical *false* or *true*. Within these margins runt pulses may occur, as illustrated in Figure 0.4. The doughnut also bounds the slope of a transition. This is significant, because different transistors may change their state of conductance at different voltage levels of the controlling gate. Transistors controlled by the same wire may then "observe" the same transition at different moments. Bounds on the slope of a transition therefore effectively limit these time differences (cf. isochronic forks in Section 8.5).

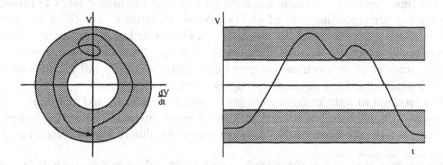

Figure 0.4: Phase and time diagram for two proper transitions in succession.

Asynchronous circuits

The method addressed in this book aims at the design of asynchronous VLSI circuits. The key question then is how to guarantee absence of interference. How to control the timing and dependencies of billions of transitions in such a way that the integrity of every single transition is assured?

The central idea is to construct a circuit from elementary circuits that indicate by means of transitions on output wires that transitions on specific input wires will not cause interference[3]. Circuits organized according to this principle are said to be *self-timed* [Sei80].

Delay-insensitive circuits are a restricted form of self-timed circuits. A circuit is delay-insensitive if the absence of interference does not depend on any assumption about delays of these elementary circuits and wires [vdS85]. In delay-insensitive circuits only point-to-point wires between elementary circuits are allowed, i.e. wires that connect one output to one input. (Forks that are not isochronic can be modeled as elementary circuits.) A major advantage of delay-insensitive circuits is their *modularity*: a delay-insensitive composition of subcircuits will operate correctly, regardless of the response times of the subcircuits and regardless of the delays introduced by the connecting wires. An appraisal of delay-insensitive circuits is given in Section 9.2.

The elementary circuits that constitute self-timed and delay-insensitive circuits may be of arbitrary size, ranging from an inverter to an embedded self-timed RAM. It is attractive to have a finite set of elementary circuits from which delay-insensitive circuits can be constructed for any specification. Such a universal basis of elementary circuits has been proposed in [Ebe89]. Unfortunately, circuits constructed on this basis tend to be impractically large.

A more practical set of elementary circuits has been proposed by Martin [Mar85b]. These elementary circuits are called *VLSI operators* and form a generalization of the traditional gates. Unfortunately, the class of delay-insensitive circuits that can be constructed from VLSI operators is severely restricted [BE92]. With the so-called *isochronic fork* as the only concession to delay insensitivity [Mar90] reasonably efficient circuits can be constructed (cf. Section 8.5).

Circuit speed

The time required for a computation is determined by the critical sequence of ordered transitions. The time needed for a single transition on a wire is the time it takes to (dis-)charge the wire via the corresponding path of pMOS (nMOS) transistors. Let C be the (parasitic) capacitance of the wire, including the transistor gates connected to it. A typical value for C is 0.1 picofarads. Charging the wire from 0 volt to the supply voltage (commonly 5 volts) involves the transfer of an electrical charge of CV from the supply rail to the wire (CV is typically 0.5 picocoulombs, equivalent to roughly 8 million electrons).

The time required to transfer these electrons is proportional to C, and also depends on the number of pMOS transistors in the charge path and their dimensions. The number of transistors in such paths is typically quite small. The main reason for this is that the (dis-)charge times

---

[3]The requirement of absence of interference restricts the behavior of the environment as well. In some cases this may be too restrictive. For instance, the handling of concurrent requests for a single resource requires a circuit that assures mutual exclusion. Inside such a mutual-exclusion circuit interference cannot be avoided. It is then a good idea to localize the interfering transitions inside elementary circuits such as arbiters.

tend to grow quadratically with this number. Observed averages for this number are very close to 2. More than 4 transistors in a path is very rare.

The (dis-)charge time is typically about 1 nanoseconds, assuming typical IC processing, a nominal power supply voltage (5 volts), and typical operating temperature (20 °C). However, for a wire of several millimeters, with a capacitance exceeding 1 picofarad, this may result in transition times of several nanoseconds, if no precautions are taken. The intrinsic switching time of a transistor is well below 1 nanoseconds. Clearly, the wires determine the operating speed of a VLSI circuit.

Energy consumption

In real systems, the cost of power, cooling, and electrical bypassing often exceeds the cost of the chips themselves. Hence any discussion of the cost of computation must include the energy cost of the individual steps of the computation process (cf. [MC80], page 322).

Following this suggestion, we shall look at the energy required for a single transition. The energy for charging a wire with capacitance C to voltage V is $\frac{1}{2}CV^2$, or $1\frac{1}{4}$ picojoules for our typical wire with 0.1 picofarads capacitance and a supply voltage of 5 volts. During each transition some charge is wasted during the time that both pMOS and nMOS transistor paths are conducting ("short-circuit dissipation" [Vee84]). For well-designed circuits this dissipation can be limited to an additional 10% of energy. A third contribution to energy consumption is leakage. Even in their blocking state, MOS transistors conduct a leakage current of, say, 0.2 nanoamperes, equivalent to an energy consumption of 1 nanojoule per second, or 1 nanowatts. Apparently, this contribution to the energy consumption pertaining to a wire can be ignored when the number of transitions involving that wire well exceeds a thousand per second. This condition is generally satisfied.

For a complete circuit, and for a given computation, the required energy can easily be computed by summing the contributions of the individual wires. Again, longer wires imply larger parasitic capacitances and hence more energy per transition.

For later reference we assume that a single transition requires about 1.5 picojoules of energy. A typical penlight battery contains 2000 joules (NiCad) to 4000 joules (Zn) (see, for example, [Cro90]), equivalent to well over 10^{15} voltage transitions. A circuit consisting of 1000 wires, each making 10,000 transitions per second, would run for 3 years on a single penlight battery! Still, for increasingly more portable consumer products the operating time can be measured in terms of hours (CD, DCC, notebooks, cellular radio), where the digital ICs consume a significant fraction of the available energy. This suggests "super computing" on a chip, involving many, many billions of transitions each second.

At this stage we may already note that asynchronous circuits potentially consume less energy, because each transition is productive: there is no energy used for clock generation and distribution, and no energy is wasted in interference.

Circuit area

A typical CMOS transistor is less than 10 μm^2 in area. This would allow for a packing density of over 100,000 transistors per mm^2. The densest practical circuits are embedded memories with about 10,000 transistors per mm². The average density in other digital VLSI circuits is well below this number. The almost two orders of magnitude difference between possible and practical transistor densities is caused by wires connecting the transistors.

We shall assume a standard-cell layout-style, in which elementary building blocks (standard cells) are lined up into rows separated by wiring areas (routing channels). The transistor density inside these standard cells is roughly constant. For moderately sized circuits that are reasonably regular, the wiring area is roughly proportional to the total cell area. Hence, the number of transistors is often a reasonable measure for the cost of a circuit. Transistor densities typically range from 3000 to 4000 transistors/mm².

The area of an IC is still a most critical resource: 20% area overhead in a competitive market is considered a serious handicap, and 50% area overhead is usually acceptable only for prototype circuits, or for small production series.

In summary: wires dominate concerns for cost and performance in every respect. The wires determine the area, the computation time and the energy consumption [SM77, Sei84]. Every VLSI design method, existing or novel, must acknowledge this fact.

Testing

The VLSI fabrication process is extremely complicated. For moderately sized circuits the yield is about 50%, i.e. 50% of the manufactured circuits function correctly. For complex circuits in an advanced technology the yield may well be below 10%. To make things worse, for larger circuits the yield decreases exponentially with the circuit area. This has two important consequences: circuit area is a most critical resource and there is a *test problem*.

The problem of testing is how to discriminate between a correct circuit and a faulty circuit. This bears no relation with software testing. It is assumed that the circuit *design* is correct and that a possible malfunctioning is caused by a defect introduced during the fabrication of the circuit. For advanced production technologies such defects cannot be avoided: their density is about 2 per cm².

The method of testing consists of two parts:

- bring the circuit into a state where an assumed fault makes a difference in the subsequent computation (controllability);

- detect this possible difference (observability).

Given the exorbitant number of possible faults and circuit states on the one hand and the limited number of pads to control and observe the circuit behavior on the other hand, it is clear testing is a hard problem, in every respect. Testing of circuits is also costly: provisions for enhancing the testability of a circuit and executing tests may account for 10 to 30% of the price of an IC.

Given the complexity of testing, the user of an IC is not in a position to test an IC effectively. It is the joint responsibility of the circuit designer and the manufacturer. A novel VLSI-circuit design method without a systematic, effective and affordable test method is simply not viable.

Chapter 1

Introduction to Tangram and handshake circuits

This book pursues a programming approach to the design of digital VLSI circuits. In such an approach the VLSI-system designer constructs a program in a suitable high-level programming language. When he is satisfied with his program, the designer invokes a so-called *silicon compiler* which translates this program into a VLSI-circuit layout.

The choice of the programming language is a crucial one, for it largely determines the application area, the convenience of design, and the efficiency of the compiled circuits. A good VLSI-programming language

0. is *general purpose* in that it allows the description of all digital functions;

1. encourages the *systematic* and *efficient* design of programs by abstracting from circuit, geometry and technology details;

2. is suitable for *automatic* translation into *efficient* VLSI circuits and test patterns.

Below follows a motivation for these requirements.

0. A wide range of applications is required to justify the investment in tools and training.

1. A major gain in design productivity can be expected by designing in a powerful high-level language. Furthermore, system designers do not need to resort to VLSI specialists. Systematic design methods, supported by mathematical reasoning, are required to deal with the overwhelming complexity involved in the design of VLSI systems.

2. Automatic translation to VLSI circuits avoids the introduction of errors at the lower abstraction levels. It also becomes attractive to design alternative programs and compare the translated circuits in costs (circuit area) and performance (speed and power).

Any such language is of necessity a compromise between convenience of design and efficiency of the result.

Traditional programming languages such as Pascal and C can be considered for this purpose. However, these languages were conceived for sequential execution on a specific architecture. It is not at all clear how to benefit from the parallelism so abundantly available in VLSI, when

11

a program describes a total order of all elementary computation steps. On the other hand, these so-called *imperative* programming languages are successful in that they are general purpose and offer a good compromise between convenience of design and efficiency of the compiled machine code.

In an effort to add parallelism to the traditional sequential programming languages, Hoare developed Communicating Sequential Processes [Hoa78]. CSP soon became an important vehicle for the (theoretical) study of *concurrency* in computing science. It was also the basis of OCCAM [INM89], a language suitable for programming networks of microprocessors. The suitability of CSP-based languages for VLSI programming has been addressed in [Mar85a, vBRS88]. In CSP terms, a VLSI circuit can be described as a fixed network of processes connected by channels. These processes are simultaneously active and co-operate by synchronization and the exchange of messages along channels. The behavior of each process can be described in a C or Pascal-like language to which proper primitives for synchronization and communication have been added.

In translating programs into circuits, it is attractive to preserve the parallelism of the program by translating each process into a subcircuit, and each channel into a set of wires. This "transparent" way of translating programs into circuits has the advantage that the programmer has control over the area, speed, and energy consumption of the circuits.

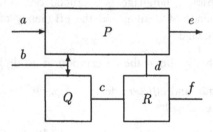

Figure 1.0: Communicating Sequential Processes.

Figure 1.0 depicts an example of a network of three communicating processes P, Q and R. The arrows indicate the directions of data transport along the channels. Channel a is an input to P, b is an input channel that forks to two processes, and e is an output channel. Channels c, d and f do not convey data: they are used for synchronization only.

One of the attractions of CSP is that it allows arbitrary numbers of processes of arbitrary complexity. The table below gives an impression of what can be realized in a single 100,000 transistor IC in terms of communicating processes. For a single IC the product of the degree of parallelism and the grain size (size of each process measured, for example, in number of transistors) is more or less constant.

degree of parallelism	# processes	# transistors / process	example
sequential	1	100k	microprocessors
coarse-grained	10	10k	digital audio (CD)
fine-grained	100	1k	systolic arrays

So far the notion "process" has been used rather loosely. In the sequel it is used to denote the set of observable communication behaviors of an object, irrespective of how the object is organized internally. The behavior of a network of processes can also be described as a single process. A program is a convenient way to define a process.

We use Tangram as a VLSI programming language. Tangram has been developed at Philips Research. It is based on Hoare's CSP [Hoa85] and includes Dijkstra's guarded-command language [Dij75].

The translation of Tangram programs into VLSI circuits has so-called *handshake circuits* as an intermediary. A handshake circuit is a network of handshake components, connected by point-to-point (handshake) channels. The only interaction among handshake components is by means of handshake signaling along these channels: there are no global signals such as clocks. The translation of Tangram programs into handshake circuits requires a modest set of different handshake components. The translation method is highly transparent, which allows the VLSI programmer to infer cost and performance of the compiled circuit fairly directly from his Tangram program.

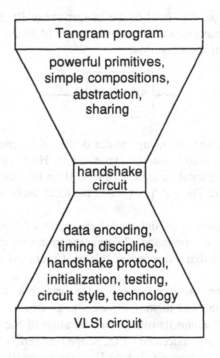

Figure 1.1: Handshake circuits: a separation of VLSI-programming and VLSI-circuit concerns.

Handshake circuits thus separate concerns for systematic and efficient VLSI-programming from concerns at the VLSI-circuit level, such as timing discipline, data encoding, initialization, and testing (see Figure 1.1). The narrow waist of the "hourglass" is intended to reflect the clear separation realized by handshake circuits.

Handshake circuits can also be considered as a VLSI *architecture.* According to Webster's

Ninth New Collegiate Dictionary [Mis87] one of the meanings of architecture is "a unifying or coherent form or structure". Handshake circuits unite control, storage, communication, logic and arithmetic in a single structure, supported by a single form of interaction: that of handshake signaling.

This chapter gives an informal introduction to Tangram and handshake circuits by means of simple examples: buffers and shift registers. Despite the simplicity of the examples, we will be able to address fundamental differences between clocked and asynchronous modes of operation. Shift registers also allow us to study the trade-offs between circuit area and energy consumption on the one hand and circuit speed on the other.

1.0   Some simple Tangram programs

One of the simplest Tangram programs is $BUF_1(a, b)$, a one-place buffer:

$$(a?W \ \& \ b!W) \cdot [\![\ x : \ \mathbf{var} \ W \ | \ \#[a?x; b!x] \ ]\!]$$

where W is an arbitrary type, e.g. *bool* or the integer range $[0..256)$. The opening pair of parentheses contains the declarations of the external ports of $BUF_1(a, b)$. Port a is an input of type W and b is an output of the same type.

The segment of Tangram text following the dot defines the behavior of the program. This behavior is described by a so-called *command* (statement). Here the behavior is described by a *block* command, in which the local variable x of type W is introduced. The brackets ' $[\![$ ' and ' $]\!]$ ' delineate the scope of x. The bar '|' separates the local declaration from the command in which it is used.

Command $\#[a?x; b!x]$ defines an unbounded repetition of input action $a?x$ followed by output action $b!x$. Execution of command $a?x$ amounts to the reception of an incoming value through a and the storage of that value in variable x. Command $b!x$ denotes the sending of the value of x through b.

In summary, $BUF_1(a, b)$ repeatedly receives a value through a and sends that value through b. Variable x is merely a container to store the incoming value between the two communication actions. The identity of x and its role in the operation of the buffer cannot be observed externally, since x is effectively concealed by the scope brackets. Only the external communications through a and b can be observed. If type W is the range $[0..10)$, a possible observation of $BUF_1(a, b)$ is:

$$a\!:\!3 \quad b\!:\!3 \quad a\!:\!9 \quad b\!:\!9 \quad a\!:\!9$$

where $a\!:\!v$ denotes the communication of value v through port a. Such a finite sequence of communications is called a trace.

A slightly more interesting program is that of two-place buffer $BUF_2(a, c)$:

$$(a?W \ \& \ c!W) \cdot [\![\ b : \ \mathbf{chan} \ W \ | \ (BUF_1(a, b) \ || \ BUF_1(b, c)) \ ]\!]$$

This two-place buffer consists of two instances of BUF_1. The output of the first instance is connected to the input of the second. Both instances operate in parallel, as denoted by '$||$'. Cascades of instances of BUF_1 are called "ripple buffers".

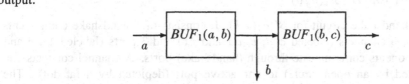

An internal communication along channel b obeys the two rules of CSP. Firstly, it requires simultaneous participation of sender and receiver. In other words, the output action of the left BUF_1 and the input action of the right BUF_1 form a single communication action. Secondly, a communication has the effect of the assignment action $xr := xl$, where xl and xr are aliases for the variable x in the left and right buffer respectively.

Communications along b are concealed by the scope brackets around the declaration of channel b. The communication behavior of $BUF_2(a,c)$ is more interesting than that of $BUF_1(a,c)$. In addition to all the traces of the one-place buffer (with their output renamed), a trace such as:

$$a:3 \quad a:9 \quad c:3 \quad c:9 \quad a:0 \quad c:0$$

may be observed. True to its name, the two-place buffer allows the number of input communications to exceed the number of output communications by two.

A quite different program is $TEE(a,b,c)$:

$$(a?W \ \& \ b!W \ \& \ c!W){\cdot}(BUF_1(a,b) \ || \ BUF_1(b,c))$$

It is a two-place buffer where the intermediate channel b is not concealed, but declared as an output:

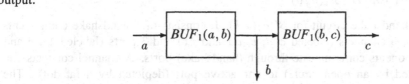

A communication along a channel that connects a single sender to multiple receivers is sometimes called a *broadcast*. A broadcast requires simultaneous participation of the sender and all receivers. A possible observation of $TEE(a,b,c)$ is:

$$a:3 \quad b:3 \quad a:9 \quad c:3 \quad b:9 \quad c:9 \quad a:0 \quad b:0 \quad c:0$$

Program $WAG(a,c)$ [vBRS88] is another tw-place buffer. Its external behavior is identical to that of $BUF_2(a,c)$. It is called a wagging buffer, because it behaves in a wagging fashion internally:

$$(a?W \ \& \ c!W){\cdot}[\![\ x,y : \ \mathbf{var} \ W \ | \ a?x; \#[(a?y \ || \ c!x); (a?x \ || \ c!y)] \ ]\!]$$

Inputs are alternately written into variables x and y. Similarly, the outputs are alternately read from the same variables. After the first input, $WAG(a,c)$ may proceed with a second input ("buffer full") or with an output ("buffer empty"). A second input must then be followed by an output or vice versa. Etcetera.

Although the observable behavior of buffer $WAG(a,c)$ cannot be distinguished from that of $BUF_2(a,c)$, the structure of the compiled circuits differ considerably, as do their cost and performance. This will be explained in the next sections.

1.1   Some simple handshake circuits

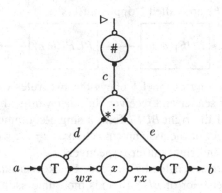

Figure 1.2: Handshake circuit for $BUF_1(a, b)$.

This section presents the handshake circuits for the various buffer programs of the previous section. Its main purpose is to develop an intuitive understanding of the operation of handshake circuits and the way they are generated from Tangram programs. The formal definition of handshake circuits is presented in Chapter 4. The translation method is described in depth in Chapter 7.

Handshake circuit for $BUF_1(a, b)$

Figure 1.2 shows a handshake circuit for $BUF_1(a, b)$. It consists of 5 handshake components (depicted by circles), 5 channels (labeled c, d, e, wx and rx) and 3 ports (labeled ▷, a and b). Handshake components communicate through (handshake) ports. A channel connects one passive port (depicted by an open circle) to one active port (depicted by a fat dot). The communication along these channels is by means of a simple two-phase handshake protocol, in which the active side requests a communication and the passive side responds by returning an acknowledgement.

In the handshake circuit for $BUF_1(a, b)$ the active ports a and b correspond to the Tangram ports with these names. The passive port ▷ (pronounced as "go") is the activation port of the handshake circuit. The environment activates the buffer by a request along ▷. Only in the case of a terminating program, which $BUF_1(a, b)$ is not, does the handshake circuit acknowledge termination through the same port.

The handshake component labeled with a semicolon is a *sequencer*. Once activated along c it sequentially performs handshakes along d and e, after which it returns an acknowledgement along c. It implements the semicolon that separates the input and output commands in the Tangram program. Unless explicitly indicated otherwise, the activation of the two active ports is counter-clockwise.

The component labeled with a '#' implements unbounded repetition and is therefore called a *repeater*. Once activated along ▷ it repeatedly executes handshakes along c, causing the repeated activation of the sequencer. The repeater never returns an acknowledgement along ▷.

Component x is a *variable*. A value can be written into x by sending it along channel wx. The acknowledgement along wx signals completion of the write action. Similarly, reading the variable starts by sending a request along rx (against the direction of the arrow). Component x responds by sending the most recently written value.

The two components labeled with a T are so-called *transferrers*. A request along d results in an active fetch of a value along a; this value is subsequently passed actively along wx. The left transferrer implements $a?x$ and the right transferrer implements $b!x$.

Observe that the structure of the handshake circuit of $BUF_1(a,b)$ clearly reflects the syntactic structure of the Tangram program.

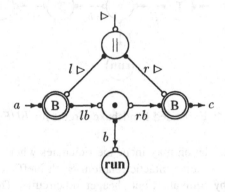

Figure 1.3: Handshake circuit for $BUF_2(a,c)$.

Handshake circuits for $BUF_2(a,c)$

A handshake circuit for $BUF_2(a,c)$ is shown in Figure 1.3. It introduces three more handshake components. The two concentric circles enclosing a B represent instances of the handshake circuit of the one-place buffer. The two one-place buffers are activated along $l \triangleright$ and $r \triangleright$ at the same time by the parallel composer after a request on $\triangleright$. Only when the parallel composer receives an acknowledgement through both its active ports will it acknowledge through $\triangleright$.

The handshake component labeled with a bullet is a *synchronizer*. It implements the concept of "communication and synchronization" of Tangram. If a request for communication arrives along both lb and rb the message arriving along lb is actively output along b. A subsequent acknowledgement along b results in a concurrent acknowledgement along lb and an output along rb.

The concealment of the Tangram channel b is realized by connecting a **run** component to handshake channel b. This component simply acknowledges each message it receives. Removing component **run** results in a handshake circuit for program $TEE(a,b,c)$, with output ports a and b.

By expanding the two one-place buffers in the circuit of Figure 1.3 the handshake circuit of Figure 1.4 is obtained. The circuit clearly reflects the syntactic structure of the original program. The applied translation method is *syntax directed* in that it closely follows the syntactic composition of the program in constructing the corresponding handshake circuit.

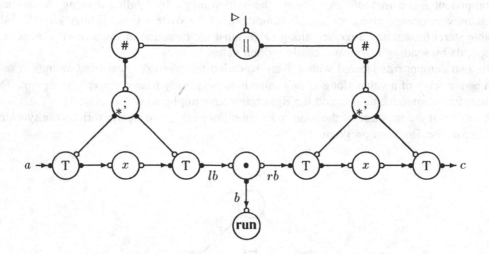

Figure 1.4: Expanded handshake circuit for $BUF_2(a, c)$.

Such a syntax-directed translation may incur inefficiencies where subcircuits are combined
in a way that only depends on their syntactic relation. Such inefficiencies can be removed by
replacing small subcircuits by equivalent but cheaper subcircuits. This form of substitution is
known as peephole optimization. One form of peephole optimization can be applied to the
buffer of Figure 1.4: the result is shown in Figure 1.5. The component labeled '•' is again a
synchronizer.

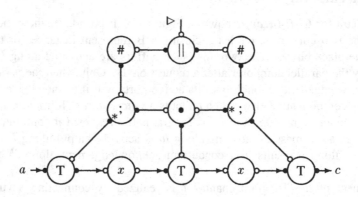

Figure 1.5: Optimized handshake circuit for $BUF_2(a, c)$.

The handshake components introduced so far all implement Tangram primitives. Given the
relatively small number of such primitives, the set of handshake components is modest in size.
By providing an "equivalent" VLSI circuit for each handshake component and by wiring
them according to the structure of the handshake circuit a VLSI circuit can be obtained. The

circuits for many handshake components are simple and fixed. For handshake components such as variables and transferrers the circuit structure depends on the number of bits required to encode the relevant data types.

Handshake circuits are clockless. All synchronization is explicit by means of handshake actions between neighboring components. The scheduling problem of assigning a time slot to every primitive action is thus avoided. Furthermore, the absence of global synchronization avoids the timing overhead of aligning all primitive actions to clock transitions. Clockless operation combined with the locality of data and control make handshake circuits potentially faster than synchronous circuits.

Although the buffers are about the simplest Tangram programs one can think of, the design of *synchronous* "elastic" buffers offers considerable challenges. In particular, the synchronization of clocked input and output actions with an asynchronous environment involves complex circuitry and fundamental reliability problems [Ano73, Sei80].

Handshake circuit for $WAG(a, c)$

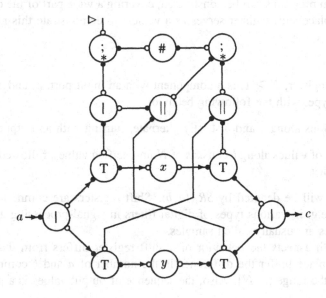

Figure 1.6: Optimized handshake circuit for $WAG(a, c)$.

A handshake circuit for $WAG(a, c)$ is presented in Figure 1.6. The three components labeled ' | ' are so-called *mixers*. They have in common that handshakes through their passive ports are passed to their active ports.

The component connected to a behaves like a demultiplexer. A request from either passive port is passed along a. The incoming message is passed to the side of the request.

The mixer connected to c passes the incoming message from one of its two passive input ports to the active output. The acknowledgement along b is passed to the side of the last incoming message (cf. multiplexer).

The third mixer is a multiplexer for synchronizing handshakes only. It allows the transferrer connected to its active side to be activated by either of the two handshake components connected to its passive ports.

These mixers make the wagging implementation of the two-place buffer more expensive in area than the ripple implementation.

1.2   Cost performance trade-offs

The programs for $BUF_2(a, c)$ and $WAG(a, c)$ in Section 1.0 are functionally identical. The corresponding handshake circuits of Figures 1.5 and 1.6, however, differ considerably. In general, a range of Tangram programs can be designed that satisfy a single functional specification. The corresponding compiled circuits will differ in cost and performance. The best Tangram program may be the one that results in the smallest compiled circuit that satisfies the specified performance requirements. Another selection criterion is consumption of the least power for the specified performance.

With this view on VLSI programming it is important that for a given functional specification a range of Tangram programs can be constructed, covering a wide part of the cost performance spectrum. An N-place shift register serves as a vehicle to demonstrate this idea.

Specification

An N-place shift register, $N \geq 1$, is a component with an input port, a, and an output port, b, of the same data type, with the following behavior:

- communications along a and b strictly alternate, starting with an output along b;

- the sequence of values along b consists of N unspecified values, followed by the sequence of input values.

This shift register will be denoted by $SR_N(a, b)$. Shift registers are common building blocks in VLSI systems, e.g. in various types of digital filters in signal-processing applications. The processed messages are usually called samples.

Note that in both aspects the behavior of a shift register differs from that of an N-place buffer. For an N-place buffer the difference in the number of a and b communications may vary in time over the range $[0..N]$. Also, the sequence of output values is a plain copy of the input sequence.

Area, speed, and energy consumption

Different shift-register programs are compared on the basis of area, speed, and energy consumption of the compiled circuits. To simplify the analysis, and to make it more concrete, we assume a fixed word width of 8 bits. The unit of costs (circuit size) is that of the circuit of an 8-bit variable. Time and energy consumption are expressed in terms of the time and energy it takes to perform an 8-bit wide (distributed) assignment. The cost and performance numbers are based on the circuit implementations of Chapter 8, combined with the area, speed, and energy analysis of Chapter 0.

For a word width of 8 the area of the (simple) control logic can be ignored safely. Alternatively, we can include some control overhead in determining the unit area. The latter results into a transistor count of 228 transistors for one area unit, corresponding to roughly 0.06 mm^2 silicon area.

The speed of the shift register is measured by the number of values it can transfer each second. This quantity is commonly referred to as *throughput* or *sample rate*. It is the reciprocal value of the average *cycle time*, the average time interval between two successive input (or output) communications. The cycle time is measured in terms of the time it takes for an 8-bit assignment. The critical path in an assignment consists of approximately 20 sequential transitions, including some overhead for control. This corresponds to 20 nanoseconds.

The energy consumption of the shift register is expressed in terms of the energy it takes one message to traverse the shift register from input to output. Again, for the unit of energy we take the 8-bit wide assignment as basis. Since about 100 transitions are involved, this corresponds to about 150 picojoules, again including some overhead for control. The power consumption of a shift register is then the product of the *actual* speed [# messages per second] and the energy per message [joules], and is measured in watts.

Low-cost realization

The simplest realization of $SR_1(a, b)$ is denoted by $SRA(a, b)$ and is defined by the Tangram program

$$(a?W \ \& \ b!W) \cdot [\![\ x : \ \textbf{var} \ W \ | \ \#[b!x; a?x] \ ]\!]$$

where W denotes the data type of the samples. Note that the repetition command closely resembles that of a 1-place buffer. The only difference is in the order of the input and output commands.

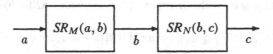

Figure 1.7: $SR_{(M+N)}(a, c)$ composed of two shift registers with a smaller capacity.

For the construction of an N-place shift register a well-known *cascade property* of shift registers is used (see Figure 1.7):

$$[\![\ b : \ \textbf{chan} \ W \ | \ SR_M(a, b) \ || \ SR_N(b, c) \ ]\!] \ = SR_{(M+N)}(a, c)$$

A realization for $SR_N(a, b)$ can now be obtained by cascading N instances of SRA. This solution will be denoted by A^N.

Note that A^N is capable of producing N outputs before doing its first input. Moreover, after these initial N outputs the behavior is that of an N-place buffer. On closer inspection, is A^N really an implementation of $SR_N(a, b)$?

It depends. If the environment relies on the alternation of b and a communications then definitely not. If the environment enforces this alternation, A^N is an acceptable realization.

In order to avoid further confusion, the first requirement of the specification of $SR_N(a,b)$ is redefined as: the following composition must not deadlock:

$$SR_N(a,b) \quad \| \quad [\![\ x,y:\ \mathbf{var}\ W\ |\ \#[b?x\ \|\ a!y]\ ]\!]$$

Note that the specification is relaxed to the extent that the ith input and the ith output may occur concurrently.

What can be said about the speed of A^N? After its first output, the last cell in the cascade is ready to do an input: "it is vacant". This vacancy then propagates backwards to the input of A^N and it takes $N-1$ successive internal assignments before an input action can occur. Including the external communications this results in a cycle time of $N+1$. For an 8-place 8-bit shift register the cycle time is then 9 time units, or 180 nanoseconds. It depends on the performance *requirements* whether 180 nanoseconds is acceptable or not. The cost of A^N is modest. It takes only N variables, which is obviously a lower bound for $SR_N(a,b)$. For $N=8$ this corresponds to approximately 0.5 mm^2. The energy consumption per message is clearly proportional to N as well. The energy required for a single message to ripple through A^8 measures 8 energy units, corresponding to 1.2 nanojoules.

Fast realizations

An alternative realization of $SR_1(a,b)$ is $SRB(a,b)$. It consists of an instance of SRA and a 1-place buffer:

$$(a?W\ \&\ b!W)\cdot [\![\ x,y:\ \mathbf{var}\ W\ \&\ c:\ \mathbf{chan}\ W\ |\ \#[c!x;a?x]\ \|\ \#[c?y;b!y]\ ]\!]$$

SRB resembles a traditional synchronous shift register composed of master slave flipflops. The SRA part assumes the role of the master, the 1-place buffer that of the slave. Input and output actions may overlap in time. In contrast with a synchronous shift register (and with SRA for that matter) SRB may start with an input. Shift register $SRB(a,b)$ can be rewritten into $SRC(a,b)$:

$$(a?W\ \&\ b!W)\cdot [\![\ x,y:\ \mathbf{var}\ W\ |\ \#[(b!y\ \|\ a?x);y:=x]\ ]\!]$$

SRB and SRC are very close in terms cost and performance (SRC is slightly cheaper, because of its simpler control structure).

By cascading N instances of SRC we obtain a second realization of $SR_N(a,b)$. This realization will be denoted by C^N. Because each SRC section has its own vacancy, the behavior of C^N is markedly different from that of A^N. For the analysis it is assumed that when the environment is ready to participate in an input or output action, it does so without delay. Then the input and output actions of each individual SRC occur simultaneously, and all N stages operate in harmony. As a result the sample rate is independent of N, and the cycle time amounts to only two time units (40 nanoseconds). The price for this nice performance is substantial: C^N requires $2N$ variables, twice that of A^N. Moreover, the energy per message also increases from N energy units to $2N$.

Given the substantial differences in cost, speed, and energy/message between A^N and C^N one may wonder if intermediate solutions exist. Indeed, by introducing one or more SRC cells in a sequence of SRA cells, intermediate solutions can be obtained of the form $C^K A^{N-K}$, with $0 \le K < N$. The cycle time can be obtained by dividing the number of successive assignments by the number of vacancies propagating backwards in parallel. We thus arrive at a cycle time of

$$\frac{N + K + 1}{K + 1}$$

These cycle times have been confirmed by simulation of the compiled handshake circuits, where the timing models of the handshake components have been calculated from the timing characteristics of their constituent VLSI operators. The solid circles in Figure 1.9 indicate the transistor counts versus throughput for five shift registers of this kind, with K equal to 0, 1, 2, 4 and 8 respectively. The energy per message for $C^K A^{N-K}$ is $N + K$ (cf. Figure 1.10). Apparently, additional throughput has its price in terms of circuit cost and in terms of energy consumption.

The realizations described so far have in common that the messages ripple through a cascade of N cells. Hence, they will be referred to as *ripple* shift registers.

Still faster realizations

One may wonder whether C^N is the fastest possible shift register. Equivalently, is two time units the minimum cycle time? By putting two shift registers in parallel, and by serving them alternatingly, faster shift registers can be constructed (see Figure 1.8). Shift registers based on this structure will be referred to as *wagging* shift registers. A similar decomposition was applied to queues in [DNS92]. In order to keep matters simple, N is restricted to even values.

$SRD(a, c, e)$ de-interleaves the incoming sequence by sending the incoming values alternatingly along c and e:

$$(a?W \,\&\, c!W \,\&\, e!W) \cdot [\![\; x, y : \; \textbf{var } W \;|\; \#[(c!x \;||\; a?y); (e!y \;||\; a?x)] \;]\!]$$

$SRE(d, f, b)$ interleaves the incoming sequences by receiving inputs alternatingly along d and f:

$$(d?W \,\&\, f?W \,\&\, b!W) \cdot [\![\; x, y : \; \textbf{var } W \;|\; \#[(b!x \;||\; d?y); (b!y \;||\; f?x)] \;]\!]$$

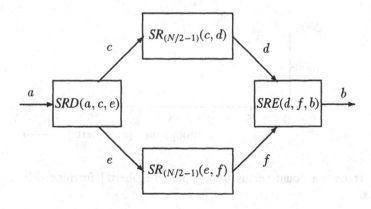

Figure 1.8: The wagging shift register.

Both *SRD* and *SRE* have a cycle time of one unit, measured at the input and output respectively. Unfortunately, due to some additional overhead in control and data routing, the real cycle time is somewhat larger. For 8-bit messages 30 nanoseconds is realistic.

For the two parallel shift registers ripple implementations can be used, e.g. composed of *SRA* and *SRC* cells. A regular communication behavior is obtained by taking identical cell sequences for $SR_{(N/2-1)}(c, d)$ and $SR_{(N/2-1)}(e, f)$.

The number of variables for this type of shift register is $N + 2K + 2$, where K is the number of C cells in each of the parallel paths. However, the cost for demultiplexing in *SRD* and multiplexing in *SRE* is not negligible. Here we shall assume 2 units for the pair, yielding a cost of $N + 2K + 4$ units.

The cycle times of the wagging solutions are determined by the cell sequences in the parallel paths. In Figure 1.9 the area and throughput are plotted for four triplets for $SR_3(c, d)$ and $SR_3(e, f)$ (from slow/small to fast/large): A^3, CA^2, C^2A and C^3. Due to the aforementioned overhead, C^2A is barely an improvement over CA^2 in speed. For the same reason C^3 offers no advantages over C^2A. The energy per message for the wagging shift registers is a clear improvement over the ripple registers, because the path for each message is about halved (cf. Figure 1.10).

Discussion

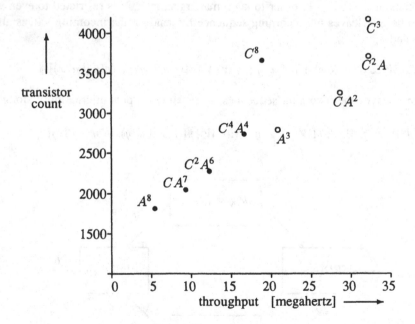

Figure 1.9: Transistor count versus throughput [megahertz] for nine different 8-place 8-bit shift registers.

From Figures 1.9 and 1.10 we can infer the following:

- Ripple shift-register A^8 is the smallest one, consisting of about 1800 transistors, covering 0.5 mm². It runs at 5 megahertz, consumes 1.2 nanojoules per message, or 6 milliwatts at the maximum rate.

- The wagging shift register based on C^2A offers the highest throughput: 32 megahertz. It measures 3700 transistors, about 1.0 mm². It consumes 1.1 nanojoules per message, corresponding to 35 milliwatts at 32 megahertz.

- The wagging shift register based on A^3 is the most energy-efficient one, consuming only 0.8 nanojoules per message. It measures 2800 transistors, or about 0.7 mm², and runs at 21 megahertz consuming 26 milliwatts.

Despite the simplicity of the specification of $SR_N(a, b)$ an interesting range of implementations has been realized. If we ignore the wagging solution based on C^3, all implementations have different area, speed, and power consumption. Among these eight solutions there is *no* best solution. Depending on throughput requirements, each of these eight implementations may be the best, except C^8, since A^3 is smaller, faster, and more energy efficient.

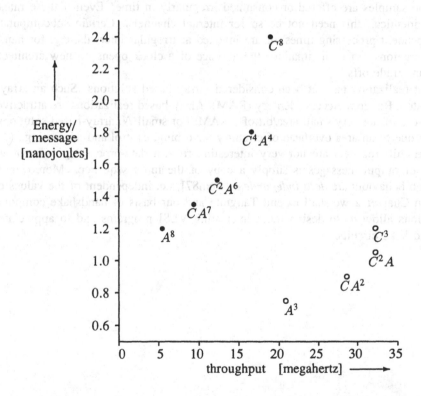

Figure 1.10: Energy/message [nanojoules] versus throughput [megahertz] for nine different 8-place 8-bit shift registers.

Shift registers are not typical VLSI circuits. Yet, the applied analysis techniques can easily be extended and refined to be of use for the analysis of general Tangram programs. Of course, more accurate estimates for size, timing and power need to be provided by the silicon compiler and simulation tools.

Concerns for cost and performance make VLSI programming different from and also more difficult than conventional programming. Especially high-performance systems (e.g. digital video systems) may require detailed performance analysis. But also for low-performance systems (e.g. digital audio systems) with critical requirements on silicon area and power consumption, balancing the performance of subsystems is important.

From a VLSI-circuit perspective, these asynchronous shift registers also provide an interesting insight. A^N requires one latch per section per bit whereas a master-slave flipflop requires two. In principle, no solution based on master slave flipflops can beat A^N in circuit size. Mimicking the behavior of A^N with synchronous circuits requires complex timing/control circuitry.

Although the sample rate of A^N is low, the vacancy travels at maximum speed from output to input. With a few *SRC* cells, the internal timing behavior becomes highly irregular. This form of irregularity is hard to capture in clocked circuits.

In complex VLSI systems different input and output ports often have different sample rates. Sometimes the samples are offered or consumed irregularly in time. Even if these rates are constant and identical, this need not be so for internal channels. Certain subcomputations have data-dependent processing times, or are invoked at irregular intervals, e.g. for handling exceptional situations. In such situations the absence of a clock opens up new architectural possibilities and trade-offs.

One type of realization has not been considered: array-based solutions. Such an array can be mapped onto a Random Access Memory (RAM). Array-based realizations are attractive for large N, because of the very small area/bit of a RAM. For small N, array-based solutions are less attractive due to an area overhead of circuitry for timing, control and addressing.

Buffers and shift registers are not very interesting from a data-processing point of view: the sequence of output messages is simply a copy of the input sequence. Moreover, their communication behaviors are *data independent* [Rem87], i.e. independent of the values communicated. In Chapter 2 we shall extend Tangram and our basis of handshake components. These extensions allow us to design more interesting VLSI programs and to appreciate the nature of handshake circuits.

Chapter 2

Examples of VLSI programs

This chapter introduces further Tangram constructs out of which more interesting programs can be described. These constructs include expressions, guarded selection, guarded repetition, and choice. The choice construct supports mixed input and output guards. Guarded selection and choice also introduce nondeterminism.

These constructs are introduced by means of concise and telling examples, namely a simple FIR filter, a median filter, a block sorter, a greatest common divisor, modulo-N counters, various stacks (including a specialization as a priority queue), and a nacking arbiter. In many cases handshake circuits are presented and explained with reference to the Tangram program text. Where relevant, circuit size, speed, and power consumption are analyzed.

2.0 FIR filter

A Finite Impulse Response (FIR) filter is a component with a single input port and a single output port. Input and output communications strictly alternate, starting with an input. For a FIR filter of order N the output values are specified as follows. The value of the ith output, $i \geq N$, is a weighted sum of the $N+1$ most recent input values. The $N+1$ weight factors are generally referred to as the filter coefficients. The first N output values are left unspecified.

A very simple FIR filter is used to introduce Tangram expressions and their translation into handshake circuits. The FIR filter is based on ADD, a simple component which repeatedly accepts two values of type W through its two input ports a and b and outputs their sum through c:

$$ADD(a, b, c) = (a?W \ \& \ b?W \ \& \ c!W) \cdot [\![\ x, y : \ \textbf{var } W \ | \ \#[(a?x \ || \ b?y); c!(x + y)] \ ]\!]$$

Expressions such as $x + y$ may occur in assignments, outputs commands and guards (see later in this chapter). It is assumed that the evaluation of an expression always terminates. However, if the result value does not "fit" its destination, the consequent behavior is not specified: the program may deadlock, or may proceed in some erratic way. ADD continues properly as long as the value of $x + y$ is of type W.

The handshake circuit for ADD is presented in Figure 2.0. The handshake component labeled '+' is an *adder*. The expression $x + y$ is evaluated in a demand-driven fashion:

    0. a request for a sum is passed to the passive output of the adder;

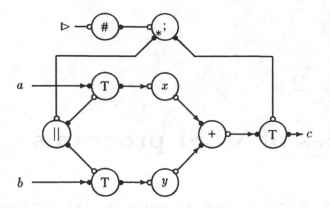

Figure 2.0: Handshake circuit for $ADD(a, b, c)$.

1. the adder forks this request to its active inputs;

2. the input values arrive at the inputs of the adder;

3. their sum is output along the output.

A very simple FIR filter of order N can now be constructed by connecting ADD with a shift register:

$$(a?W \ \& \ c!W) \cdot [\![\ b : \ \textbf{chan} \ W \mid ADD(a, b, c) \parallel SR_N(a, b) \ ]\!]$$

The ith output, $i \geq N$, is the sum of the ith input and the input with index $i - N$. This composition is depicted in Figure 2.1. Input channel a is connected to both ADD and SR. In general, any number of receivers may be connected to a channel. The connected receivers must all participate in each communication along that channel. This is another example of broadcast (cf. program *TEE* in Section 1.0). There may be at most one sender.

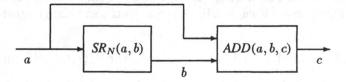

Figure 2.1: A simple FIR filter constructed from $SR_N(a, b)$ and $ADD(a, b, c)$.

A more general FIR filter program is discussed in [vBRS88], in which the degree of parallelism is parameterized. The program is a linear systolic array of $N \, \textbf{div} \, M$ cells, where M is a measure of the grain size of the parallelism. If $M = N$ the program is sequential and requires a single multiplier. The other extreme solution is $M = 1$: an array of N cells guarantees maximum throughput, but requires N multipliers.

2.1 Median filter

A median filter repeatedly outputs the median value of the three most recent inputs. (Similar to a FIR filter, the sequence of output messages starts with a few unspecified values.) The median filter can be described with the guarded selection construct, as in the following Tangram program:

$$(a?W \ \& \ b!W).$$
$$[\![\ x, y, z : \textbf{var} \ W \ \& \ xy, yz, zx : \textbf{var} \ bool$$
$$| \ \#[\ (z := y; y := x; a?x \ || \ yz := xy)$$
$$; xy := x \le y \ || \ zx := z \le x$$
$$; \textbf{if} \quad zx = xy \quad \rightarrow \quad b!x$$
$$[\!] \quad xy = yz \quad \rightarrow \quad b!y$$
$$[\!] \quad yz = zx \quad \rightarrow \quad b!z$$
$$\textbf{fi}$$
$$]$$
$$]\!]$$

The Tangram segment **if** ... **fi** is a *guarded selection* [Dij75]. The bracket pair **if fi** encloses three so-called guarded commands. A guarded command has the form $B \rightarrow S$, where B is a Boolean expression and S a command. Execution of a selection command starts with the evaluation of the guards. If all guards are *false*, the subsequent behavior of the program is unspecified. If at least one guard evaluates to *true*, the command corresponding to a *true* guard is executed. If more than one guard of a selection command evaluates to *true*, the choice of which command to execute is not specified. This nondeterminism can be resolved at compile time, or even at run time. Of course, for reasons of efficiency, the programmer may decide to strengthen the guards.

The Tangram description of the median filter can be understood as follows. Just prior to the execution of the selection command, the variables x, y and z contain the three most recent input values, in increasing age. At that point the three Boolean variables xy, yz and zx have the values $x \le y$, $y \le z$ and $z \le x$. The expression $zx = xy$ is then equivalent to "x is the median value". The two other guards can be read similarly.

Note that if $x = y = z$ all three guards evaluate to *true*, one of the output commands will be selected nondeterministically. (In this case the choice does not affect the value output.) Either the Tangram compiler or the VLSI circuit itself will have to introduce asymmetry in order that a choice can be made.

The median filter nicely demonstrates an advantage of this form of command selection. The symmetry among the three guards can only be captured in a language with explicit and overlapping guards for the three alternatives. An **if-then-else** command would break the symmetry.

The handshake circuit for the selection command of the median filter program is depicted in Figure 2.2. The write ports of the variables are shown unconnected. After an activation along $\triangleright$ the selection command is executed in two phases.

In the first phase the **if** component actively collects the disjunction of the guards. The component labeled ' $[\!]$ ' passes on a request on its output to both its Boolean inputs; upon reception of these Booleans their disjunction is transmitted along its output. Note that the guards are evaluated in parallel.

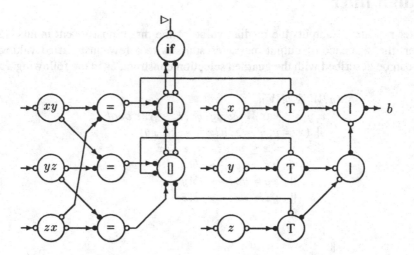

Figure 2.2: Handshake circuit for the **if fi** section of the median filter.

The effect of the second phase depends on the collected disjunction of the guards. If this value equals *false*, the **if** component halts and the circuit deadlocks. If the value equals *true*, as is always the case for the median filter, component **if** activates the topmost [] component. This component activates the circuit corresponding to an input from which it received the value *true*. In this solution the nondeterminism is resolved in the [] component.

This implementation scheme works for an arbitrary number of guards. If the [] components are organized according to a binary tree, the computation of the disjunction of the guards and the selection of the appropriate command can be done in $O(\log N)$ time, where N denotes the number of guards.

The handshake component labeled '=' is another example of a binary operator. Variables xy, yz and zx have two read ports each, from which concurrent read actions are allowed.

The median filter is an instance of a so-called rank-order filter. After each input value the rank-order filter outputs the value with rank K among the last N inputs ($0 \leq K < N$). A value has rank k among N values if it has position k in the ascendingly ordered list of these N values. The median filter is a rank-order filter with $N = 3$ and $K = 1$. [KU92] present programs for rank-order filters. Their solutions are linear systolic arrays of N cells. Except for the two end cells, all cells are identical. The cells communicate with neighboring cells in a regular, systolic manner.

FIR filters and rank-order filters are examples of so-called window computations. A window is a consecutive segment of sequence of values ("stream"). The window size for the FIR filter is $N+1$ and for the median filter it equals 3. In [Str92] other examples of window computations are described.

2.2 Block sorter

A block sorter has a single input port of type W (a range of integers) and a single output port of the same type. It accepts integers, grouped in blocks of size N, $N \geq 1$, and outputs them so that each block is sorted in ascending order. Unlike window computations, so-called block computations assume that the input stream has been partitioned into fixed-sized blocks.

The VLSI-programming challenge comes with the required performance: the input and output rates must be independent of N. The block sorter provides a first application of the N-fold repetition construct.

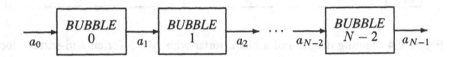

Figure 2.3: A block sorter composed of $N - 1$ *BUBBLE* cells.

The constant sort rate clearly suggests a systolic solution. The block sorter is realized by an array of $N - 1$ *BUBBLE* cells numbered from 0 to $N - 2$. Let i range over the cell numbers. The input port and output port of *BUBBLE* i are named a_i and a_{i+1} respectively (cf. Figure 2.3).

The array of *BUBBLE*s sorts each block by moving larger values towards the end of the block. Each *BUBBLE* extends the length of the sorted tail segment of each block by one. That is, *BUBBLE* 0 puts the largest value in position $N - 1$; *BUBBLE* 1 puts the one-but-largest value in position $N - 2$ *and* leaves the largest value in place. In general, *BUBBLE* i puts the value with rank $N - i - 1$ in place and passes the sorted tail sequence of length i as is. In other words, a block communicated along channel a_i has its tail of length i sorted. After a block has passed an array of $N - 1$ *BUBBLE*s, $N - 1$ values are in place, and hence the block is sorted.

A Tangram program for *BUBBLE* is

```
(a?W & b!W).
‖   x, y :  var W
|   #[  a?y
    ;   #(N − 1)[a?x ;  if x > y  →  b!y ;  y := x [] ¬(x > y)  →  b!x fi ]
    ;   b!y
    ]
]‖
```

where $\#(N - 1)[S]$ is used to denote the $(N - 1)$-fold repetition of command S. Note that the guards of the selection command are complementary (cf. **if-then-else**), resulting in a deterministic selection of one of the guarded commands.

Variable y is used to store the largest value of the current block input so far. An input value not exceeding y is simply passed. A larger input value replaces y, after the current value of y has been output. Notice that extending the array with additional *BUBBLE*s would not change its function, since sorting is idempotent. Fewer than $N - 1$ *BUBBLE*s results in a partial sorter.

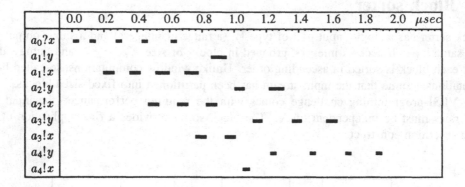

Figure 2.4: Timing diagram of a block sorter with $N = 5$ for an anti-sorted block.

The highest throughput is achieved if anti-sorted blocks (sorted in descending order) are offered, as is shown in Figure 2.4. A sorted block is processed at a lower rate, because of the more frequent execution of $y := x$ (c.f. Figure 2.5). The *latency* of the block sorter, i.e. the lead of input communications over output communications is bounded between 0 and $2(N-1)$. The maximum throughput of this block sorter occurs when the odd *BUBBLE*s operate more or less synchronously, as do the even ones. Then the latency is approximately $\frac{3}{2}N$ communications.

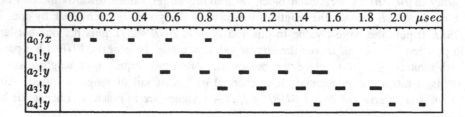

Figure 2.5: Timing diagram of a block sorter with $N = 5$ for a sorted block.

Formal specifications of the block sorter and of *BUBBLE* can be found in [vBRS88]. That article also contains a few optimizations and modifications, including one that trades the throughput with the overall number of variables.

A handshake circuit for *BUBBLE* is depicted in Figure 2.6. Notice that it resembles that of the wagging buffer in Figure 1.6. The top two rows of handshake components control the data transfers in the "data path", i.e. the network of handshake components of the bottom three rows. The handshake circuit introduces three new handshake components:

- An $(N-1)$-fold repeater, the component labeled '#$N-1$'. A handshake through its passive port encloses $N-1$ handshakes through its active port.

- A *comparator*, labeled with '>'. Its communication behavior is that of the adder component in Figure 2.0, but instead of outputting the sum it outputs the boolean result of comparing the two input values.

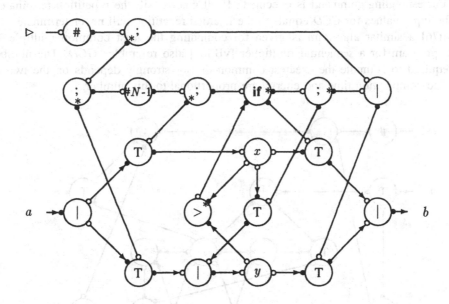

Figure 2.6: Handshake circuit for *BUBBLE*.

- An **if-then-else** component, labeled 'if'. A handshake through its passive port encloses the fetching of a boolean value and a subsequent handshake through the '∗'-labeled active port (after a *true* input) or one through the other active port (after a *false* input).

The **if**-component actually implements an **if-then-else** command. Its application here takes advantage of the complementarity of the guards in the selection command of *BUBBLE*.

2.3 Greatest common divisor

GCD repeatedly computes and outputs the greatest common divisor of the two most recent inputs. Its Tangram program introduces the guarded repetition construct:

$$
\begin{aligned}
&(a?W \ \& \ b?W \ \& \ c!W). \\
&[\![\ x, y : \textbf{var} \ W \\
&| \ \#[\ (a?x \ || \ b?y) \\
&\quad ; \ \textbf{do} \ \ x > y \ \rightarrow \ x := x - y \\
&\quad \quad \ \ [\!] \ \ y > x \ \rightarrow \ y := y - x \\
&\quad \quad \ \ \textbf{od} \\
&\quad ; c!x \\
&\quad] \\
&]\!]
\end{aligned}
$$

The algorithm goes back to Euclid; this particularly elegant version is based on [Dij76]. The program segment **do .. od** is a *guarded repetition*, a generalization of the well-known **while**

command.   As long as at least one guard evaluates to *true*, one of the *true* guards is selected
and the corresponding command is executed. If all guards fail, the repetition terminates. If
one of the input values for *GCD* equals 0, the guarded repetition will never terminate.

In [Dij76] a similar algorithm is given for computing the least common multiple. The
Tangram program for a sequential multiplier [vBS88] also resembles *GCD*. The number of
cycles required to compute the greatest common divisor strongly depends on the two input
values. The computation time and energy are proportional to this number.

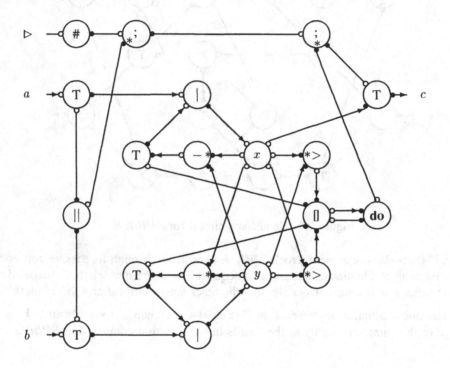

Figure 2.7: Handshake circuit for *GCD*.

A handshake circuit for *GCD* is given in Figure 2.7. The **do**-component, labeled '**do**',
implements the guarded repetition. A handshake through its passive port encloses a sequence
of handshakes:

  0. fetch a boolean value;

  1. if this value is *false* the sequence terminates; if *true* a handshake follows through its
     other active port, and both steps are repeated.

Note that the communication behavior of *GCD* is identical to that of *ADD*. The handshake
circuits have the same external ports, viz. an activation port, two input ports and one output
port. The fact that *GCD* contains an iterative algorithm is completely hidden for the user of the
circuits. The proposed method of compiling Tangram programs into handshake circuits leads
to a form of distributed control. Information is kept local, with the associated advantages of
shorter wires, minimum timing overhead, and reduced power consumption.

2.4 Modulo-N counters[0]

A modulo-N counter $COUNT_N$, $N \geq 1$, is a component with external ports a and b, whose behavior is specified by the regular expression $(a^N \; b)^*$, where exponentiation with N denotes N-fold repetition. It is a useful primitive in VLSI design, where it can be applied to control the N-fold execution of some finite computation (cf. the block sorter of Section 2.2).

The modulo-N counter is included for two reasons. Firstly, it allows the introduction of the choice command in its simplest form, i.e. a non-arbitrated binary choice via two undirected channels. Secondly, it provides an example where asynchronous circuits consume inherently less energy than their synchronous counter parts.

The idea for a systolic implementation of the modulo-N counter as a linear array of $O(\log N)$ cells is described in [Kes91a]. An attractive property of this solution is its constant response time. A variation on this idea can be found in [EP92].

The main differences between the solution presented below and [Kes91a] are:

- neighboring cells interact via two undirected channels, as opposed to a single channel of type *Boolean*;

- the *initial* response time is not constant, but $O(\log N)$.

These differences result in a cheaper and faster circuit. We are also interested in the power consumption of the modulo-N counter as a function of N, when it operates in an environment that has a constant response time. A circuit with parameter N consumes *constant power* if this power consumption has a constant upperbound, independent of N. For a modulo-N counter with constant response time this amounts to a constant amount of energy per external communication, independent of N.

The behavior of a modulo-N counter $COUNT_N$, with $N \geq 1$, is specified by the regular expression

$$(a^N \; b)^* \tag{2.0}$$

This can be rewritten as

$$(a^{N \bmod 2} \; (a \; a)^{N \operatorname{div} 2} \; b)^* \tag{2.1}$$

$COUNT_1$ can be implemented by the Tangram command #[a ; b]. For $N > 1$, Expression 2.1 suggests a decomposition of the counter into a modulo-(N **div** 2) counter and cell *HEAD* as in

where the behavior of *HEAD* is given by the regular expression

$$(a^{N \bmod 2} \; (\underline{a} \; a \; a)^* \; \underline{b} \; b)^* \tag{2.2}$$

The head cell effectively doubles each $\underline{a}$ communication of the modulo-(N **div** 2) counter and passes $\underline{b}$ along b after exactly N communications along a. Regular expression 2.2 is

---

[0]This section is adapted from [vB93]

used to derive the Tangram descriptions for the head component. We shall derive different implementations for odd and even N. The head cell for odd N is named CO and behaves as

$$(a \ (\underline{a} \ a \ a)^* \ \underline{b} \ b)^* \tag{2.3}$$

As the inner finite repetition cannot be expressed in Tangram directly, some rewriting is required:

$(a \ (\underline{a} \ a \ a)^* \ \underline{b} \ b)^*$

$=$

$((a \ \underline{a} \ a)^* \ a \ \underline{b} \ b)^*$

$=$

$(a \ \underline{a} \ a + a \ \underline{b} \ b)^*$

$=$

$(a \ (\underline{a} \ a + \underline{b} \ b))^*$

Casting this regular expression into Tangram syntax yields:

$$CO(a, b, \underline{a}, \underline{b}) \ = \ \#[a \ ; [\underline{a} \ ; a \mid \underline{b} \ ; b]] \tag{2.4}$$

Operator ';' binds more strongly than '|'. The environment is repeatedly offered the choice between a synchronization by $\underline{a}$ or by $\underline{b}$. These two synchronization commands act as *guards* in the choice command. For each $\underline{a}$, process CO performs a synchronization through a; likewise, for each $\underline{b}$, it performs only one through b.

Similarly, the cell for even N is named CE and is specified by:

$$CE(a, b, \underline{a}, \underline{b}) \ = \ \#[[\underline{a} \ ; a \ ; a \mid \underline{b} \ ; b]] \tag{2.5}$$

A program for a modulo-N counter can now be constructed with the cells $COUNT_1$, CE and CO for any value of N. This requires $\lfloor \log_2 N \rfloor + 1$ cells. For instance, the number 11 can be written as $1 + 2 * (1 + 2 * (2 * 1))$, corresponding with the following Tangram program for a modulo-11 counter:

$$
\begin{array}{ll}
[\![\quad a_1, b_1, a_2, b_2, a_3, b_3 : \textbf{chan} & \tag{2.6} \\
| \quad CO \ (a, b, a_1, b_1) \ \| \ CO \ (a_1, b_1, a_2, b_2) \ \| \ CE \ (a_2, b_2, a_3, b_3) \ \| \ COUNT_1(a_3, b_3) \\
]\!]
\end{array}
$$

The analysis of the response time can be based on sequence functions [Rem87]. Here we shall present an informal analysis, in which time is viewed as a linear sequence of discrete time slots, numbered from 0 onwards. Let the communications of $HEAD$ along a and b be assigned to successive odd-numbered time slots. The expressions for CO, and CE permit a consistent assignment of $\underline{a}$ and $\underline{b}$ to even-numbered time slots. (Since external communications outnumber internal communications, some of the even-numbered time slots remain "vacant".) The distance between two successive external communications of the sub-counter is therefore at least two. The modulo-$(N$ **div** $2)$ counter can match this schedule. Notice that the first external communication of $COUNT_N$ may occur after $O(\log N)$ internal communications, because CE starts with an internal communication.

Figure 2.8 shows the simulated timing of $COUNT_{50}$. Each bar represents a communication. The sub-counters clearly run at exponentially lower rates.

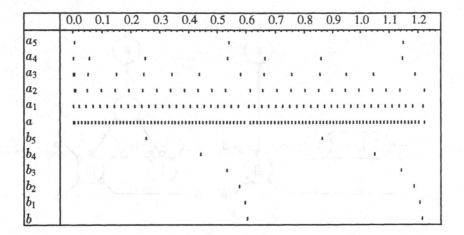

	0.0	0.1	0.2	0.3	0.4	0.5	0.6	0.7	0.8	0.9	1.0	1.1	1.2

rows: a_5, a_4, a_3, a_2, a_1, a, b_5, b_4, b_3, b_2, b_1, b

Figure 2.8: The simulated timing of the communications between the cells of a modulo-50 counter. Time is in μ seconds.

Handshake circuits

Figure 2.9 depicts handshake circuits for *CE* and *CO*. The activation channels of the cells of the modulo-N counter are connected by a tree of parallel composers. The root of that tree is the activation channel of the complete counter.

The *selectors* (labeled '[]') implement the choice constructs. After activation through its topmost passive port, the choice component is prepared to participate in a handshake through one of the other two passive ports. The choice between the two is made by the environment. Subsequently, the choice component actively handshakes on the active port opposite to the selected passive port, and then returns an acknowledgement along its activation channel.

The circuits have been obtained by a systematic syntax-directed decomposition of the respective Tangram expressions, as becomes evident by comparing the connectivity of the handshake circuits with the syntactic structure of these expressions. Notice that both handshake circuits consist of the same four handshake components, albeit connected differently.

The sequencers guarantee mutually exclusive use of the channels connected to the passive ports of the mixers. Also, communications along $\underline{a}$ and $\underline{b}$ are kept sequential by the sub-counters. Hence, there is no need to address the issue of arbitration here.

Cost and performance analysis

A modulo-N counter can be built using one *COUNT*$_1$ cell (requiring 26 CMOS transistors) and $\lfloor \log_2 N \rfloor$ cells of type *CO* or *CE* (each requiring 120 transistors). Hence, a modulo-N counter can be realized using

$$26 + 120 \lfloor \log_2 N \rfloor \tag{2.7}$$

transistors. For large N the number of transistors can be reduced by employing cheaper non-systolic sub-counters, since the constant-response time of the "less significant" sub-counters

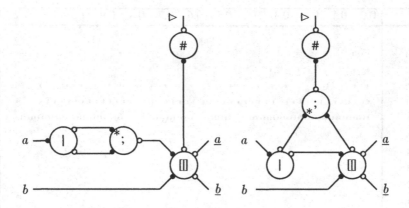

Figure 2.9: Handshake circuits for *CE* and *CO*.

is not utilized.

Our analysis of the power and energy consumption of the counter starts with the observation that the employed handshake-component implementations have a bounded physical extent, and that the number of internal voltage transitions is proportional to the number of external transitions. Hence, the energy consumption of a handshake component is proportional to the number of handshakes in which it is involved. By the same reasoning we can see that the energy consumption of each of the cells $COUNT_1$, *CE*, and *CO* is proportional to the number of external handshakes.

The array of cells can be laid out in such a way that the wires connecting neighbor cells have bounded lengths. The power analysis therefore reduces to counting handshakes: $N + 1$ for the head cell plus N **div** $2 + 1$ for the next cell, etc. The total number of handshakes required for $a^N b$, denoted by E_N, is given by (cf. Figure 2.8)

$$E_N = \sum_{i=0}^{M} (N \textbf{ div } 2^i + 1) \tag{2.8}$$

where $M = \lfloor \log_2 N \rfloor$.

E_N is a measure for the energy required for executing the sequence $a^N b$ once. Because of the constant response time of the counter, E_N/N is a measure of the power consumption. This quotient is less than 3, and we may therefore conclude that the power consumption as function of N has a constant upper bound.

A modulo-100 counter has been realized on silicon in a 1μ CMOS process [vBBK$^+$93] (see also Section 9.1). In this circuit the output wire b_0 is fed back to b_1 via an *AND* gate. The observed count rate exceeds 80 megahertz at a 5 volts supply voltage. Discounting the above *AND* gate would result in a count rate of approximately 100 megahertz.

Simulation of the energy consumption of a modulo-100 counter yields 6 nanojoule for $a^{100} b$, about 60 picojoules per a handshake. These simulations have been confirmed by measurements. At a count rate of 80 megahertz this corresponds to a power consumption of less than 5 milliwatts.

Discussion

The presented modulo-N counter has been used to implement the Tangram construct $\#N[S]$: repeat command S exactly N times.

It takes four wires to connect neighboring cells by two undirected channels. This can be reduced to three wires by merging the two channels into a single directed channel of type *bool*, because the undirected channels are used strictly sequentially. The specification of the modulo-N counter becomes:

$$((c.true)^N \ c.false)^* \tag{2.9}$$

A suitable Tangram expression for cell CO is:

$$[\![\ x : \ \textbf{chan} \ bool \,|\, \#[c!true; \underline{c}?x; c!x] \ ]\!] \tag{2.10}$$

and for cell CE:

$$[\![\ x : \ \textbf{chan} \ bool \,|\, \#[\underline{c}?x; c!x; \ \textbf{if} \ x \rightarrow c!x \ [\!] \ \neg x \rightarrow skip \ \textbf{fi} \ ] \ ]\!] \tag{2.11}$$

The resulting counter circuit is slightly slower and larger.

An interesting property of the presented asynchronous realization of the modulo-N counter is that it features *constant power*: the power consumption as function of N has a constant upper bound. This property is unique to asynchronous realizations of the counter: any synchronous circuit uses at least $O(\log N)$ clocked flipflops and hence consumes $O(\log N)$ power.

Furthermore, the power consumption is proportional to the *actual* rate of counting. In particular, when standing-by the counter consumes no power at all, except for leakage. The power consumption of a synchronous circuit is proportional to the clock frequency, and may be substantial, even when the counter is inactive.

We take both properties as evidence that asynchronous circuits are potentially more power efficient than their synchronous counterparts.

2.5   Stacks

A stack is a *last-in, first-out* (LIFO) data structure, also known as a *push-down* stack. In its simplest form a stack has two ports, an input port through which a message can be *pushed* onto the stack, and an output port through which a message can be *popped* from the stack. We consider stacks of finite capacity N, with $N \geq 0$. In each state the stack shall be ready to engage in either a push or a pop operation. If the stack is empty, some appropriate value will be output after a pop request. If the stack is full, we are not interested in the stack content after a push.

After a simple version of a stack, two specializations will be described, viz. a low-power version and a priority queue. These examples introduce directed guards in choice commands: an input and an output guard combined into a single choice.

We intend to implement a stack of capacity $N + 1$ by extending a stack of capacity N with a *HEAD* cell, similar to the modulo-N counter. With a and b as input and output ports of $STACK_N$ and $\underline{a}$ and $\underline{b}$ as ports of $STACK_{N-1}$, this can be visualized as

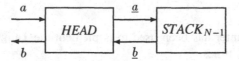

This decomposition yields a linear arrangement of N *HEAD* cells, connected to a cell for *STACK₀*. Similar decompositions can be found in [MC80, Mar89, KR90, JU90b]. For *STACK₀* we propose the program

$$(a?W \,\&\, b!W).[\![\; x : \textbf{var } W \mid \#[a?x] \mid\mid \#[b!C] \;]\!]$$

where C is some appropriate constant. A simple Tangram program for *HEAD* is

$$
\begin{aligned}
&(a?W \,\&\, b!W).\\
&[\![\quad x, y : \textbf{var } W\\
&\mid \quad \#[\quad [\; a?x \;;\; \underline{a}!y \;;\; y := x\\
&\qquad\qquad \mid b!y \;;\; \underline{b}?y\\
&\qquad\qquad]\\
&\qquad\quad]\\
&]\!]
\end{aligned}
$$

The current content of *HEAD* is stored in variable y. After an input through a, the current content is passed to the sub-stack, making y free to store the newly input value. As external and internal communications alternate, we may expect constant response time, as in [KR90]. Unlike the stacks of [KR90], the above stack does not have *maximum storage utilization*: the stack requires $2N + 1$ variables, as opposed to the logical minimum N.

Neither is the stack very efficient in its energy consumption. As *HEAD* responds to each external communication with an internal communication, a push or pop request to *STACK$_N$* results in N internal communications, similar to the stack of [MC80]. Unlike the clocked Mead & Conway stack, our stack does not consume energy when not being operated upon.

A handshake circuit for *HEAD* is given in Figure 2.10. Ports a and b are implemented as passive ports. The circuit introduces the *guard* handshake component, labeled 'G', in two versions, one for input guards (connected to a) and one for output guards (connected to b).

The output-guard component acts like a connector from b to i. However, the request for output through b is first passed to the selector through r. After this, the guard component waits for a grant along g. Only then the b request is passed along i. The subsequent incoming data through i is then passed through b, and is also used as a signal to produce an acknowledge through g. The operation of the input-guard component is similar.

Low-power version

A first specialization of the above stack is concerned with reducing the energy consumption, by avoiding transfers of the values stored in empty cells. We realize this by introducing a special value $\perp$ to denote "empty". The program for *STACK₀* requires only a minor modification:

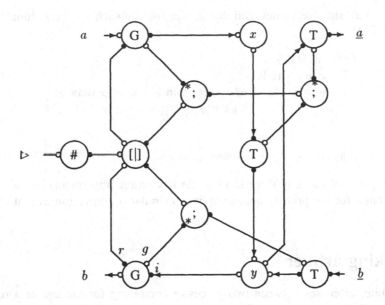

Figure 2.10: Handshake circuit for *HEAD*.

the constant C is to be replaced by the reserved value $\bot$. The program for *HEAD* becomes

```
(a?W & b!W).
[  x, y : var W
|  y := ⊥ ;#[  [ a?x ;   if y = ⊥ → skip [] y ≠ ⊥ → a!y fi ; y := x
           | b!y ;    if y = ⊥ → skip [] y ≠ ⊥ → b?y fi
           ]
]
]|
```

By assigning $\bot$ to variable y, cell *HEAD* is initialize to "empty". Communications with the sub-stack are guarded by the non-emptyness of *HEAD*. As a bonus, the stack indicates its empty status by outputting $\bot$.

The number of internal communications is reduced to the degree of filling of the stack. If we assume that the stack is half full in average, we have reduced the energy consumption per access by about a factor two. This reduction comes at the expense of additional hardware and delay to test the value of y.

Priority queue

A priority queue is a bag of values. It allows two operations: adding a new value, and removing the *maximum* value. Again, we restrict the capacity to N.

The implementation of the priority queue is actually a specialization of our first stack. Again, $\bot$ is used as a special value to denote the empty status of a cell. Moreover, we require that $\bot$

is comparable to all storable values, and that $\perp < x$ for any such value. A suitable Tangram program for *HEAD* is

$$(a?W \ \& \ b!W).$$
$$\textbf{[\!\![} \quad x, y : \textbf{var } W$$
$$\textbf{|} \quad y := \perp \ ; \#\textbf{[} \quad \textbf{[} \ a?x \ ; \ \underline{a}!(x \ \textbf{min} \ y) \ ; \ y := (x \ \textbf{max} \ y)$$
$$\textbf{|} \ b!y \ ; \ \underline{b}?y$$
$$\textbf{]}$$
$$\textbf{]}$$
$$\textbf{]\!\!]}$$

For a priority queue of capacity 0 we can use the low-power implementation of $STACK_0$. A low-power version for the priority queue requires a similar modification as that made to our original stack.

2.6   Nacking arbiter

A nacking arbiter arbitrates between two processes competing for the use of a resource. A request by one of the processes is either granted ("resource is free") or rejected ("resource is in use by the other process"). After a request has been granted the process can return the privilege by making a second request. After a request has been rejected the process may repeat the request --- if it still wants the resource --- or continue with something else instead. Hence, this arbiter is also known as non-blocking arbiter [JU90a] or arbiter with reject [ND91]. The problem was originally posed by Al Davis and Ken Stevens of Hewlett-Packard Laboratories, Palo Alto.

The nacking arbiter has been specified at the level of individual wires and voltage transitions on these wires, using a Delay Insensitive calculus [JU90a] or using a specialized form of Petri nets [ND91]. The purpose of our exercise is to show that the specification can be captured using synchronized communications as well, by presenting a Tangram program.

Our nacking arbiter has Boolean output ports a and b, to be connected to the two competing processes A and B. Grant and rejection are encoded by the values *true* and *false* respectively. The three states of the nacking arbiter are encoded in the Boolean variables na and nb, denoting "resource is *not* in use by A" and "resource is *not* in use by B" respectively. Both variables are initialized to *true*, corresponding to "resource is free". Based on the above choices, the Tangram program can be readily obtained:

$$(a!bool \ \& \ b!bool).$$
$$\textbf{[\!\![} \quad na, nb : \textbf{var } bool$$
$$\textbf{|} \quad na, nb := true, true$$
$$; \#\textbf{[} \quad \textbf{[} \ a!nb \ ; \ na := na \neq nb$$
$$\textbf{|} \ b!na \ ; \ nb := nb \neq na$$
$$\textbf{]}$$
$$\textbf{]}$$
$$\textbf{]\!\!]}$$

Notice that output commands are used as guards in the binary choice. The Tangram program for the nacking arbiter is both simple and remarkably concise. An initial asymmetry in the access privilege can be realized by initializing either *na* or *nb* to *false*.

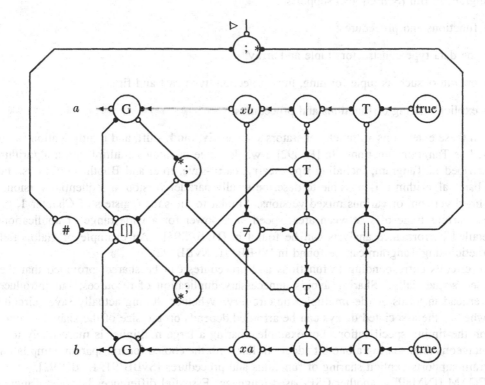

Figure 2.11: Handshake circuit for nacking arbiter.

The handshake circuit for the nacking arbiter is depicted in Figure 2.11. Output ports *a* and *b* are implemented as passive ports. The circuit requires two output-guard components.

Three wires suffice to implement each output channel: one for the request, one for granting the resource, and one for signaling the rejection, as in the circuits for the other published nacking arbiters. Obviously, arbitration between requests through *a°* and *b°* is required. Arbitration is resolved in the select component, labeled '[|]' in the handshake circuit of Figure 2.11.

2.7 Discussion

The programs and handshake circuits of this chapter give an impression of Tangram and its compilation into handshake circuits. The following remarks place the preceding examples in a wider perspective.

The programs presented so far are written in a subset of Tangram. We have seen the assignment, input, output, and synchronization as basic commands. In Chapter 1 we used sequential and parallel composition, as well as unbounded repetition to obtain structured commands. A block structure was used to restrict the scope of variable and channel names. This chapter introduced guarded selection, guarded repetition, and choice as further structuring primitives. Expressions were either of type *bool* or of a finite range of integers.

Tangram in full [Sch93] also supports:

- functions and procedures;

- the data type constructors tuple and array;

- operators such as tuple forming, tuple selection, type cast and fit;

- explicit sharing of functions and procedures.

With these extensions arithmetic operators such as **div**, **mod**, shift, and multiplication can be defined as Tangram functions. In [Haa92] a whole range of integer multiplication algorithms is described in Tangram, including ripple-carry, carry-save, tree, and Booth multipliers. For each basic algorithm it is possible to describe a fully parallel version, a sequential version, a pipe-lined version, or various mixed versions. Similar to the shift registers of Chapter 1, this allows various trade offs between area, speed, and power for a wide range of applications. A detailed performance analysis can be found in [HvBPS93]. An example of Galois-field arithmetic using Tangram can be found in [SvBB+91, KvBB+92].

The circuits corresponding to functions and procedures can be shared, provided that they are used sequentially. Sharing avoids unnecessary duplication of resources, but introduces an overhead in terms of (de-)multiplexing circuitry. Whether sharing actually saves circuitry and whether the associated delays can be afforded depends on the size of the shared resource and on the timing specification. For example, sharing a large multiplier is more likely to be advantageous than sharing a one-bit adder. In line with the choice for transparent compilation, Tangram supports explicit sharing of functions and procedures [SvBB+91, KvBB+92].

OCCAM [INM89] is another CSP-based language. Essential differences between Tangram and OCCAM are related to differences in the target implementation: VLSI circuits versus Transputer networks. In particular, OCCAM does not support output guards, broadcast, and sharing, and has limited facilities for type construction and operators.

To what extent are Tangram and handshake circuits general purpose? Neither Tangram nor handshake circuits contain constructs or notions that are specific to certain application areas. Applications range from very small circuits (e.g. the buffers of Section 1.0) to quite sizable circuits (e.g. a graphics processor [SvB88], or a high-throughput RSA encryptor [Kes91b]). Tangram and handshake circuits support fine-grained parallelism (as for instance in systolic arrays [Rem87]), as well as coarse-grained parallelism (e.g. in Compact Disc subsystems [KS90, KvBB+92]).

Many diverse applications were cited along with the programs in this chapter. Other examples of programs in CSP-based notations include: a micro-processor [MBL+89] and a regular-expression recognizer [KZ90]. A Tangram program for a very simple processor, together with an evaluation of the compiled and processed circuit can be found in Section 9.1.

Chapter 3

Handshake processes

3.0 Introduction

A handshake is a means of synchronization among communicating mechanisms. In its simplest form it involves two mechanisms connected by a pair of so-called *links*, one for sending signals and one for receiving signals. The sending of a signal and the reception of a signal are atomic actions, and constitute the possible events by which a mechanisms can interact with its environment.

A signal sent by one mechanism is bound to arrive at the other mechanism, after a finite, *non-zero* amount of time. Hence, this form of communication is asynchronous; the sending and the arrival of a signal correspond to two distinct events. It is assumed that a link allows at most one signal to be on its way. Consequently, a signal sent must arrive at the other end of the link before the next one can be sent. When the traveling time of a signal along the link is unknown, the *only* way to know that a signal has arrived at the other side is to be so informed by the other mechanism. The other link in the pair performs the acknowledgement.

Such a causally ordered sequence of events is called a handshake. The two mechanisms involved play different (dual) roles in a handshake. One mechanism has the *active* role: it starts with the sending of a request and then waits for an acknowledgement. The other mechanism has the *passive* role: it waits for a request to arrive and responds by acknowledging. A handshake realizes synchronization among mechanisms; it can and will occur only if both mechanisms are ready to participate.

Some useful terminology is introduced next. The pair of links forms a so-called *channel*; the two terminals of a channel are called *ports*. This study only considers channels with a fixed division of the passive and active roles during handshakes. Hence, a port is either passive or active, depending on its handshake role.

In a more general setting, a channel consists of two finite, non-empty sets of links. A handshake then consists of a request along a link of one set, acknowledged by a signal along a link from the other set. By choosing a particular link, a mechanism can convey additional information. For instance, a pair of output links suffices to communicate a Boolean value with each handshake. A mechanism may be connected to several other mechanisms, by an arbitrary number of channels, and may therefore have multiple ports, of different activities.

This chapter presents a formalism for mechanisms that interact exclusively by means of handshakes. The central notion is that of *handshake process*, a mathematical object that can be used to specify all possible behaviors of such a handshake mechanism. In Chapter 4 it is shown that handshake processes can also be used to describe the external behavior of handshake circuits, i.e. of networks of handshake processes. In Chapter 6 the semantics of a subset of Tangram is expressed in terms of handshake processes.

In the context of VLSI circuits, a mechanism may correspond to a CMOS circuit, a link to a wire and a signal to a voltage transition. The requirement that at most one signal may be on its way on a single link ensures the absence of transmission interference (cf. Section 0.1). Chapter 8 discusses in more detail the relationship between handshake processes and VLSI circuits.

Before delving into the mathematics of handshake processes we shall review some notational conventions used in this book.

3.1   Notational conventions

Functions

A function f in $A \rightarrow B$ has domain A and range B. Function application is denoted with an infix '$\cdot$' as in $f \cdot x$, instead of the more traditional $f(x)$. Operator '$\cdot$' binds more strongly than all other operators except for subscription and superscription (e.g. exponentiation). Furthermore, the '$\cdot$' is right-binding, that is $f \cdot g \cdot x = f \cdot (g \cdot x)$.

Guarded selection

An expression may have the form of a *guarded selection* as in:

$$
\begin{array}{lll}
\textbf{if} & B_0 & \rightarrow & E_0 \\
[] & B_1 & \rightarrow & E_1 \\
& \vdots & \\
[] & B_{N-1} & \rightarrow & E_{N-1} \\
\textbf{fi}
\end{array}
$$

Guarded expression $B_i \rightarrow E_i$ consists of *guard* B_i and *expression* E_i. A guard is a Boolean expression. The order of the alternatives is irrelevant. In the guarded selections of this book we shall see to it that at least one of the guards evaluates to *true*, and that if both B_i and B_j evaluate to *true* expressions E_i and E_j have the same value. For instance, the minimum of two integers, denoted by x **min** y may be defined as

$$
\begin{array}{lll}
\textbf{if} & x \leq y & \rightarrow & x \\
[] & y \leq x & \rightarrow & y \\
\textbf{fi}
\end{array}
$$

The notation for guarded selection strongly resembles that of guarded commands [DS90] (cf. the median filter in Section 2.1).

Quantified expressions

Universal quantification is a generalization of conjunction. Its format [DS90] is

$$(\forall \text{ dummies} : \text{range} : \text{term})$$

where

- "dummies" stands for an unordered list of local variables whose scope is delineated by the parenthesis pair;

- "range" is a predicate that delineates the domain of the dummies; and

- "term" denotes the quantified expression.

Similarly, existential quantification (with quantifier $\exists$) is a generalization of disjunction. Quantification over an empty range yields the unit element of the quantifier: *true* for $\forall$ and *false* for $\exists$. When the range is evident from the context it is usually omitted.

The above format is also applied to generalizations of other symmetric and associative binary operators. For instance, the continued union of the set of sets A is denoted by $(\cup a : a \in A : a)$. If $A = \emptyset$ this expression yields $\emptyset$, the unit element of set union.

For set construction a similar format is used, viz

$$\{\text{dummies} : \text{range} : \text{term}\}$$

For instance, the image of function f with domain D can be written as

$$\{x : x \in D : f \cdot x\}$$

Derivations

Let $\preceq$ be a partial order, i.e. $\preceq$ is a reflexive, antisymmetric and transitive relation on some set. For convenience' sake, we often abbreviate a conjunction of the form $(E = F) \wedge (F \preceq G)$ to $E = F \preceq G$. In particular, a proof of $E \preceq G$ may take the form (cf. [DS90])

$$
\begin{array}{ll}
\quad E & \\
= & \{ \text{ hint why } E = F \ \} \\
\quad F & \\
\preceq & \{ \text{ hint why } F \preceq G \ \} \\
\quad G &
\end{array}
$$

for some judiciously chosen F. The above example naturally generalizes to a list of (in-) equalities. From a derivation of the form $E \preceq F \preceq \cdots \preceq E$ it may be concluded that all related elements are equal, on account of transitivity and antisymmetry of $\preceq$. Note that implication ('$\Rightarrow$') and set inclusion ('$\subseteq$') are examples of partial orders. An example of a derivation is given below.

Closures

Let $(A, \preceq)$ be a preordered set, i.e. $\preceq$ is a reflexive and transitive relation on A. We shall often base a closure operator and a closedness predicate on such a preorder as follows.

Definition 3.0   (closure, closed)

   0. For any subset B of A the $\preceq$-*closure* of B in A, denoted by $B^{\preceq}$, is defined by

$$B^{\preceq} = \{a : a \in A \wedge (\exists b : b \in B : a \preceq b) : a\}$$

   This closure is also known as the *downward* closure of B.

   1. B is called $\preceq$-*closed*, denoted by $(\preceq) \cdot B$, if $B = B^{\preceq}$.

□

Operator $^{\preceq}$ is indeed a closure operation, since ([DP90] page 36):

Property 3.1

   0. $B \subseteq B^{\preceq}$ (extensive)

   1. $B^{\preceq} = (B^{\preceq})^{\preceq}$ (idempotent)

   2. $B \subseteq C \Rightarrow B^{\preceq} \subseteq C^{\preceq}$ (order preserving)

□

The closure operation binds more strongly than any other operation. As an example of the proof style applied, we prove idempotence of the above closure operation.

Proof   of idempotency :

   $(B^{\preceq})^{\preceq}$

$=$ { definition of $\preceq$-closure (twice) }

   $\{a : a \in A \wedge (\exists b : b \in \{c : c \in A \wedge (\exists d : d \in B : c \preceq d) : c\} : a \preceq b) : a\}$

$=$ { calculus }

   $\{a : a \in A \wedge (\exists b : b \in A \wedge (\exists d : d \in B : b \preceq d) : a \preceq b) : a\}$

$=$ { trading }

   $\{a : a \in A \wedge (\exists b, d : b \in A \wedge d \in B : a \preceq b \wedge b \preceq d) : a\}$

$=$ { $\preceq$ is reflexive and transitive }

   $\{a : a \in A \wedge (\exists d : d \in B : a \preceq d) : a\}$

$=$ { definition of $\preceq$-closure }

   $B^{\preceq}$

□

For later use we mention without proof:

Property 3.2

0. $\emptyset^{\preceq} = \emptyset$, hence $(\preceq)\cdot\emptyset$.

1. $B^{\preceq} \cup C^{\preceq} = (B \cup C)^{\preceq}$.

2. Hence, $(\preceq)\cdot B \wedge (\preceq)\cdot C \Rightarrow (\preceq)\cdot(B \cup C)$.

□

3.2 Handshake structures

Ports and port structures

A handshake through a port consists of two events: a request followed by an acknowledgement. We shall identify these events by symbols, such as r and a. A port consists of a set of request symbols and a set of acknowledgement symbols. These two symbol sets of port p must be non-empty, disjoint and finite, and will be denoted by $\mathbf{0}p$ and $\mathbf{1}p$ respectively. A handshake consists of an occurrence of an event from $\mathbf{0}p$ followed by an occurrence of an event of $\mathbf{1}p$. A port structure is a set of ports, partitioned into a set of passive ports and a set of active ports.

Definition 3.3 (port structure)

0. A *port* p is a pair of disjoint, finite, and non-empty sets of symbols $\langle \mathbf{0}p, \mathbf{1}p \rangle$. $\mathbf{a}p$ denotes the symbol set of p, viz. $\mathbf{0}p \cup \mathbf{1}p$.

1. A *port set* P is a finite (possibly empty) set of ports. $\mathbf{a}P$ is the set of symbols of P, viz. $(\cup p : p \in P : \mathbf{a}p)$.

2. A *proper port set* P is port set with disjoint symbol sets:

$$(\forall a, b : a \in P \wedge b \in P : a = b \vee \mathbf{a}a \cap \mathbf{a}b = \emptyset)$$

3. A *port structure* A is a pair $\langle A^{\circ}, A^{\bullet} \rangle$, of port sets, such that $A^{\circ} \cup A^{\bullet}$ is a proper port set. A° is called the *passive* port set of A and $A^{\bullet}$ the *active* port set of A. Note that $\mathbf{a}A^{\circ} \cap \mathbf{a}A^{\bullet}$ need not be empty.

   $\mathbf{a}A$ denotes the set of symbols of A, viz. $\mathbf{a}A^{\circ} \cup \mathbf{a}A^{\bullet}$. Set $\mathbf{a}A$ is called the *alphabet* of A.

4. Elements of $A^{\circ} \cap A^{\bullet}$ are the *internal* ports of port structure A, and elements of set $(A^{\circ} \setminus A^{\bullet}) \cup (A^{\bullet} \setminus A^{\circ})$ are the *external* ports of A.

5. Port structures A and B are *compatible* if $A^{\circ} \cup A^{\bullet} \cup B^{\circ} \cup B^{\bullet}$ is a proper port set.

6. The *union* of compatible port structures A and B, denoted by $A \cup B$, is the port structure $\langle A^{\circ} \cup B^{\circ}, A^{\bullet} \cup B^{\bullet} \rangle$.

7. The *difference* of compatible port structures A and B, denoted by $A \setminus B$, is the port structure $\langle A^\circ \setminus B^\circ, A^\bullet \setminus B^\bullet \rangle$.

□

The symbols $^\circ$ and $^\bullet$ are used as postfix operators on port structures; they bind more strongly than any other operator. If p is a passive port, $\mathbf{0}p$ is the set of the input symbols of p and $\mathbf{1}p$ the set of output symbols of p. For active ports this is the other way around:

Definition 3.4   (input and output symbols)

Let A be a port structure and let $a \in A$. Then

0. $\mathbf{i}a$ denotes the set of input symbols of port a:

$$
\begin{aligned}
\mathbf{i}a = \ &\mathbf{if} \ \ a \in A^\circ \ \ \rightarrow \ \ \mathbf{0}a \\
&[] \ \ a \in A^\bullet \ \ \rightarrow \ \ \mathbf{1}a \\
&\mathbf{fi}
\end{aligned}
$$

1. Operator $\mathbf{i}$ is lifted to port structures by $\mathbf{i}A = (\cup a : a \in A : \mathbf{i}a)$.

2. $\mathbf{o}a$ denotes the set of output symbols of port a:

$$
\begin{aligned}
\mathbf{o}a = \ &\mathbf{if} \ \ a \in A^\circ \ \ \rightarrow \ \ \mathbf{1}a \\
&[] \ \ a \in A^\bullet \ \ \rightarrow \ \ \mathbf{0}a \\
&\mathbf{fi}
\end{aligned}
$$

3. Operator $\mathbf{o}$ is lifted to port structures by $\mathbf{o}A = (\cup a : a \in A : \mathbf{o}a)$.

□

Obviously, we have $\mathbf{i}A \cup \mathbf{o}A = \mathbf{a}A$. If A has no internal ports then $\mathbf{i}A \cap \mathbf{o}A = \emptyset$.
Ports may be directed as well. An *input port* is a port that consists of multiple input symbols and a single output symbol. Accordingly, an *output port* is a port that consists of a single input symbol and multiple output symbols. A port that consists of two singleton sets will be referred to as a *nonput port*; it serves for mere synchronization. If both symbol sets contain more than one symbol, the port permits bidirectional transfer of data during each handshake; it may be referred to as a *biput port*. Bidirectional data transfer will not recur in the sequel.

Definition 3.5   (port definition)

A port definition defines a port structure that consists of a single port; it may have one of the six forms below. Let a be a name and T be a type, i.e. a non-empty set of values.

0. a°, $a^\circ?T$ and $a^\circ!T$ define port structures of the form $\langle \{p\}, \emptyset \rangle$, where p is a single (passive) port. For the three port definitions p denotes $\langle \{a_0\}, \{a_1\} \rangle$, $\langle \{a_0\} \times T, \{a_1\} \rangle$, and $\langle \{a_0\}, \{a_1\} \times T \rangle$ respectively.

1. Likewise, $a^\bullet$, $a^\bullet?T$ and $a^\bullet!T$ define port structures of the form $\langle \emptyset, \{p\} \rangle$, where p is a single (active) port. For the three port definitions p denotes $\langle \{a_0\}, \{a_1\} \rangle$, $\langle \{a_0\}, \{a_1\} \times T \rangle$, and $\langle \{a_0\} \times T, \{a_1\} \rangle$ respectively.

2. The name in the port definition will be used as *port name*.

3. A list of port definitions separated by commas defines a port structure, provided that the port names are distinct. The port structure is obtained by taking the union of the port structures specified by the individual port definitions.

□

Note that $a°$ and $a•$ define nonput ports, that $a°?T$ and $a•?T$ define input ports and that $a°!T$ and $a•!T$ define output ports.

Example 3.6

0. $a°?bool$ defines a port structure consisting of a single passive input port of type *bool*, viz. the port $\langle\{a_0 : false, a_0 : true\}, \{a_1\}\rangle$. The input symbols are $a_0 : false$ and $a_0 : true$ and the output symbol is a_1, the acknowledgement to an input.

1. $a°!bool$ defines a port structure consisting of a single passive output port of type *bool*, viz. the port $\langle\{a_0\}, \{a_1 : false, a_1 : true\}\rangle$. The input symbol a_0 denotes a request for an output. The output symbols are $a_1 : false$ and $a_1 : true$.

□

The alphabet of port structure A, denoted by $\mathbf{a}A$, was defined as the set of symbols that occur in the port definitions of port structure A. The symbols of an alphabet are used to denote individual communications between a mechanism and its environment. Finite symbol sequences are called traces.

Definition 3.7 (trace)

0. A *trace* is a finite sequence of symbols.

1. The *empty trace* is denoted by ε.

2. $len \cdot t$ denotes the length of t.

3. The *concatenation* of traces s and t is obtained by juxtaposition, as in st.

4. Trace s is called a *prefix* of t, denoted by $s \leq t$, if there exists a trace u such that $su = t$.

5. The set of all traces over alphabet B is denoted by B^*.

6. The *projection* of trace t on alphabet B, denoted by $t\lceil B$, is defined by

$$
\begin{aligned}
\varepsilon\lceil B &= \varepsilon \\
(at)\lceil B &= \mathbf{if} \quad a \notin B \quad \rightarrow \quad t\lceil B \\
&\quad\;[] \quad a \in B \quad \rightarrow \quad a(t\lceil B) \\
&\quad \mathbf{fi}
\end{aligned}
$$

If A is a port structure, $t\lceil A$ is used as a shorthand for $t\lceil(\mathbf{a}A)$.

□

Sets of traces will be used to characterize mechanisms. Each trace records a possible sequence of communication events in which a mechanism has engaged up to some moment in time. Prefix order is a partial order on traces. Hence, in accordance with Section 3.1, the *prefix closure* of trace set B is denoted by $B^{\leq}$, and the *prefix closedness* of trace set B by $(\leq)\cdot B$.

Given a port structure A, we consider traces over alphabet $\mathbf{a}A$. A *handshake trace* is a trace in which the occurrences of $\mathbf{0}$-symbols and $\mathbf{1}$-symbols of each port strictly alternate, and in which the first symbol occurrence of each port is a $\mathbf{0}$-symbol.

Definition 3.8   (handshake trace)

The set of handshake traces with port structure A is denoted by A^H and is defined as

$$\{t : t \in (\mathbf{a}A)^* \wedge (\forall a, s : a \in A \wedge s \leq t : 0 \leq len\cdot(s\lceil\mathbf{0}a) - len\cdot(s\lceil\mathbf{1}a) \leq 1) : t\}$$

□

Property 3.9

  0. $\langle\emptyset,\emptyset\rangle^H = \{\varepsilon\}$

  1. $(\leq)\cdot A^H$

  2. $\langle A^\circ, A^\bullet\rangle^H = \langle A^\bullet, A^\circ\rangle^H$

□

Definition 3.10   (handshake structure)

  0. A *handshake structure* S is a pair $\langle\mathbf{p}S, \mathbf{t}S\rangle$, in which $\mathbf{p}S$ is a port structure and $\mathbf{t}S$ a set of handshake traces, i.e. $\mathbf{t}S \subseteq (\mathbf{p}S)^H$.

  1. The prefix closure is extended to handshake structures by

$$S^{\leq} = \langle\mathbf{p}S, (\mathbf{t}S)^{\leq}\rangle$$

  2. Similarly, a handshake structure is $\leq$-closed if its trace set is.

□

Symbols $\mathbf{p}$ and $\mathbf{t}$ are used as operators on handshake structures. In the sequel R and S denote handshake structures. Also, the following shorthands are used:

  0. $\mathbf{p}^\circ S = (\mathbf{p}S)^\circ$

  1. $\mathbf{p}^\bullet S = (\mathbf{p}S)^\bullet$

  2. $\mathbf{a}S = \mathbf{a}(\mathbf{p}S)$

  3. $\mathbf{i}S = \mathbf{i}(\mathbf{p}S)$

  4. $\mathbf{o}S = \mathbf{o}(\mathbf{p}S)$

3.3 Handshake processes

A handshake process will be defined as a handshake structure that satisfies five conditions. Handshake processes are used to represent the external behavior of a mechanism. Hence, handshake process $\langle \mathbf{p}P, \mathbf{t}P \rangle$ has no internal ports, i.e. $\mathbf{p}^\circ P \cap \mathbf{p}^\bullet P = \emptyset$ (condition 0). Furthermore, trace set $\mathbf{t}P$ is required to be non-empty (condition 1).

In addition to the absence of internal ports and the presence of at least one handshake trace, three more conditions will be imposed, relating to progress, insensitivity to delays, and readiness to accept further inputs.

So far, we clearly distinguished physical objects such as mechanisms and events, from mathematical objects such as processes and symbols. Following Hoare [Hoa85] and others, this distinction will be adhered to less strictly. Whenever convenient, we use phrases such as "After process P has engaged in trace t, it is ready to accept input a".

Quiescence

Let t be a trace of handshake process P. After engaging in t, the environment may be unable to obtain further output from P. Usually, this happens simply because the behavior of P does not permit P to extend t with any output symbol. Even if t can be extended with an output symbol, P may (nondeterministically) choose not to do so, and remain idle. In either case, t is called a *quiescent trace* [Mis84, Jon85]. Process P may leave quiescence after the environment has supplied further input.

A handshake process will be represented by its quiescent traces. Following [Jos92], the set of all (observable) traces is then the prefix closure of the set of quiescent traces. The quiescent-trace set of a handshake process must include the traces that have no output successors, i.e. it must include all its *passive traces*.

Definition 3.11   (passive traces)

Let S be a handshake structure ($\mathbf{p}S$ may have internal ports), and let t be a trace of $\mathbf{t}S^{\leq}$.

  0. The *successor set* of t with respect to S, denoted by $suc\cdot(t, S)$, is

$$\{a : a \in \mathbf{a}S \wedge ta \in \mathbf{t}S^{\leq} : a\}$$

  1. t *is passive in* S, denoted by $pas\cdot(t, S)$, when $suc\cdot(t, S) \cap \mathbf{o}S = \emptyset$.

  2. S *is passive* when $pas\cdot(\varepsilon, S)$.

  3. The *passive restriction of* S, denoted by $Pas\cdot S$, is the handshake structure

$$\langle \mathbf{p}S, \{t : t \in \mathbf{t}S^{\leq} \wedge pas\cdot(t, S) : t\} \rangle$$

□

The following property follows directly from the above definition.

Property 3.12

For handshake structure S we have $Pas \cdot S = Pas \cdot S^{\leq}$.

□

For handshake process P, tP represents the set of quiescent traces. Condition 2 in the definition of a handshake process is therefore $tPas \cdot S \subseteq tS$.

An alternative way to look at the notion of quiescence is suggested by the following property.

Property 3.13

Let S be a handshake structure such that $tPas \cdot S \subseteq tS$. Then

$$t \in tS^{\leq} \;=\; (\exists u : u \in (oS)^{*} : tu \in tS)$$

Or put into words, for any trace t in $tS^{\leq}$, there is a trace u consisting of output symbols only, such that tu is in tS. Phrased differently, a handshake process can always become quiescent by producing outputs only.

Sketch of proof

Trace tu can be constructed as follows. Consider the successor set of t with respect of S. If this set does not contain any outputs, t is passive and therefore a member of tS. If this successor set contains an output, say a, then $ta \in tS^{\leq}$.

This extension is to be repeated until $suc \cdot (t, S) \subseteq iS$. The u thus obtained is indeed of finite length, because oS is finite, and u contains at most one symbol of each port. The resulting tu is passive by definition, and hence in tS.

□

Reordering

Let P be a handshake process and let t be an element of $tP^{\leq}$. Assume that, after engaging in t, the environment sends signals along links a and b to P, in that order, and that P is ready to receive them, that is, tab is also in $tP^{\leq}$. When no assumptions are made about the delays involved, a and b may arrive in the opposite order. Under such circumstances it is reasonable to require that tba is also in $tP^{\leq}$. Trace tba is said to *reorder* trace tab [Mis84, JHJ89]. A similar reordering must be allowed for two output symbols of P: for outputs c and d, trace tdc reorders tcd.

A slightly more subtle reordering is relevant when two symbols of opposite direction are involved, say input a and output c. Suppose tca is an element of $tP^{\leq}$. Apparently the input a was not required by P in order to output c. If a had experienced less delay it would have arrived before the output of c. Hence, trace tac reorders tca, *provided* that both tac and tca are handshake traces. The converse, tca reorders tac, does not hold, because input a may be a prerequisite for output c. A formalization of reordering of handshake traces is given by means of a binary relation r_B, where B is a port structure (B may have internal ports).

Definition 3.14 (reorders)

$\mathbf{R}_B$ is the smallest binary relation on $(iB \cup oB)^*$ with for all symbols $a, b \in (iB \setminus oB)$, all symbols $c, d \in (oB \setminus iB)$, and all symbols $e \in (iB \cap oB)$:

0. $ab \mathbf{R}_B ba$

1. $cd \mathbf{R}_B dc$

2. $ac \mathbf{R}_B ca$

3. $ae \mathbf{R}_B ea$

4. $ec \mathbf{R}_B ce$

and for all traces $r, s, t, u \in (iB \cup oB)^*$:

5. $t \mathbf{R}_B t$

6. $r \mathbf{R}_B s \wedge s \mathbf{R}_B t \Rightarrow r \mathbf{R}_B t$

7. $r \mathbf{R}_B s \wedge t \mathbf{R}_B u \Rightarrow rt \mathbf{R}_B su$

The sole purpose of introducing relation $\mathbf{R}_B$ is to define relation $\mathbf{r}_B$ on B^H as the restriction of $\mathbf{R}_B$ to handshake trace set B^H, i.e. for handshake traces $s, t \in B^H$ we define $s\mathbf{r}_B t$ as $s\mathbf{R}_B t$.

□

Relation $\mathbf{R}_B$ is the reorder relation "$\sqsubseteq$" of [JHJ89] *extended* to alphabets with common input and output symbols. Properties 3 and 4 are derived from 0 to 2 by requiring e to assume both the role of input and that of output. When $iB \cap oB = \emptyset$, relation $\mathbf{R}$ reduces to $\sqsubseteq$ cited above. This extension will appear useful when analyzing parallel compositions of handshake processes in Chapter 4. Note that $s \mathbf{R} t \Rightarrow len \cdot s = len \cdot t$. In the sequel we shall only use relation $\mathbf{r}_B$, which will usually be shortened to $\mathbf{r}$ when B is obvious from the context.

Since $\mathbf{r}$ is a preorder on B^H, $T^{\mathbf{r}}$ denotes the *reorder closure* of handshake-trace set T and $(\mathbf{r}) \cdot T$ denotes the reorder closedness of T (cf. Section 3.1). Both operators are lifted to handshake structures in the obvious way.

Property 3.15

Let B and C be compatible port structures, let $s, t \in B^H$, and let S be a handshake structure. Then

0. $(\mathbf{r}) \cdot B^H$

1. $s \ \mathbf{r}_{B \cup C} \ t \Rightarrow s \ \mathbf{r}_B \ t$

2. $s \mathbf{r} t \Rightarrow s \lceil C \ \mathbf{r} \ t \lceil C$

3. $(\mathbf{r}) \cdot S \Rightarrow (\mathbf{r}) \cdot (S \lceil C)$

4. $(\mathbf{r}) \cdot S \Rightarrow (\mathbf{r}) \cdot S^{\leq}$

□

Property 1 is a consequence of the judicious choice of the extension of **r**. Property 2 follows from 3.14.7, and Property 3 is a corollary of 2.

Proof   of 4. Let $t \in \mathbf{t}S^{\leq}$ and $u \in (\mathbf{p}S)^H$. We derive:

$$t \in \mathbf{t}S^{\leq} \wedge u \, \mathbf{r} \, t$$

=   { definition of $\leq$-closure }

$$(\exists v : v \in (\mathbf{a}S)^* : tv \in \mathbf{t}S) \wedge u \, \mathbf{r} \, t$$

⇒   { definition of **r** ; calculus }

$$(\exists v : v \in (\mathbf{a}S)^* : tv \in \mathbf{t}S \wedge uv \, \mathbf{r} \, tv)$$

⇒   { (**r**)$\cdot S$ }

$$(\exists v : v \in (\mathbf{a}S)^* : uv \in \mathbf{t}S)$$

=   { definition of $\leq$-closure }

$$u \in \mathbf{t}S^{\leq}$$

□

Example 3.16

The implication $(\leq)\cdot S \Rightarrow (\leq)\cdot S^{\mathbf{r}}$ does not hold in general, as shown by the following S. $\mathbf{p}S$ consists of two passive ports, viz. a° and b°. By definition, $\mathbf{i}S = \{a_0, b_0\}$ and $\mathbf{o}S = \{a_1, b_1\}$. The trace set of S is given by $\mathbf{t}S = \{a_0 b_0\}^{\leq}$.

Obviously, we have $(\leq)\cdot S$ and $a_0 b_0 \in \mathbf{t}S$. Also, with $u = b_0 a_0$, we have $u \in S^{\mathbf{r}}$. However, prefix b_0 of u is not an element of $S^{\mathbf{r}}$.

□

Condition 3 in the definition of a handshake process states that $\mathbf{t}P$ must be closed under reordering. By Property 3.15.4, $\mathbf{t}P^{\leq}$ is then reorder closed as well.

Receptiveness

A non-empty set of handshake traces that includes all its passive prefixes and that is closed under reordering is a good candidate for the definition of handshake processes. However, it turns out that certain operations on such handshake processes, including parallel composition, are complicated in their definitions and usage. A useful class of handshake processes with surprisingly simple properties is obtained by imposing an additional requirement.

Definition 3.17   **(input extension)**

Let B be a port structure, and let $t, tu \in B^H$. Handshake trace tu is an input extension of t in B, denoted by $tu \, \mathbf{x}_B \, t$, if $u \in (\mathbf{i}B \setminus \mathbf{o}B)^*$.

□

When B is obvious from the context, $\mathbf{x}_B$ will be shortened to $\mathbf{x}$. Also $\mathbf{x}$ is a clearly a preorder. Hence, $T^{\mathbf{x}}$ denotes the input-extension closure of handshake-trace set T, and $(\mathbf{x})\cdot T$ denotes input-extension closedness. Both operators are lifted to handshake structures in the obvious way. A handshake structure whose *prefix closure* is closed under input extension is called *receptive*. The notion of receptiveness is similar to that of [Dil89, JHJ89], albeit restricted to handshake traces.

Property 3.18

Let B and C be compatible port structures, let $s, t \in B^H$, and let S be a handshake structure. Then:

0. $(\mathbf{x})\cdot B^H$

1. $s \; \mathbf{x}_{B \cup C} \; t \;\Rightarrow\; s \; \mathbf{x}_B \; t$

2. $s \, \mathbf{x} \, t \;\Rightarrow\; s{\lceil}C \; \mathbf{x} \; t{\lceil}C$

3. $(\mathbf{x})\cdot S \;\Rightarrow\; (\mathbf{x})\cdot (S{\lceil}C)$

4. $(\mathbf{x})\cdot S \Rightarrow (\mathbf{x})\cdot S^{\mathbf{r}}$

5. $(\leq)\cdot S \Rightarrow (\leq)\cdot S^{\mathbf{x}}$

6. $(\mathbf{x})\cdot S^{\leq} \;\Rightarrow\; (\mathbf{x})\cdot (Pas\cdot S)^{\leq}$

□

Condition 4 in the definition of a handshake process states that its trace set must be receptive. As a result, the *only* obligation to be met by the environment is that it must adhere to the handshake protocol.

Handshake processes

By collecting the conditions stated so far, we obtain the complete definition of handshake processes:

Definition 3.19   (handshake process)

A handshake process is a handshake structure $\langle A, T \rangle$ that satisfies the following conditions:

0. $A^{\circ} \cap A^{\bullet} = \emptyset$ (no internal ports)

1. $T \neq \emptyset$ (non-empty trace set)

2. $t(Pas\cdot \langle A, T \rangle) \subseteq T$ (quiescence for passive traces)

3. $(\mathbf{r})\cdot T$ (reorder closed)

4. $(\mathbf{x})\cdot T^{\leq}$ (receptive)

$\prod \cdot A$ denotes the set of all handshake processes with port alphabet A.

□

Like CSP, handshake-process theory has no notion of fairness. Unlike CSP, there is not a notion of divergence. Consequently, the various causes for quiescence cannot be distinguished. In the sequel P and Q (possibly subscripted) denote handshake processes. Unless stated otherwise, the word process is used as a shorthand for handshake process.

For a port structure A the following generic processes are defined.

Definition 3.20

    0. *CHAOS·A* is the least predictable handshake process. It can engage in a handshake through any port at any time, and it can become quiescent at any time:

$$CHAOS \cdot A = \langle A, A^H \rangle$$

    1. *STOP·A* never engages in a handshake communication through any of its ports. Nevertheless, it does not refuse any input through a passive port; it simply does not respond to such an input:

$$STOP \cdot A = \langle A, \{\varepsilon\}^{\mathbf{X}} \rangle$$

    2. *RUN·A* is always willing to engage in a handshake through any of its ports:

$$RUN \cdot A = Pas \cdot CHAOS \cdot A$$

□

Note that $CHAOS \cdot \langle \emptyset, \emptyset \rangle = RUN \cdot \langle \emptyset, \emptyset \rangle = STOP \cdot \langle \emptyset, \emptyset \rangle = \langle \langle \emptyset, \emptyset \rangle, \{\varepsilon\} \rangle$. There is only one process with the empty port structure. More examples of handshake processes are presented next.

Example 3.21

    0. P_0 is prepared to engage once in a handshake through a°:

$$\langle a^\circ, \{\varepsilon, a_0 a_1, a_0 a_1 a_0\} \rangle$$

    1. P_1 is prepared to engage once in a handshake through $a^\bullet$:

$$\langle a^\bullet, \{a_0, a_0 a_1\} \rangle$$

    2. P_2 behaves like P_0: it participates in a handshake through a°, but it refuses to acknowledge an input through b°:

$$\langle a^\circ \cup b^\circ, \{\varepsilon\} \cup \{a_0 a_1\}^{\mathbf{X}\,\mathbf{r}} \rangle$$

which equals

$$\langle a^\circ \cup b^\circ, \quad \{\varepsilon, b_0$$
$$, a_0 a_1, a_0 a_1 b_0, a_0 b_0 a_1, b_0 a_0 a_1$$
$$, a_0 a_1 a_0, a_0 a_1 a_0 b_0, a_0 a_1 b_0 a_0, a_0 b_0 a_1 a_0, b_0 a_0 a_1 a_0\} \rangle$$

□

Even for such a simple behavior as P_2 the number of traces becomes considerable (11 quiescent traces!).

State graphs

A pictorial representation useful for handshake processes of modest complexity is the *state graph* accompanied by a port structure. A state graph is a directed graph in which arcs are labeled by symbols of the alphabet of the process. The nodes of a state graph are partitioned into a set of *quiescent* nodes and a set of *transient* nodes. Different arcs emanating from a node must have different labels.

A non-empty subset of the nodes contains the so-called start nodes; often there is exactly one start node. A path from a start node corresponds to the trace that is obtained by listing the labels of the consecutive arcs in the path. The empty path corresponds to the empty trace. A path ending in a quiescent node corresponds to a quiescent trace. A state graph is said to represent handshake process P if:

0. its accompanying port structure equals $\mathbf{p}P$;

1. each path that ends in a quiescent node corresponds to a trace in $\mathbf{t}P$, and vice versa;

2. each path that ends in a transient node corresponds to a prefix of a quiescent trace.

Note that:

0. if there are no outputs from a node, the node must be quiescent;

1. if there are several outputs from a transient node, it is nondeterministic which output occurs;

2. if there are one or more outputs from a quiescent node, it is nondeterministic whether an output occurs or the process refuses to output.

The following conventions are used when drawing state graphs:

0. Quiescent nodes are depicted by open circles, and transient nodes by filled ones.

1. A start node is enclosed by a concentric circle.

2. To avoid clutter, a node is occasionally depicted more than once. These multiple occurrences are labeled with a number unique to that node.

3. For clarity's sake, a question mark (exclamation mark) is attached to labels denoting input (output) symbols.

4. In some regularly drawn state graphs, the labeling of the arcs is incomplete. Arcs forming two opposite sides of a rectangle are then assumed to have the same label.

Example 3.22

0. Process P_2 of the previous example is depicted by the following state graph:

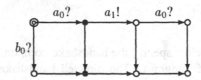

1. Process P_3 is prepared to engage once in a handshake through either a° or b°:

$$\langle a^\circ \cup b^\circ, \{\varepsilon\} \cup \{a_0a_1, b_0b_1\}^{\mathbf{x\,r}} \rangle$$

P_3 contains 19 quiescent traces as depicted by:

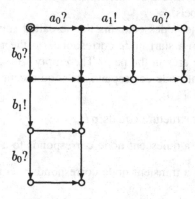

2. Process P_4 is like P_3, except that the choice between the two handshakes is made by the process itself:

$$\langle a^\circ \cup b^\circ, \{\varepsilon, a_0, b_0\} \cup \{a_0a_1, b_0b_1\}^{\mathbf{x\,r}} \rangle$$

P_4 contains 21 quiescent traces as depicted by:

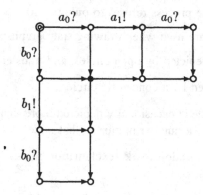

Trace a_0 is a quiescent trace. If P_4 choses internally for a handshake through b°, no progress is made after trace a_0. Similarly, P_4 may refuse to complete a handshake through b°.

□

Example 3.23

The handshake processes below specify the handshake components required for the translation of the undirected subset of Tangram. The directed handshake components are presented in

Example 5.37. Two examples, viz. *NMIX* and *NVAR*, describe *non-receptive* handshake structures, i.e. the environment may not always provide inputs. *NMIX* and *NVAR* will be used in Chapter 8 as cheaper substitutes for *MIX* and *VAR*.

Each handshake process is parameterized by a list of port names enclosed by parentheses. The ° and • postfixes indicate at the activity of these ports. The behavior of most components is represented by a state graph. The graphic symbol introduced for each component will be used in handshake-circuit diagrams in later chapters.

Let a, b and c be distinct names.

0. $STOP \cdot (a°)$ has port structure $a°$. It does not respond to a request through port $a°$.

1. $RUN \cdot (a°)$ has port structure $a°$. It acknowledges a request through $a°$ and returns to its initial state.

2. $CON \cdot (a°, b•)$ is a *connector*. It has port structure $a° \cup b•$ and each handshake through $a°$ encloses a handshake through $b•$.

3. $OR \cdot (a°, b•, c•)$ has port structure $a° \cup b• \cup c•$. Each handshake through $a°$ encloses either a handshake through $b•$ or one through $c•$.

4. $SEQ \cdot (a°, b•, c•)$ is a *sequencer*. It has port structure $a° \cup b• \cup c•$. A handshake through $a°$ encloses both a handshake through $b•$ and one through $c•$, in that order.

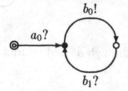

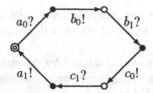

The asterisk marks the active port which handshakes first.

5. $DUP \cdot (a^\circ, b^\bullet)$ is a *duplicator*.   It has port structure $a^\circ \cup b^\bullet$. A handshake through a° encloses two handshakes through $b^\bullet$. The state graph can be obtained from the state graph of the sequencer by renaming events c_0 and c_1 to b_0 and b_1 respectively.

6. $REP \cdot (a^\circ, b^\bullet)$ is a *repeater*.   It has port structure $a^\circ \cup b^\bullet$. A handshake through a° encloses an unbounded repetition of handshakes through $b^\bullet$.

Note that the handshake through port a is never completed.

7. $PAR \cdot (a^\circ, b^\bullet, c^\bullet)$ has port structure $a^\circ \cup b^\bullet \cup c^\bullet$. A handshake through a° encloses both a handshake through $b^\bullet$ and one through $c^\bullet$, in parallel.

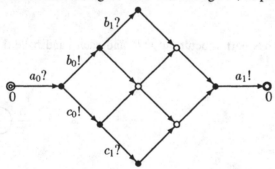

8. $NMIX \cdot (a^\circ, b^\circ, c^\bullet)$ has port structure $a^\circ \cup b^\circ \cup c^\bullet$. A handshake through $c^\bullet$ is enclosed by a handshake through either a° or b°. The environment must decide.

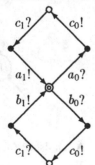

Note that $NMIX \cdot (a^\circ, b^\circ, c^\bullet)$ is *not* a handshake process, because it is not receptive: trace a_0 may not be extended with b_0 and vice versa. (*NMIX* stands for Non-receptive Mixer; cf. Section 8.2.)

9. $MIX \cdot (a^\circ, b^\circ, c^\bullet)$ has the same port structure as $NMIX \cdot (a^\circ, b^\circ, c^\bullet)$ and is obtained by ''making'' *NMIX* receptive as follows. First we take the input-extension closure of the prefix closure of *MIX*. The result is receptive, but also excessively nondeterministic, because it is prefix closed (cf. Property 3.18.4). By taking the passive restriction and then the reorder closure we obtain handshake process *MIX*. This transformation can be formalized as

$$(Pas \cdot NMIX \cdot (a^\circ, b^\circ, c^\bullet)^{\leq \mathbf{X}})^{\mathbf{r}}$$

Process $MIX \cdot (a^\circ, b^\circ, c^\bullet)$ is receptive on account of Property 3.18.6.

The trace set of *MIX* contains that of *NMIX*, but allows simultaneous handshakes on a° and b°. After trace $a_0 b_0 c_0 c_1$ *MIX* decides nondeterministically whether it will continue with a_1 or b_1. In environments where handshakes through a° and b° never overlap, $MIX \cdot (a^\circ, b^\circ, c^\bullet)$ may be replaced by a $NMIX \cdot (a^\circ, b^\circ, c^\bullet)$ (cf. Section 8.2).

10. $PAS \cdot (a^\circ, b^\circ)$ has two passive ports, viz. a° and b°. It synchronizes each handshake through a° with a handshake through b°.

In [Kal86] $PAS \cdot (a^\circ, b^\circ)$ was introduced as a *passivator*.

11. $JOIN \cdot (a^\circ, b^\circ, c^\bullet)$ resembles $PAS \cdot (a^\circ, b^\circ)$, but has an additional active port $c^\bullet$. A handshake through $c^\bullet$ is enclosed by handshakes through both a° and b°.

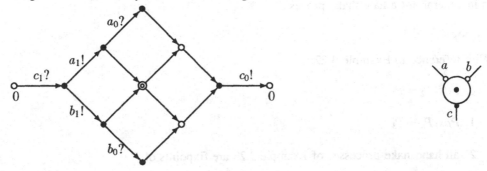

Note that $JOIN \cdot (a^\circ, b^\circ, c^\bullet)$ and $PAR \cdot (a^\circ, b^\bullet, c^\bullet)$ only differ in their arc labelings and in their start nodes.

12. $NVAR_{bool} \cdot (a^\circ, b^\circ)$ is a Boolean variable with write port $a^\circ?bool$ and read port $b^\circ!bool$. In the state graph below, the symbol names $a_0 : false$, $a_0 : true$, $b_1 : false$ and $b_1 : true$ are abbreviated by a_f, a_t, b_f and b_t respectively.

(x is used here as an instance name of the *NVAR* component; the type of the ports is assumed to be clear from the context.) Note that the state diagram has two initial states. The environment may start with a read request. *NVAR* then chooses nondeterministically between the values *false* and *true*.

For the same reason as *NMIX*, *NVAR* is not a handshake component: it is not receptive. The receptive counterpart of *NVAR* is obtained by the same transformation

$$VAR_{bool} \cdot (a^\circ, b^\circ) = (Pas \cdot NVAR_{bool} \cdot (a^\circ, b^\circ)^{\leq \mathbf{x}})^{\mathbf{r}}$$

Process *VAR* allows simultaneous read and write handshakes. Their order is nondeterministic.

□

Note that all handshake processes of Example 3.23 are passive.

Pas **and** *after*

The passive restriction of P, denoted $Pas \cdot P$, has been defined as a handshake structure with port structure $\mathbf{p}P$; the quiescent traces of $Pas \cdot P$ are those prefixes of $\mathbf{t}P$ that have input successors only (see Definition 3.11). *Pas* is clearly idempotent, and the passive restriction of a handshake process cannot have an empty trace set. Furthermore, it preserves receptiveness (Property 3.18.6). However, *Pas* does not always preserve reorder closedness. Hence, $Pas \cdot P$ is in general *not* a handshake process.

Example 3.24

With reference to Example 3.22:

0. $Pas \cdot P_2 = P_2$

1. $Pas \cdot P_4 = P_3$

2. all handshake processes of Example 3.23 are fixpoints of *Pas*

□

Next we define the behavior of a handshake process after trace t has been observed.

Definition 3.25   (after)

Let t be a handshake trace. The handshake structure $after \cdot (t, S)$ is defined by:

$$after \cdot (t, S) = \langle \mathbf{p}S, \{u : tu \in \mathbf{t}S : u\} \rangle$$

$\square$

Clearly, $P = after \cdot (\varepsilon, P)$. In general, however, $after \cdot (t, P)$ is not a handshake process. For instance, a trace of $after \cdot (t, P)$ may start with an acknowledgement to a request that occurred in t. For *closed* traces this is not a problem. A handshake trace is closed if every handshake started has also been completed.

Definition 3.26   (closed trace)

Handshake trace t, $t \in A^H$ is *closed*, denoted by $closed \cdot t$, if $len \cdot (t \lceil 0a) = len \cdot (t \lceil 1a)$ for all ports $a \in A$.

$\square$

Property 3.27

If $t \in \mathbf{t}P^{\leq}$ and $closed \cdot t$ then $after \cdot (t, P)$ is a handshake process.

$\square$

Example 3.28

With reference to Examples 3.22 and 3.23:

   0. $after \cdot (a_0 a_1, P_2) = STOP \cdot (a^{\circ} \cup b^{\circ})$

   1. $after \cdot (a_0 a_1, RUN \cdot a^{\bullet}) = RUN \cdot a^{\bullet}$ and

   2. $after \cdot (a_0 b_0 b_1 a_1, CON \cdot (a^{\circ}, b^{\bullet})) = CON \cdot (a^{\circ}, b^{\bullet})$

$\square$

3.4   The complete partial order $(\Pi \cdot A, \sqsubseteq)$

In this section we analyze the structure of $\prod \cdot A$, i.e. the set of all processes with port structure A. All processes in this section have port structure A. For convenience, $CHAOS \cdot A$ will be abbreviated to $CHAOS$. This section follows the lead of [BHR84, Hoa85].

Refinement order

First we introduce an order relation $\sqsubseteq$ among handshake structures.

Definition 3.29   (refinement)

Let S and T be handshake structures. S refines to T, denoted by $S \sqsubseteq T$, if $\mathbf{t}S \supseteq \mathbf{t}T$.

□

Let P and Q be handshake processes. Paraphrasing Hoare ([Hoa85], page 132) we may say that $P \sqsubseteq Q$ now means that Q is equal to P or better in that it is less likely to become quiescent. Q is more predictable than P, because if Q can do something undesirable, P can do it too; and if Q can become quiescent, so can P. *CHAOS* can do anything at any time, and can become quiescent at any time. True to its name, it is the least predictable and controllable of all handshake processes; or in short the worst. Refinement $\sqsubseteq$ is clearly a partial order on $\prod \cdot A$, with *CHAOS* as least element.

Expression $P \sqsubseteq Q$ can also be read as ''P specifies Q'', ''Q satisfies P'', or ''Q implements P''. One of the main reasons to choose a nondeterministic specification is to allow the implementor to select the cheapest or otherwise most attractive implementation that satisfies the specification. Conversely, nondeterminism in specifications permits the specifier to abstract from many of the implementation details.

Example 3.30

    0. $P \sqsubseteq Pas \cdot P$.

And with reference to Example 3.22:

    1. $P_4 \sqsubseteq P_2$, and $P_4 \sqsubseteq P_3$.

    2. $P_3 \not\sqsubseteq P_2$, and $P_2 \not\sqsubseteq P_3$. Neither P_2 nor P_3 can be refined any further.

□

Process P is maximal under $\sqsubseteq$ if any proper subset of $\mathbf{t}P$ violates the conditions of the definition of handshake process. With the aid of a state graph, this maximality can be easily checked. In terms of state graphs, there are two ways to reduce the trace set of the process it represents. One way is to turn a quiescent node into a transient node. This is allowed only when at least one output arc leaves that node (for instance the node reachable by trace a_0 in P_4). So, in the state graph of a maximal process all outputs must leave from a transient node. The other way to reduce the trace set is to remove one or more arcs. However, elimination of an input arc always results in a process that violates receptiveness. Elimination of an output arc is allowed only if its source node is quiescent, or if it shares its transient source node with another output arc. (Arc b_1 leaving the node reached by trace b_0 in process P_4 may be removed.) Of course, the removal of one or more arcs must also leave the process reorder closed.

The behavior of an assembly in which process P is one of the components may be described as a function F from processes (with port structure $\mathbf{p}P$) to processes. If P can be refined into Q, it is only reasonable to require that $F \cdot Q$ is at least as good as $F \cdot P$. In other words, F must then be *order preserving*.

Definition 3.31 (order preserving)

Function F from handshake structures to handshake structures is order preserving (alternatively called *monotone* or *isotone*), if it preserves refinement ordering, i.e. if

$$S \sqsubseteq T \;\Rightarrow\; F\!\cdot\!S \sqsubseteq F\!\cdot\!T$$

$\square$

Property 3.32

    0. Let $\preceq$ be a preorder on traces. Then the $\preceq$-closure on handshake structures is order preserving.

    1. Corollary: prefix closure, reorder closure and input-extension closure are order preserving.

$\square$

    A property of handshake processes that proves useful in the implementation of handshake components and handshake circuits is the following.

Definition 3.33 (initial when closed)

A handshake process P is *initial-when-closed* if for all *closed* traces $t \in tP^{\leq}$ we have

$$P \sqsubseteq after\!\cdot\!(t, P)$$

$\square$

When a closed trace of such a process has been observed, we may assume that the process is in an initial state. All processes of Example 3.23 are initial-when-closed. None of the processes of Example 3.22 are.

Complete partial order

The greatest lower bound of a set of handshake processes is obtained by taking the union of the respective trace sets.

Definition 3.34 (union)

The union of handshake structures S and T, denoted by $S \sqcap T$, is defined as $\langle A, tS \cup tT \rangle$.

$\square$

Property 3.35

If P and Q are handshake processes, then $P \sqcap Q$ is also a handshake process.

$\square$

In Section 3.5 we shall interpret $P \sqcap Q$ as the nondeterministic composition of processes P and Q. The least upper bound of a set of handshake processes does not in general exist in $\prod \cdot A$. If it exists, it is obtained by intersecting the trace sets.

Definition 3.36   (intersection)

The intersection of handshake structures S and T, denoted by $S \sqcup T$, is defined as $\langle A, \mathbf{t}S \cap \mathbf{t}T \rangle$.

□

For a chain of processes, it will be shown that the continued $\sqcup$ is a process.

Definition 3.37   (chain, limit)

0. An (ascending) *chain* is defined as an infinite sequence $(i : 0 \le i : S_i)$ of handshake structures, such that $S_i \sqsubseteq S_{i+1}$.

1. For chain $(i : 0 \le i : S_i)$ the *limit* is defined as the the continued intersection of the handshake structures in the chain, viz.

$$(\sqcup i : 0 \le i : S_i)$$

    which equals

$$\langle A, \{t : (\forall i : 0 \le i : t \in \mathbf{t}S_i) : t\}\rangle$$

□

The following properties of limits are useful.

Property 3.38

0. Let $\preceq$ be a preorder on traces, and let $(i : 0 \le i : S_i)$ be a chain of $\preceq$-closed processes. Then the limit $(\sqcup i : 0 \le i : S_i)$ is $\preceq$-closed as well.

1. Corollary: the above applies specifically for prefix closedness, reorder closedness, and input-extension closedness.

2. Let chain $(i : 0 \le i : S_i)$ be such that $\mathbf{t}Pas \cdot S_i \subseteq \mathbf{t}S_i$. Then

$$\mathbf{t}Pas \cdot (\sqcup i : 0 \le i : S_i) \subseteq \mathbf{t}(\sqcup i : 0 \le i : S_i)$$

Proof   of 0 (i ranges over the natural numbers). We derive:

$t \in (\sqcup i :: S_i)$

$=$ { definition of limit }

$(\forall i :: t \in S_i)$

$=$ { S_i are closed under $\preceq$ }

$(\forall i :: (\forall u : u \preceq t : u \in S_i))$

=   { calculus }

   $(\forall u : u \preceq t : (\forall i :: u \in S_i))$

=   { definition of limit }

   $(\forall u : u \preceq t : u \in (\sqcup i :: S_i))$

□

Another property of functions related to limits is continuity.

Definition 3.39   (continuous)

Let F be a function from handshake structures to handshake structures and let $(i : 0 \leq i : S_i)$ be a chain of handshake structures. F is (upward) *continuous* if it satisfies:

$$(\sqcup i : 0 \leq i : F \cdot S_i) \;=\; F \cdot (\sqcup i : 0 \leq i : S_i)$$

□

Continuity of a function from handshake structures to any CPO is defined similarly. The predicate $\preceq$-closedness is generally not continuous. For some preorders the $\preceq$-closures are continuous (see e.g. Property 3.41), but *not* for all, as shown by the following example.

Example 3.40

Consider the chain $(i : 0 \leq i : S_i)$, with $S_i = \langle a^\circ, \{j : i \leq j : (a_0 a_1)^j\} \rangle$. Then $(\sqcup i :: S_i^{\leq}) = \langle a^\circ, (a^\circ)^H \rangle$ and $(\sqcup i :: S_i)^{\leq} = \langle a^\circ, \emptyset \rangle$.

□

The following property claims continuity for two specific preorders on traces.

Property 3.41

   0. **r**-closure is continuous.

   1. **x**-closure is continuous.

Proof   of 0. Let $(i : 0 \leq i : S_i)$ be a chain and let t be a trace of $(\sqcup i :: S_i^{\mathbf{r}})$. Furthermore, let U_i be the set $\{u : u \in S_i \land t \mathbf{\,r\,} u : u\}$. Note that U_i depends on t. Clearly, $(i : 0 \leq i : U_i)$ is also a chain. We derive:

   $t \in (\sqcup i :: S_i^{\mathbf{r}})$

=   { definitions of **r**-closure and of limit }

   $(\forall i :: (\exists u : t \mathbf{\,r\,} u : u \in S_i))$

=   { definition of U_i }

   $(\forall i :: (\exists u :: u \in U_i))$

=   { $(i : 0 \leq i : U_i)$ is chain; $|\, U_i \,|$ is finite }

$(\exists u :: (\forall i :: u \in U_i))$

=   { definition of U_i }

$(\exists u : t \mathbf{\, r \,} u : (\forall i :: u \in S_i))$

=   { definitions of limit and of r-closure }

$t \in (\sqcup i :: S_i)^{\mathbf{r}}$

$\square$

The above limit properties form the introduction to the following theorem.

Theorem 3.42

The limit of a chain of processes is a process.

Proof   Follows from Properties 3.38 and 3.41.

$\square$

Definition 3.43   (complete partial order, CPO)

Partial order $\langle Z, \preceq \rangle$ is complete if

   0. Z contains a least element, and

   1. every chain in Z has a limit.

$\square$

   From Theorem 3.42 we infer:

Corollary 3.44

Partial order $(\prod \cdot A, \sqsubseteq)$ is a CPO with $CHAOS \cdot A$ as least element and $(\sqcup i : 0 \leq i : P_i)$ as limit of chains $(i : 0 \leq i : P_i)$.

$\square$

Property 3.45

For chain $(i : 0 \leq i : S_i)$ we have for all j: $P_j \sqsubseteq (\sqcup i : 0 \leq i : S_i)$.

$\square$

   One reason why we took all the trouble to prove that $(\prod \cdot A, \sqsubseteq)$ is a CPO, is that the least fixpoint for equations of the form $P = F \cdot P$, with F a continuous function, can be constructed straightforwardly within a CPO. This allows the definition of handshake processes by means of recursion. Recursive process definitions will be discussed in Chapter 5.

3.5   Nondeterminism

In contrast to CSP, the maximal elements of the partial order $\sqsubseteq$ are not necessarily deterministic. Nondeterministic behavior may exhibit itself in two forms:

0. a process may have the choice of performing an output or becoming quiescent;

1. a process may choose between two outputs, where the choice of one of the outputs disables the other.

This is formalized below.

Definition 3.46   (deterministic handshake process)

Handshake process $\langle A, T \rangle$ is deterministic if for all distinct output symbols a and b:

0. $ta \in T^{\leq} \Rightarrow t \notin T$

1. $ta \in T^{\leq} \wedge tb \in T^{\leq} \Rightarrow tab \in T^{\leq}$

□

Example 3.47

All processes presented so far are deterministic, except P_3 and P_4 in Example 3.22 and $OR \cdot (a^{\circ}, b^{\bullet}, c^{\bullet})$, $MIX \cdot (a^{\circ}, b^{\circ}, c^{\bullet})$, $NVAR_{bool} \cdot (a^{\circ}, b^{\circ})$ and $VAR_{bool} \cdot (a^{\circ}, b^{\circ})$ in Example 3.23, and, of course, $CHAOS \cdot A$. $RUN \cdot A$ is deterministic only if A consists exclusively of nonput ports and input ports. Note that $NMIX \cdot (a^{\circ}, b^{\circ}, c^{\bullet})$ is deterministic, albeit not receptive. $NVAR_{bool} \cdot (a^{\circ}, b^{\circ})$ is nondeterministic, because after a trace b_0 the variable may reply with either $b_0 : false$ or $b_0 : true$.

□

An interesting and useful classification of *non*-deterministic asynchronous processes has been suggested by Tom Verhoeff [Ver89], on which we base the following definition.

Definition 3.48   (static and dynamic nondeterminism)

Nondeterministic process P is *statically* nondeterministic if it can be refined into a deterministic process, and *dynamically* nondeterministic otherwise.

□

Example 3.49

With reference to Examples 3.22 and 3.23:

0. P_4 and $OR \cdot (a^{\circ}, b^{\bullet}, c^{\bullet})$ are statically nondeterministic; the former can be refined into (for instance!) P_2 and the latter to $CON \cdot (a^{\circ}, b^{\bullet})$ with $c^{\bullet}$ added to its port structure.

1. P_3 and $MIX \cdot (a^{\circ}, b^{\circ}, c^{\bullet})$ are dynamically nondeterministic, in spite of their maximality under $\sqsubseteq$.

2. Note that the statically nondeterministic P_4 can also be refined into the dynamically nondeterministic P_3 .

□

Dynamically nondeterministic processes require arbiters for their implementation.

Nondeterministic composition

Process $P \sqcap Q$ ("P or Q") behaves exactly like P *or* like Q. The choice between P and Q is nondeterministic.

Property 3.50

  0. Nondeterministic composition is idempotent, order preserving, commutative, associative, distributive, and continuous.

  1. $P \sqcap Q \sqsubseteq P$.

□

If a process is specified by $P \sqcap Q$, the implementor is free to select either P or Q as an implementation. For order preserving F we obviously have

$$F \cdot (P \sqcap Q) \sqsubseteq F \cdot P \sqcap F \cdot Q$$

A stronger property of functions on handshake processes is [BHR84] is *distributivity*:

Definition 3.51 (distributivity)

  0. A function F from handshake processes to handshake processes is *distributive* if

$$F \cdot (P \sqcap Q) = F \cdot P \sqcap F \cdot Q$$

  1. A function of two or more arguments is called distributive if it is distributive in each argument separately.

□

Distributive functions are clearly order preserving. Nondeterministic composition is distributive, since

$$P \sqcap (Q \sqcap R) = (P \sqcap Q) \sqcap (P \sqcap R)$$

Example 3.52

  0. Let $\preceq$ be a preorder on traces. Then the $\preceq$-closure on handshake structures is distributive.

  1. Corollary: prefix closure, reorder closure and input-extension closure are distributive.

□

Chapter 4

Handshake circuits

4.0 Introduction

The most interesting operation on handshake processes is parallel composition. Parallel composition is defined only for *connectable* processes. Connectability of handshake processes captures the idea that ports form the unit of connection (as opposed to individual port symbols), and that a passive port can only be connected to a single active port and vice versa. A precise definition will be given later.

The communication between connectable handshake processes is asynchronous: the sending of a signal by one process and the reception of that signal by another process are two distinct events. Asynchronous communication is more complicated than synchronized communication, because of the possible occurrence of *interference*. The concept of interference with respect to voltage transitions has been mentioned in Section 0.1. Interference with respect to symbols occurs when one process sends a symbol and the other process is not ready to receive it. The receptiveness of handshake processes and the imposed handshake protocol exclude the possibility of interference. We are therefore allowed to apply the simpler synchronized communication in the definition of parallel composition of handshake processes.

Another complication is, however, the possibility of *divergence*: an unbounded amount of internal communication, which cannot be distinguished externally from deadlock. From an implementation viewpoint divergence is undesirable: it forms a drain on the power source, without being productive.

The external behavior of the parallel composition of connectable P and Q will be denoted by $P \parallel Q$, which is again a handshake process. Both internal and external behavior of the parallel composition of two processes will be analyzed in detail in Section 4.1.

Section 4.2 introduces handshake circuits. A handshake circuit is a finite set of pairwise connectable handshake processes. The external behavior of a handshake circuit is again a handshake process, and is uniquely defined by $\parallel$, due to the associativity and commutativity of $\parallel$.

Handshake processes form a special class of so-called *delay-insensitive* processes. Delay-insensitive processes and their parallel (de-)compositions have been studied extensively (references will be given later). Some facts about handshake processes and their compositions are stated in terms of the existing theory on delay-insensitivity in Appendix A, including:

- handshake processes are delay-insensitive;

73

- ports of handshake processes are *independent*;

- handshake circuits are free of interference.

4.1   Parallel composition

First we must agree on how to specify connectivity between two handshake processes, say P and Q. A convenient way to specify connectivity is by identity of ports, that is, port a of P is connected to port b of Q if a and b consist of the same sets of symbols. In order to exclude various forms of "partial connections", we require that ports of P and Q are either identical, or have disjoint symbol sets: the port structures of P and Q must be compatible (cf. Definition 3.3). Furthermore, we exclude connections between two passive ports or two active ports, because this would imply the connection of outputs to outputs. In short, P and Q must be *connectable*. This notion is defined together with the *reflection* of a port structure next.

Definition 4.0   (connectability, reflection)

0. Port structures A and B are *connectable*, denoted by $A \bowtie B$, if

   (a) A and B are compatible, and

   (b) $A^\circ \cap B^\circ = \emptyset$ and $A^\bullet \cap B^\bullet = \emptyset$

1. Two handshake structures are connectable if their respective port structures are connectable.

2. The *reflection* of port structures A, denoted by $\overline{A}$, is defined by:

$$\overline{\langle A^\circ, A^\bullet \rangle} = \langle A^\bullet, A^\circ \rangle$$

□

Connectability and reflection enjoy the following obvious properties.

Property 4.1

0. $A \bowtie \emptyset$

1. $A \bowtie B = B \bowtie A$

2. $\mathbf{a}A \cap \mathbf{a}B = \emptyset \;\Rightarrow\; A \bowtie B$

3. $A \bowtie \overline{A}$

4. $A = \overline{\overline{A}}$

□

Example 4.2

0. $a^\circ \bowtie a^\bullet$

1. $a^\circ?bool \bowtie a^\bullet!bool$

2. $P \bowtie CHAOS \cdot \overline{\mathbf{p}P}$

3. $SEQ \cdot (a^\circ, b^\bullet, c^\bullet) \bowtie MIX \cdot (b^\circ, c^\circ, d^\bullet)$

4. $MIX \cdot (a^\circ, b^\circ, c^\bullet) \bowtie SEQ \cdot (c^\circ, d^\bullet, e^\bullet)$

$\Box$

In what follows we assume that P and Q are connectable handshake processes. Now we are ready to analyze the interaction between P and Q. Let C be the set of internal ports, viz. $(\mathbf{p}^\circ P \cap \mathbf{p}^\bullet Q) \cup (\mathbf{p}^\bullet P \cap \mathbf{p}^\circ Q)$, let port $p \in C$, and let a be an element of $\mathbf{a}p$, such that $a \in (iP \cap oQ)$. Furthermore, let $t \in \mathbf{t}P^\leq$ and $u \in \mathbf{t}Q^\leq$, and let this pair of traces specify the current state.

In general, $t\lceil C \neq u\lceil C$, because symbols sent by one process need not have arrived at the other process yet. Even if all sent symbols have arrived, t and u may differ due to reordering. Assume that event a may occur next as an output of Q, i.e. trace $ua \in \mathbf{t}Q^\leq$. By outputting a, process Q either starts a handshake (if $a \in \mathbf{0}p$), or acknowledges a handshake (if $a \in \mathbf{1}p$). Because at most one symbol can be on its way in a channel, we may conclude that $u\lceil p = t\lceil p$. The question now is: is P ready to input a? I.e., is ta in $\mathbf{t}P^\leq$?

The following simple reasoning shows that this is so. Since Q is a handshake process, trace ua must be a handshake trace, and therefore $ua\lceil p$ and $ta\lceil p$ are also handshake traces. With t a handshake trace, ta must be a handshake trace as well. Because P is receptive, it must be prepared to extend t with a. Hence, $ta \in \mathbf{t}P^\leq$: the arrival of a at P does not cause interference. Similar reasoning holds for $a \in (oP \cap iQ)$, because of symmetry. Absence of interference for sets of processes is defined in Appendix A.

The interaction through common ports restricts the behavior of P and Q; not all traces of P can occur in the presence of Q and vice versa. Let the prefix-closed trace sets P' and Q' denote the respective restricted behaviors. The above reasoning suggests that $P'\lceil C = Q'\lceil C$. It is because of this that the *weave* [vdS85] of P and Q is useful in the definition of $P \parallel Q$.

Definition 4.3   (weave)

For connectable handshake structures R and S, we define the *weave* of R and S, denoted by $R \mathbf{w} S$, as

$$\langle A, \{t : t \in A^H \wedge t\lceil \mathbf{p}R \in \mathbf{t}R \wedge t\lceil \mathbf{p}S \in \mathbf{t}S : t\} \rangle$$

where $A = \mathbf{p}R \cup \mathbf{p}S$.

$\Box$

The following properties will be used. See [vdS85] for similar properties and proofs.

Property 4.4

Let R, S and T be three mutually connectable handshake structures.

　0. $R \mathbf{w} \, CHAOS \cdot \langle \emptyset, \emptyset \rangle = R$

　1. $R \mathbf{w} \, S = S \mathbf{w} \, R$

　2. $(R \mathbf{w} \, S) \mathbf{w} \, T = R \mathbf{w} \, (S \mathbf{w} \, T)$

□

Some properties of handshake structures are preserved with weaving.

Property 4.5

Let R and S be connectable handshake structures.

　0. $(\le) \cdot R \wedge (\le) \cdot S \;\Rightarrow\; (\le) \cdot (R \mathbf{w} \, S)$

　1. $(\mathbf{r}) \cdot R \wedge (\mathbf{r}) \cdot S \;\Rightarrow\; (\mathbf{r}) \cdot (R \mathbf{w} \, S)$

　2. $(\mathbf{x}) \cdot R \wedge (\mathbf{x}) \cdot S \;\Rightarrow\; (\mathbf{x}) \cdot (R \mathbf{w} \, S)$

Proof

　0. Similar to Property 1.17 in [vdS85].

　1. Let $\mathbf{r}_R$, $\mathbf{r}_S$ and $\mathbf{r}_{RS}$ denote $\mathbf{r} \, \mathbf{p}_R$, $\mathbf{r} \, \mathbf{p}_S$ and $\mathbf{r} \, \mathbf{p}_{R \cup pS}$ respectively. We derive:

$$t \in \mathbf{t}(R \mathbf{w} \, S) \wedge s \, \mathbf{r}_{RS} \, t$$

$=$　　{ Definition 4.3 (weaving) }

$$t \lceil \mathbf{a}R \in \mathbf{t}R \wedge t \lceil \mathbf{a}S \in \mathbf{t}S \wedge s \, \mathbf{r}_{RS} \, t$$

$\Rightarrow$　　{ Property 3.15.2 (twice) }

$$t \lceil \mathbf{a}R \in \mathbf{t}R \wedge s \lceil \mathbf{a}R \, \mathbf{r}_{RS} \, t \lceil \mathbf{a}R \wedge t \lceil \mathbf{a}S \in \mathbf{t}S \wedge s \lceil \mathbf{a}S \, \mathbf{r}_{RS} \, t \lceil \mathbf{a}S$$

$\Rightarrow$　　{ Property 3.15.1 (twice) }

$$t \lceil \mathbf{a}R \in \mathbf{t}R \wedge s \lceil \mathbf{a}R \, \mathbf{r}_R \, t \lceil \mathbf{a}R \wedge t \lceil \mathbf{a}S \in \mathbf{t}S \wedge s \lceil \mathbf{a}S \, \mathbf{r}_S \, t \lceil \mathbf{a}S$$

$\Rightarrow$　　{ R and S are reorder closed }

$$s \lceil \mathbf{a}R \in \mathbf{t}R \wedge s \lceil \mathbf{a}S \in \mathbf{t}S$$

$=$　　{ definition of weaving }

$$s \in \mathbf{t}(R \mathbf{w} \, S)$$

　2. Similar to 1.

□

Property 4.6

Let R and S be connectable handshake structures.

   0. $t(R \mathbf{w} S)^{\leq} \subseteq t(R^{\leq} \mathbf{w} S^{\leq})$

   1. $tPas \cdot (R \mathbf{w} S) \subseteq t(Pas \cdot R \mathbf{w} Pas \cdot S)$

Proof

   0. Similar to Property 1.18 in [vdS85].

   1. Similar to Property 4.5.1.

□

The following property of weaving will be used as a lemma in Theorem 4.12.

Property 4.7

Let P and Q be handshake processes. Then

$$t \in t(P^{\leq} \mathbf{w} Q^{\leq})$$
$$\Rightarrow \ t \in t(P \mathbf{w} Q) \vee (\exists u : u \in (oP \cup oQ)^* \ \wedge \ tu \in t(P^{\leq} \mathbf{w} Q^{\leq}) : u \neq \varepsilon)$$

Proof   Let $t \in (\mathbf{p}P \cup \mathbf{p}Q)^H$. We derive:

   $t \in t(P^{\leq} \mathbf{w} Q^{\leq})$

$=$ { definition of weaving }

   $t \lceil \mathbf{a}P \in tP^{\leq} \ \wedge \ t \lceil \mathbf{a}Q \in tQ^{\leq}$

$\Rightarrow$ { Property 3.13 (twice) }

   $(\exists v, w : v \in (oP)^* \wedge w \in (oQ)^* : (t \lceil \mathbf{p}P)v \in tP \ \wedge \ (t \lceil \mathbf{p}Q)w \in tQ)$

$\Rightarrow$ { P and Q are receptive; $Q^{\leq}$ is reorder closed }

      $(t \lceil \mathbf{p}P \in tP \ \wedge \ t \lceil \mathbf{p}Q \in tQ)$
   $\vee \ \ (\ \exists v, w : v \in (oP)^* \wedge w \in (oQ)^*$
      $:\ tvw \lceil \mathbf{p}P \in tP^{\leq} \ \wedge \ tvw \lceil \mathbf{p}Q \in tQ^{\leq} \ \wedge \ (v \neq \varepsilon \vee w \neq \varepsilon)$
      $)$

$\Rightarrow$ { $u = vw$; definition of weaving (twice); calculus; trading }

   $t \in t(P \mathbf{w} Q) \vee (\exists u : u \in (oP \cup oQ)^* \ \wedge \ tu \in t(P^{\leq} \mathbf{w} Q^{\leq}) : u \neq \varepsilon)$

□

So far we have ignored quiescence in analyzing the parallel composition of two processes, by looking at the prefix closures of the trace sets only. Fortunately, the weave also captures quiescence, because a parallel composition is quiescent if and only if both components are. This makes the weave an attractive composition operator. However, the weave of two processes is *not* a handshake process, because of its internal ports. By concealing the internal ports and projection of the quiescent traces of the weave on the external ports, we obtain a handshake structure that represents the externally observable behavior of a parallel composition, in most cases. This form of parallel composition is known as *blending* [vdS85].

Definition 4.8   (blending; external port structure)

    0. The *blend* of handshake processes P and Q, denoted by P **b** Q, is defined as

$$(P \ \mathbf{w}\ Q)\lceil \mathbf{e}(\mathbf{p}P \cup \mathbf{p}Q)$$

    where $\mathbf{e}(\mathbf{p}P \cup \mathbf{p}Q)$ is the external port structure, defined next.

    1. The *external port structure* of port structure A, denoted by $\ \mathbf{e}\ A$, is the port structure $A \setminus \overline{A}$, which is equivalent to $\langle A^\circ \setminus A^\bullet, A^\bullet \setminus A^\circ \rangle$ (cf. Definition 3.3).

□

Unfortunately, the blend of two handshake processes is not a handshake process in general, as shown by the following example.

Example 4.9

Consider the parallel composition of $REP{\cdot}(a^\circ, b^\bullet)$ and $RUN{\cdot}b^\circ$. The former includes the traces $\varepsilon, a_0 b_0$ and $a_0 b_0 b_1 b_0$, the latter includes $\varepsilon, b_0 b_1$ and $b_0 b_1 b_0 b_1$.

    The handshake structure $REP \cdot (a^\circ, b^\bullet) \ \mathbf{w}\ RUN \cdot b^\circ$ contains exactly one trace, viz. ε. No other trace is quiescent: after trace a_0 processes $REP{\cdot}(a^\circ, b^\bullet)$ and $RUN{\cdot}b^\circ$ "play ping-pong" indefinitely. Concealment of b has of course no effect on this trace set. However, the resulting blend $\langle a^\circ, \{\varepsilon\}\rangle$ is *not* a handshake process, because it is not receptive. Trace a_0 does occur, and is quiescent as far as the environment is concerned. If we ignore handshakes along b, we apparently must accept $\langle a^\circ, \{\varepsilon, a_0\}\rangle$ as the behavior of $REP{\cdot}(a^\circ, b^\bullet) \ \| \ RUN{\cdot}b^\circ$.

□

The occurrence of an unbounded sequence of internal events is known as *infinite chatter* (cf. [vdS85], page 52) or *infinite overtaking* (cf. [Hoa85], page 80). The traces that lead to such a bothersome state of affairs are called *divergences*.

Definition 4.10   (divergences)

For handshake structure $\langle A, T \rangle$ we define the *divergences* of $\langle A, T \rangle$, denoted by $div \cdot \langle A, T \rangle$, as the trace set

$$\{t : (\forall n : 0 \leq n : (\exists u : u \in (A^\circ \cap A^\bullet)^* \wedge tu \in T : n < len{\cdot}u)) : t\}$$

□

Recall that $A^\circ \cap A^\bullet$ is the set of internal ports of A. Note that a handshake structure without internal ports cannot have divergences. The set of divergences of a reorder-closed handshake structure is also closed under reordering, as we shall prove next.

Property 4.11

0. Let R be a prefix-closed handshake structure. Then $div \cdot R \subseteq tR$.

1. Let R be a reorder-closed handshake structure. Then $div \cdot R$ is also reorder closed.

Proof

0. Follows immediately from the definition of *div*.

1. Let $R = \langle A, T \rangle$. We derive:

$$t \in \mathbf{t} div \cdot \langle A, T \rangle \wedge s \mathbf{r} \, t$$

$= \quad \{ \text{ Definition 4.10 (divergences) } \}$

$$(\forall n : 0 \le n : (\exists u : u \in X^* \wedge tu \in T : n < len \cdot u)) \wedge s \mathbf{r} \, t$$

$= \quad \{ \text{ calculus; Definition 3.14.7 } \}$

$$(\forall n : 0 \le n : (\exists u : u \in X^* \wedge tu \in T \wedge su \mathbf{r} \, tu : n < len \cdot u))$$

$= \quad \{ \ T \text{ is reorder closed } \}$

$$(\forall n : 0 \le n : (\exists u : u \in X^* \wedge su \in T : n < len \cdot u))$$

$= \quad \{ \text{ definition of } div \ \}$

$$s \in \mathbf{t} div \cdot \langle A, T \rangle$$

□

Theorem 4.12

Let P and Q be handshake processes. Then

$$\mathbf{t}(P^{\le} \mathbf{w} \, Q^{\le}) \ = \ (\mathbf{t}(P \mathbf{w} Q) \ \cup \ div(P^{\le} \mathbf{w} \, Q^{\le}))^{\le}$$

Proof by mutual set inclusion.

Case $(\mathbf{t}(P \mathbf{w} Q) \ \cup \ div(P^{\le} \mathbf{w} \, Q^{\le}))^{\le} \ \subseteq \ \mathbf{t}(P^{\le} \mathbf{w} \, Q^{\le})$.

$\quad t \in (\mathbf{t}(P \mathbf{w} Q) \cup div \cdot (P^{\le} \mathbf{w} \, Q^{\le}))^{\le}$

$\Rightarrow \quad \{ \text{ prefix closure distributes over } \cup; \text{ Property 4.11.0 } \}$

$\quad t \in (\mathbf{t}(P \mathbf{w} Q)^{\le} \ \cup \ \mathbf{t}(P^{\le} \mathbf{w} \, Q^{\le})^{\le})$

$= \quad \{ \ \mathbf{t}S \subseteq \mathbf{t}S^{\le}; \text{ weaving is monotonic } \}$

$\quad t \in \mathbf{t}(P^{\le} \mathbf{w} \, Q^{\le})^{\le}$

$= \quad \{ \text{ Property 4.5.0 } \}$

$\quad t \in \mathbf{t}(P^{\le} \mathbf{w} \, Q^{\le})$

Case $\mathbf{t}(P^{\leq} \mathbf{w} Q^{\leq}) \subseteq (\mathbf{t}(P \mathbf{w} Q) \cup div(P^{\leq} \mathbf{w} Q^{\leq}))^{\leq}.$

Let trace $t \in \mathbf{t}(P^{\leq} \mathbf{w} Q^{\leq})$ and let predicate X_n be defined as

$$t \in \mathbf{t}(P \mathbf{w} Q)^{\leq} \vee (\exists u : u \in (\mathbf{o}P \cup \mathbf{o}Q)^* \wedge tu \in \mathbf{t}(P^{\leq} \mathbf{w} Q^{\leq}) : n \leq len \cdot u)$$

Predicate X_0 holds trivially. Using Property 4.7 it follows that $(\forall n : 0 \leq n : X_n \Rightarrow X_{n+1})$
Hence, by induction, we have $(\forall n : 0 \leq n : X_n)$. Equivalently:

$$t \in \mathbf{t}(P \mathbf{w} Q)^{\leq}$$
$$\vee (\forall n : 0 \leq n : (\exists u : u \in (\mathbf{o}P \cup \mathbf{o}Q)^* \wedge tu \in \mathbf{t}(P^{\leq} \mathbf{w} Q^{\leq}) : n \leq len \cdot u))$$

The second term brings us very close to the definition of *div* (cf. Definition 4.10). However,
u ranges over all outputs and not exclusively over internal symbols. Fortunately, the number
of external outputs in u is bounded, because of handshaking and the finite number of ports
involved. Hence, as far as the second term is considered, t is a prefix of a divergence of
$P^{\leq} \mathbf{w} Q^{\leq}$. Q.e.d.

□

Corollary 4.13

Let P and Q be connectable handshake processes such that $div \cdot (P^{\leq} \mathbf{w} Q^{\leq}) = \emptyset$.

0. $(P \mathbf{w} Q)^{\leq} = P^{\leq} \mathbf{w} Q^{\leq}$

1. $(P \mathbf{b} Q)^{\leq} = P^{\leq} \mathbf{b} Q^{\leq}$

□

Having dealt with interference, quiescence, concealment, and divergence, we have done all the
groundwork needed for the definition of $P \parallel Q$.

Definition 4.14   (parallel composition)

The parallel composition of connectable handshake processes P and Q is denoted by $P \parallel Q$
and defined as

$$\langle A, (\mathbf{t}(P \mathbf{w} Q) \cup div \cdot (P^{\leq} \mathbf{w} Q^{\leq})) \lceil A \rangle$$

with $A = \mathbf{e}(\mathbf{p}P \cup \mathbf{p}Q)$.

□

As a corollary to Theorem 4.12 we may conclude:

Property 4.15

$(P \parallel Q)^{\leq} = P^{\leq} \mathbf{b} Q^{\leq}$

□

Theorem 4.16

The parallel composition of connectable handshake processes P and Q, as denoted by $P \parallel Q$, is a handshake process.

Proof Since $P \parallel Q$ is clearly a handshake structure, it remains to prove that $P \parallel Q$ satisfies the five conditions of Definition 3.19. The proof is structured accordingly.

0. According to Definition 4.14 we have $\mathbf{p}(P \parallel Q) = \mathbf{e}(\mathbf{p}P \cup \mathbf{p}Q)$. From Definition 4.8.1 it can directly be seen that $\mathbf{e}(\mathbf{p}P \cup \mathbf{p}Q)$ has no internal ports.

1. We derive:

   true
   $\Rightarrow$ { $\mathbf{t}P$ and $\mathbf{t}Q$ are non-empty }
        $\varepsilon \in \mathbf{t}P^{\leq} \wedge \varepsilon \in \mathbf{t}Q^{\leq}$
   $\Rightarrow$ { definition of blend }
        $\varepsilon \in \mathbf{t}(P^{\leq} \mathbf{b} \ P^{\leq})$
   $=$ { Property 4.15 }
        $\varepsilon \in \mathbf{t}(P \parallel Q)^{\leq}$
   $\Rightarrow$ { calculus }
        $\mathbf{t}(P \parallel Q) \neq \emptyset$

2. We derive:

   $\mathbf{t}Pas \cdot (P \parallel Q)$
   $=$ { Property 3.12 }
        $\mathbf{t}Pas \cdot (P \parallel Q)^{\leq}$
   $=$ { Property 4.15 }
        $\mathbf{t}Pas \cdot (P^{\leq} \mathbf{b} \ Q^{\leq})$
   $\subseteq$ { Property 4.6.1 }
        $\mathbf{t}(Pas \cdot P^{\leq} \mathbf{b} \ Pas \cdot Q^{\leq})$
   $=$ { Property 3.12 (twice) }
        $\mathbf{t}(Pas \cdot P \mathbf{b} \ Pas \cdot Q)$
   $\subseteq$ { P and Q are quiescent for passive traces; property of $\mathbf{b}$ }
        $\mathbf{t}(P \mathbf{b} Q)$
   $\subseteq$ { property of $\parallel$ }
        $\mathbf{t}(P \parallel Q)$

Hence, $P \parallel Q$ is quiescent for passive traces.

3. We derive:

   true

   $\Rightarrow$ $\{$ P and Q are reorder closed $\}$

   $(\mathbf{r}){\cdot}P \,\wedge\, (\mathbf{r}){\cdot}Q$

   $\Rightarrow$ $\{$ Properties 3.2.1 (twice) and 4.5.1 (twice) $\}$

   $(\mathbf{r}){\cdot}(P \mathbf{\,w\,} Q) \,\wedge\, (\mathbf{r}){\cdot}(P^{\le} \mathbf{\,w\,} Q^{\le})$

   $\Rightarrow$ $\{$ Properties 4.11.1 and 3.15.3 $\}$

   $(\mathbf{r}){\cdot}(P \mathbf{\,w\,} Q) \,\wedge\, (\mathbf{r}){\cdot}div{\cdot}(P^{\le} \mathbf{\,w\,} Q^{\le})$

   $\Rightarrow$ $\{$ Properties 3.2.1 and 3.15 $\}$

   $(\mathbf{r}){\cdot}((P \mathbf{\,w\,} Q) \cup div{\cdot}(P^{\le} \mathbf{\,w\,} Q^{\le})) \lceil \mathbf{e}(\mathbf{A}P \cup \mathbf{A}Q))$

   $=$ $\{$ definition of $P \parallel Q$ $\}$

   $(\mathbf{r}){\cdot}(P \parallel Q)$

4. We derive:

   true

   $\Rightarrow$ $\{$ P and Q are receptive $\}$

   $(\mathbf{x}){\cdot}P^{\le} \,\wedge\, (\mathbf{x}){\cdot}Q^{\le}$

   $\Rightarrow$ $\{$ Property 4.5.2 $\}$

   $(\mathbf{x}){\cdot}(P^{\le} \mathbf{\,w\,} Q^{\le})$

   $\Rightarrow$ $\{$ Property 3.18.3 $\}$

   $(\mathbf{x}){\cdot}(P^{\le} \mathbf{\,b\,} Q^{\le})$

   $=$ $\{$ Property 4.15 $\}$

   $(\mathbf{x}){\cdot}(P \parallel Q)^{\le}$

$\square$

Property 4.17

0. Parallel composition is commutative, associative, distributive and continuous.

1. $CHAOS{\cdot}\langle \emptyset, \emptyset \rangle \parallel P \,=\, P$.

2. $(\mathbf{p}P = \overline{\mathbf{p}Q}) \,=\, (P \parallel Q = CHAOS{\cdot}\langle \emptyset, \emptyset \rangle)$.

3. In particular, $P \parallel CHAOS{\cdot}\overline{\mathbf{p}P} = CHAOS{\cdot}\langle \emptyset, \emptyset \rangle$.

$\square$

In the remainder of this book, examples involving parallel composition are free of infinite overtaking. Parallel composition then reduces to the conceptually simpler blending.

The way two processes are connected can be pictured by means of a *connection diagram*. These diagrams are also a convenient means to display the connectivity pattern of handshake circuits (see, for example, the circuits of Section 1.1). In a connection diagram, processes are drawn as circles with their ports drawn as small circles attached to their periphery. Passive ports are represented by open circles, active ports by filled ones. A channel is represented by a line connecting *exactly* one passive port to one active port of two *distinct* processes. The direction of a channel is represented by an arrow indicating the direction of data transport (when applicable).

Example 4.18

The parallel compositions below refer to handshake processes of Example 3.23.

   0. The parallel composition of two connectors connected "tail to head" is again a connector:

$$CON \cdot (a^\circ, b^\bullet) \;||\; CON \cdot (b^\circ, c^\bullet) = CON \cdot (a^\circ, c^\bullet)$$

   1. Connecting a connector to a process has the effect of renaming the port it connects to:

$$REP \cdot (a^\circ, b^\bullet) \;||\; CON \cdot (b^\circ, c^\bullet) = REP \cdot (a^\circ, c^\bullet)$$

   2. A port of a handshake process can effectively be concealed by connecting it to a *RUN* component:

$$JOIN \cdot (a^\circ, b^\circ, c^\bullet) \;||\; RUN \cdot (c^\circ) = PAS \cdot (a^\circ, b^\circ)$$

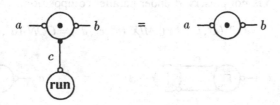

   Also:

$$SEQ \cdot (a^\circ, b^\bullet, c^\bullet) \;||\; RUN \cdot (c^\circ) = CON \cdot (a^\circ, b^\bullet)$$

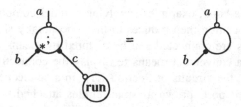

3. An active port can be turned into a passive port by connecting it to a passivator:

$$RUN \cdot a^\bullet \parallel PAS \cdot (a^\circ, b^\circ) = RUN \cdot b^\circ$$

4. A duplicator can be constructed from a sequencer and a mixer:

$$SEQ \cdot (a^\circ, b^\bullet, c^\bullet) \parallel MIX \cdot (b^\circ, c^\circ, d^\bullet) = DUP \cdot (a^\circ, d^\bullet)$$

$$a \ \text{—} \ \boxed{\begin{smallmatrix} ; \\ * \end{smallmatrix}} \ \overset{c}{\underset{b}{\rule{0pt}{0pt}}} \ \boxed{|} \ \text{—} \ d \qquad = \qquad a \ \text{—} \ \boxed{\textbf{dup}} \ \text{—} \ d$$

A duplicator can also be constructed from a *PAR* component and a mixer:

$$PAR \cdot (a^\circ, b^\bullet, c^\bullet) \parallel MIX \cdot (b^\circ, c^\circ, d^\bullet) = DUP \cdot (a^\circ, d^\bullet)$$

$$a \ \text{—} \ \boxed{\parallel} \ \overset{c}{\underset{b}{\rule{0pt}{0pt}}} \ \boxed{|} \ \text{—} \ d \qquad = \qquad a \ \text{—} \ \boxed{\textbf{dup}} \ \text{—} \ d$$

It is interesting to compare the respective weaves. Trace $a_0 b_0 c_0 d_0$ is a trace of $PAR \cdot (a^\circ, b^\bullet, c^\bullet)$ **w** $MIX \cdot (b^\circ, c^\circ, d^\bullet)$ but not of $SEQ \cdot (a^\circ, b^\bullet, c^\bullet)$ **w** $MIX \cdot (b^\circ, c^\circ, d^\bullet)$. For trace $a_0 b_0 d_0$ the converse is true: it is quiescent only in the sequencer-based duplicator.

However, these differences in internal behavior are concealed for the external observer.

5. Nondeterminism is not preserved under parallel composition:

$$OR \cdot (a^\circ, b^\bullet, c^\bullet) \parallel MIX \cdot (b^\circ, c^\circ, d^\bullet) = CON \cdot (a^\circ, d^\bullet)$$

$$a \ \text{—} \ \boxed{\sqcap} \ \overset{c}{\underset{b}{\rule{0pt}{0pt}}} \ \boxed{|} \ \text{—} \ d \qquad = \qquad a \ \text{—} \ \bigcirc \ \text{—} \ d$$

6. Another realization of $CON \cdot (a^\circ, d^\bullet)$ is suggested by:

$$PAR \cdot (a^\circ, b^\bullet, c^\bullet) \parallel JOIN \cdot (b^\circ, c^\circ, d^\bullet) = CON \cdot (a^\circ, d^\bullet)$$

In Chapter 7 we shall recognize examples 0, 1, 4 and 6 as instances of property 7.23. Each of the above examples can also be viewed as a substitution or rewrite rule: the composition at the left-hand side of an equality may be replaced by the component at the right-hand side. These substitutions therefore also suggest optimizations of handshake circuits (cf. Section 8.1).

□

We conclude this section with two properties of parallel composition that prove useful for the initialization of handshake circuits (Section 8.6).

Property 4.19

0. The property "being passive" is preserved under parallel composition, that is, $P \parallel Q$ is passive if P and Q are passive.

1. The property "initial-when-closed" is preserved under parallel composition.

□

4.2   Handshake circuits

Handshake circuits at last!

Definition 4.20   (handshake circuit)

0. A *handshake circuit* is a finite *connectable* set of handshake processes.

1. Let H be a finite set of handshake structures. H is *connectable*, denoted by $\bowtie H$, if all handshake structures are pairwise connectable, that is:

$$\bowtie H \;=\; (\forall S, T : S \in H \wedge T \in H \wedge S \neq T : S \bowtie T)$$

□

In particular, the empty set and the singleton set are handshake circuits. Note that the required connectability excludes "broadcast" among handshake processes: a port may occur in the port structures of at most two processes of a given handshake circuit. Consistent with the terminology of Chapter 1 we shall refer to the handshake processes of a handshake circuit as its *handshake components*.

Most of the operators of the previous section can be generalized to handshake circuits in a straightforward fashion.

Definition 4.21

   0. The *external port structure* of handshake circuit H, denoted by $\mathbf{e}H$, is the port structure

$$\mathbf{e}(\cup \, P : P \in H : \mathbf{p}P)$$

   1. $H^{\leq} = \{P : P \in H : P^{\leq}\}$

   2. $\mathbf{W} \cdot H = (\, \mathbf{w} \;\; P : P \in H : P)$

   3. $\mathbf{B} \cdot H = (\, \mathbf{b} \;\; P : P \in H : P)$

   4. $\| \cdot H = (\| \;\; P : P \in H : P)$

□

The first definition relies on

$$A \bowtie B \;\wedge\; B \bowtie C \;\wedge\; C \bowtie A \;\Rightarrow\; \mathbf{e}(A \cup B) \bowtie C$$

The last three definitions rely on the associativity and commutativity of weaving, blending, and parallel composition, as well as on the existence of the identity $CHAOS \cdot \langle \emptyset, \emptyset \rangle$ for all three operators. Many of the properties of the previous section generalize similarly:

Corollary 4.22

For handshake circuit H we have:

   0. $div \cdot (\mathbf{W} \cdot H^{\leq}) = \emptyset \quad \Rightarrow \quad (\mathbf{W} \cdot H)^{\leq} = \mathbf{W} \cdot (H^{\leq})$

   1. $div \cdot (\mathbf{W} \cdot H^{\leq}) = \emptyset \quad \Rightarrow \quad \| \cdot H = \mathbf{B} \cdot H$

   2. $\mathbf{e}H = \mathbf{p}(\| \cdot H)$

   3. $\| \cdot H$ is a handshake process.

   4. $(\| \cdot H)^{\leq} = \| \cdot H^{\leq}$

□

The following properties relate to the set nature of a handshake circuit.

Property 4.23

   0. $\emptyset$ is a handshake circuit. Since $STOP \cdot \langle \emptyset, \emptyset \rangle$ is the unit of parallel composition of handshake processes, we have $\| \cdot \emptyset = STOP \cdot \langle \emptyset, \emptyset \rangle$.

   1. Let H and I be handshake circuits, such that $\bowtie(H \cup I)$. Then $H \cup I$ is a handshake circuit, and

$$\begin{aligned}\mathbf{e}(H \cup I) \;\; &= \mathbf{e}(\mathbf{e}H \cup \mathbf{e}I) \\ \| \cdot (H \cup I) \;\; &= (\| \cdot H) \;\; \| \;\; (\| \cdot I)\end{aligned}$$

□

As a corollary to Property 4.19, we may conclude that the behavior of a handshake circuit constructed from passive components is also passive. The same holds for the property initial-when-closed.

Example 4.24

0. A three-way mixer is the natural generalization of the two-way mixer *MIX*. A three-way mixer with $a°$, $b°$ and $c°$ as passive ports and $d^\bullet$ as active port can be realized by

$$MIX \cdot (a°, b°, d^\bullet) \parallel MIX \cdot (c^\upsilon, d°, e^\bullet)$$

which is equivalent to

$$MIX \cdot (b°, c°, d^\bullet) \parallel MIX \cdot (a°, d°, e^\bullet)$$

Pictorially this can be expressed as:

An N-way mixer ($N \geq 2$) can be realized as a tree of $N-1$ two-way mixers. Although all trees exhibit the same behavior (i.e. define the same N-way mixer process), response times to requests through different passive ports may differ considerably. The degenerate case, with all $N-1$ mixers linked into a list, is an extreme in this respect.

1. Similar to the N-way mixer, we may consider N-way generalizations of *SEQ*, *PAR* and *OR*. These three handshake circuits have one passive port and N active ports, and can be constructed from $N-1$ instances of their two-way counterparts.

2. $DUP_N \cdot (a°, b^\bullet)$ is one way to generalize the duplicator, with $DUP_1 \cdot (a°, b^\bullet) = DUP \cdot (a°, b^\bullet)$, and for $N > 1$:

$$DUP_N \cdot (a°, b^\bullet) = DUP_{N-1} \cdot (a°, b^\bullet_{N-1}) \parallel DUP \cdot (b°_{N-1}, b^\bullet)$$

For each handshake through a we may expect 2^N handshakes through port b. With $N = 90$ and a rate of one handshake through b per nanosecond, it takes approximately 10^{18} seconds to complete a single handshake through $a°$. This is about the estimated life time of the universe, and may present a slight problem for the testing of a VLSI circuit that implements this chain (see Section 8.7).

□

Chapter 5

Sequential handshake processes

5.0 Introduction

So far the quiescent trace set of a handshake process was specified in one of the following forms: by enumeration, by a predicate, by a state graph, or by parallel composition of other handshake processes.

For many handshake processes none of the above forms may be convenient. An example of such a process is the process that first behaves like P and then, "after successful termination of P", behaves like Q. Of course, such *sequential composition* of the handshake processes P and Q requires a notion of successful termination of a process. A *sequential handshake process* is a handshake process in which that notion is incorporated.

The aim of this chapter is to develop a model for sequential handshake processes and a calculus for these processes. An important application of this calculus is the description of the handshake components required for the compilation of Tangram. Another application is the semantics of Tangram itself.

5.1 Sequential handshake processes

A sequential handshake process is a handshake process, some of whose traces are designated as *terminal* traces, i.e. traces that lead to successful termination. In a sequential composition these terminal traces can be prefixed to traces of the subsequent sequential handshake process.

Let T denote the set of quiescent traces and let U denote the set of terminal traces of sequential handshake process P. Sets T and U must satisfy a number of conditions, which are introduced informally.

For terminal handshake trace u, we require that for any handshake trace v, trace uv is a handshake trace as well. Therefore, we require that all terminal traces are closed.

Traces that are both terminal and quiescent form a special class of traces. After such a trace, a nondeterministic choice is made whether to terminate successfully or not. Hence, $T \cap U$ does not need to be empty.

Proper input extensions of terminal trace u, and reorderings thereof, form another special class of traces. Since they are not closed, they cannot be terminal. They are not necessarily quiescent either. We choose not to record these traces explicitly, but to require that handshake

89

structure $\langle A, T \cup U^{\mathbf{x}\,\mathbf{r}} \rangle$ is a handshake process.

Reordering should of course not have an effect on termination. Hence, both T and U must be closed under reordering. Combining the above leads to the following definition.

Definition 5.0   (sequential handshake process)

Let P be a triple $\langle A, T, U \rangle$, in which A is a port structure, and T and U are subsets of A^H. Furthermore, let V denote $T \cup U^{\mathbf{x}\,\mathbf{r}}$. Triple P is a *sequential handshake process* if the following conditions are satisfied (cf. Definition 3.19):

   0. $A^\circ \cap A^\bullet = \emptyset$

   1. $V \neq \emptyset$

   2. $\mathbf{t}(Pas \cdot \langle A, V \rangle) \subseteq V$

   3. $(\mathbf{r}) \cdot T \wedge (\mathbf{r}) \cdot U$

   4. $(\mathbf{x}) \cdot V^{\leq}$ and

   5. $(\forall u : u \in U : closed \cdot u)$

Trace set U is the set of *terminal* traces and T is the set of quiescent traces. Sequential handshake process P may be written as $\langle \mathbf{p}P, \mathbf{t}P, \mathbf{u}P \rangle$. The set of all sequential handshake processes with port structure A is denoted by $\sum \cdot A$.

□

Note that Conditions 0 to 4 closely mirror the corresponding conditions of the definition of handshake processes. For brevity's sake, the word handshake may be omitted in "sequential handshake process". In the remainder of this section P and Q denote sequential handshake processes. The following property shows their relation to (non-sequential) handshake processes.

Property 5.1

   0. If $\langle A, T, U \rangle$ is a sequential handshake process then $\langle A, T \cup U^{\mathbf{x}\,\mathbf{r}} \rangle$ is a handshake process.

   1. Corollary: if $\langle A, T, \emptyset \rangle$ is a sequential handshake process then $\langle A, T \rangle$ is a handshake process.

□

These properties inspire the following definition.

Definition 5.2   (permanent sequential process)

   0. A sequential handshake process is *permanent* if its set of terminal traces is empty.

   1. A handshake process $\langle A, T \rangle$ is said to *correspond to* the permanent sequential process $\langle A, T, \emptyset \rangle$, and vice versa.

□

When P is a permanent sequential process, and no confusion can arise, we will sometimes use P as if it is a handshake process and omit the phrase "the handshake process corresponding to". In particular, permanent sequential processes are used to define the behavior of handshake components and handshake circuits.

In [Hoa85] a symbol $\sqrt{}$ is appended to terminal traces, indicating successful termination. A clear advantage of such an encoding is the absence of the need to introduce another process model. To some extent, this advantage is eroded when the extra rules that govern the use of $\sqrt{}$ have to be taken into account. Moreover, the recording of the terminal traces in a separate set simplifies the definition of the various operators on sequential processes.

For a port structure A the following generic sequential processes are defined.

Definition 5.3

0. *CHAOS $\cdot$ A* is the least predictable sequential handshake process. It can engage in a handshake through any port at any time, it can become quiescent at any time, and it may terminate successfully after any closed trace:

$$CHAOS \cdot A = \langle A, A^H, \{t : t \in A^H \wedge closed \cdot t : t\} \rangle$$

1. *RUN $\cdot$ A* is always willing to engage in a handshake through any of its ports. However, it never terminates:

$$RUN \cdot A = \langle A, \mathbf{tPas} \cdot \langle A, A^H \rangle, \emptyset \rangle$$

2. *STOP $\cdot$ A* never engages in a handshake communication through any of its ports. Neither does it ever terminate successfully:

$$STOP \cdot A = \langle A, \{\varepsilon\}^{\mathbf{X}}, \emptyset \rangle$$

3. *SKIP $\cdot$ A* never engages in a handshake communication through any of its ports. All it does is terminate successfully:

$$SKIP \cdot A = \langle A, \emptyset, \{\varepsilon\} \rangle$$

□

CHAOS $\cdot$ A, *RUN $\cdot$ A*, and *STOP $\cdot$ A* have also been defined as handshake processes and have the same set of quiescent traces as their non-sequential counterparts (cf. Definition 3.20). In the sequel the context indicates which variant is intended. *RUN $\cdot$ A* and *STOP $\cdot$ A* are permanent sequential processes. Also note that:

- $CHAOS \cdot \langle \emptyset, \emptyset \rangle = \langle \langle \emptyset, \emptyset \rangle, \{\varepsilon\}, \{\varepsilon\} \rangle$

- $RUN \cdot \langle \emptyset, \emptyset \rangle = \langle \langle \emptyset, \emptyset \rangle, \{\varepsilon\}, \emptyset \rangle$

- $STOP \cdot \langle \emptyset, \emptyset \rangle = \langle \langle \emptyset, \emptyset \rangle, \{\varepsilon\}, \emptyset \rangle$

- $SKIP \cdot \langle \emptyset, \emptyset \rangle = \langle \langle \emptyset, \emptyset \rangle, \emptyset, \{\varepsilon\} \rangle$

Thus there are three sequential processes with the empty port structure.

CPO of sequential handshake processes

The set of sequential handshake processes with port structure A, denoted by $\sum\cdot A$, can be analyzed in a way similar to our analysis of $\prod\cdot A$. The respective definitions, properties and theorems then bear close resemblance. In this subsection we rephrase the more significant results of Section 3.4 in terms of sequential processes. All sequential processes in this sub-section have port structure A. First we introduce a partial order relation $\sqsubseteq$ among sequential processes.

Definition 5.4   (refinement)

Let P and Q be sequential processes with the same port structure. P refines to Q, denoted by $P \sqsubseteq Q$, if

$$\mathbf{t}P \supseteq \mathbf{t}Q \quad \text{and} \quad \mathbf{u}P \supseteq \mathbf{u}Q$$

□

Again, $P \sqsubseteq Q$ may be read as P refines to Q, P specifies Q, or Q implements P. The least element in this order is $CHAOS\cdot A$. A function from $\sum\cdot A$ to $\sum\cdot A$ is *order preserving* if it preserves refinement ordering.

Definition 5.5   (nondeterministic composition)

The nondeterministic composition of P and Q, denoted by $P \sqcap Q$, is defined as $\langle A, \mathbf{t}P \cup \mathbf{t}Q, \mathbf{u}P \cup \mathbf{u}Q \rangle$.

□

$P \sqcap Q$ is the greatest lower bound of P and Q in the partial order $\langle \sum\cdot A, \sqsubseteq \rangle$. Later $\sqcap$ is generalized to sequential processes with unequal port structures. A function from $\sum\cdot A$ to $\sum\cdot A$ is *distributive* if it distributes over nondeterministic composition.

Definition 5.6   (intersection)

The intersection of P and Q, denoted by $P \sqcup Q$, is defined as

$$\langle A, \mathbf{t}P \cap \mathbf{t}Q, \mathbf{u}P \cap \mathbf{u}Q \rangle$$

□

The intersection of two sequential processes is generally not a sequential process. However, with limit and chain defined as in Section 3.4 we arrive at the following, hardly surprising, theorem.

Theorem 5.7

Partial order $(\sum\cdot A, \sqsubseteq)$ is a CPO with $CHAOS\cdot A$ as least element
and $(\sqcup i : 0 \le i : P_i)$ as limit of chain $(i : 0 \le i : P_i)$.

□

In accordance with Definition 3.39, function F from $\sum\cdot A$ to $\sum\cdot A$ is *continuous* if it commutes with the limit operation.

Recursion

One way to define a sequential handshake process is by recursion, for example as a fixpoint of a given function F, i.e. a solution of the equation $P = F \cdot P$. We conclude this section by instancing the well-known fixpoint construction in CPO's [BHR84, DP90].

Theorem 5.8

Let F be a continuous function from $\sum \cdot A$ to $\sum \cdot A$, and let the n-fold composition of F be denoted by F^n. Then

$$(\sqcup n : 0 \leq n : F^n \cdot CHAOS)$$

is the *least fixpoint* of F.

Proof   First we prove that the above limit is a fixpoint of F:

$$F \cdot (\sqcup n : 0 \leq n : F^n \cdot CHAOS)$$

$=$ { continuity of F }

$$(\sqcup n : 0 \leq n : F \cdot (F^n \cdot CHAOS))$$

$=$ { calculus }

$$(\sqcup n : 1 \leq n : F^n \cdot CHAOS)$$

$=$ { $CHAOS \sqsubseteq F^n \cdot CHAOS$ }

$$(\sqcup n : 0 \leq n : F^n \cdot CHAOS)$$

It is also the least fixpoint, since (let Q be a fixpoint):

$$(\sqcup n : 0 \leq n : F^n \cdot CHAOS)$$

$\sqsubseteq$ { $CHAOS \sqsubseteq Q$ and F is order preserving }

$$(\sqcup n : 0 \leq n : F^n \cdot Q)$$

$=$ { Q is a fixpoint }

$$(\sqcup n : 0 \leq n : Q)$$

$=$ { calculus }

$$Q$$

$\square$

An application of this fixpoint theorem is given in the next section.

5.2   Handshake process calculus

This section develops a calculus for sequential handshake processes. It is restricted to sequential processes with nonput ports, thereby excluding input and output of data. Extensions to this calculus, including data communication and assignments, are described informally in Section 5.4. The calculus includes the following operations: parallel composition, extension, concealment, nondeterministic composition, sequential composition, N-fold repetition, unbounded repetition, enclosure, and choice. The choice of the operators is inspired by the syntax of Tangram.

Basic sequential processes

The following definition introduces four basic sequential processes.

Definition 5.9   (*stop, skip,* $a°$, **and** $a^•$)

Let a be a name.

   0. $stop = STOP \cdot \langle \emptyset, \emptyset \rangle = \langle \langle \emptyset, \emptyset \rangle, \{\varepsilon\}, \emptyset \rangle$

   1. $skip = SKIP \cdot \langle \emptyset, \emptyset \rangle = \langle \langle \emptyset, \emptyset \rangle, \emptyset, \{\varepsilon\} \rangle$

   2. $a° = \langle a°, \{\varepsilon\}, \{a_0 a_1\} \rangle$

   3. $a^• = \langle a^•, \{a_0\}, \{a_0 a_1\} \rangle$

   □

Note that $a°$ may both denote a port structure and a sequential process; the same holds for $a^•$. Generally, the context indicates which denotation is intended.

Parallel composition

Definition 5.10   (**parallel composition**)

Let P and Q be two connectable sequential processes, and let $A = \mathbf{e}(\mathbf{p}P \cup \mathbf{p}Q)$. The parallel composition of P and Q is denoted by $P \parallel Q$ and defined by

   0. $\mathbf{p}(P \parallel Q) = A$

   1. $\mathbf{t}(P \parallel Q) =$
      $(\mathbf{t}P \mathbf{\ w\ } \mathbf{t}Q \ \cup \ (\mathbf{u}P)^{\mathbf{x\,r}} \mathbf{\ w\ } \mathbf{t}Q \ \cup \ \mathbf{t}P \mathbf{\ w\ } (\mathbf{u}Q)^{\mathbf{x\,r}} \ \cup \ div \cdot (\mathbf{t}P^{\leq} \mathbf{\ w\ } \mathbf{t}Q^{\leq})) \lceil A$

   2. $\mathbf{u}(P \parallel Q) = (\mathbf{u}P \mathbf{\ w\ } \mathbf{u}Q) \lceil A$

where the weave of trace sets V and W in the context of $\mathbf{p}P$ and $\mathbf{p}Q$ is shorthand for

$$\{t : t \in (\mathbf{p}P \cup \mathbf{p}Q)^H \land t \lceil \mathbf{p}P \in V \land t \lceil \mathbf{p}Q \in W : t\}$$

   □

This definition closely resembles Definition 4.14. The main addition is the requirement that both P and Q must agree on successful termination. If one process is ready to terminate when the other is quiescent, then the composition is quiescent.

Property 5.11

    0. $P \parallel Q$ is a sequential process.

    1. Parallel composition is commutative, associative, distributive, and continuous.

    2. $a^\circ \parallel a^\bullet = skip$.

    3. $skip \parallel P = P$.

    4. For permanent P we have $stop \parallel P = P$.

□

Conformant port structures

Connectability of port structures is a requirement for the parallel composition of (sequential) handshake processes. In such a composition, two processes may only share the opposite side of a channel. Other operators require sequential processes to share the same side of a channel. A different requirement is imposed on the respective port structures: they must be *conformant*.

Definition 5.12   (conformance)

Port structures A and B are *conformant*, denoted by $A \bowtie\!\!\!\triangle B$, if

    0. A and B are *compatible*, and

    1. $A^\circ \cap B^\bullet = \emptyset$ and $A^\bullet \cap B^\circ = \emptyset$.

Two handshake structures are conformant if their respective port structures are. Conformance of sequential processes is defined similarly.

□

Conformance is related to connectability by the following property.

Property 5.13

$A \bowtie\!\!\!\triangle B = A \bowtie \overline{B}$

□

Conformance enjoys the following obvious properties.

Property 5.14

    0. $A \bowtie\!\!\!\triangle B = B \bowtie\!\!\!\triangle A$.

    1. $B \subseteq A \Rightarrow B \bowtie\!\!\!\triangle A$. Consequently, $A \bowtie\!\!\!\triangle \emptyset$ and $A \bowtie\!\!\!\triangle A$.

    2. $\mathbf{p}A \cap \mathbf{p}B = \emptyset \wedge A$ and B are compatible $\Rightarrow A \bowtie\!\!\!\triangle B$.

□

Extension

Some relations and operations on processes are defined only for processes with equal port structures. Under such circumstances, the extension of the port structure of a process may be useful. The extension of P with conformant port structure A is a sequential process that has port structure $\mathbf{p}P \cup A$, and behaves like P. The following definition relies on the fact that disjoint port structures are both conformant and connectable.

Definition 5.15   (extension)

Let $A \bowtie \mathbf{p}P$. The extension of P by A is denoted by $(A) \cdot P$ and defined as

$$P \parallel SKIP \cdot (A \setminus \mathbf{p}P)$$

□

Property 5.16

Let A, B and $\mathbf{p}P$ be mutually conformant. Then

0. $(A) \cdot P$ is a sequential process.

1. $(\langle \emptyset, \emptyset \rangle) \cdot P = P$

2. $(A) \cdot P = (A \setminus \mathbf{p}P) \cdot P$

3. $(\mathbf{p}P) \cdot P = P$

4. $(B) \cdot (A) \cdot P = (A) \cdot (B) \cdot P = (A \cup B) \cdot P$

5. $(A) \cdot stop = STOP \cdot A$

6. $(A) \cdot skip = SKIP \cdot A$

□

The following property is helpful in translating Tangram programs into handshake circuits.

Property 5.17

Let A be a port structure and P a permanent sequential process. Then

$$(A) \cdot P = P \parallel STOP \cdot (A \setminus \mathbf{p}P)$$

Of course, $(A) \cdot P$ is then also permanent.

□

Concealment

Concealment of a subset of the ports of sequential process P has the effect that handshakes through these concealed ports occur without participation of the environment, and are even invisible to the environment. This concealment may have the effect of hiding unbounded sequences of handshakes through the concealed ports. These possible divergences are taken into account in the following definition.

Definition 5.18   (concealment)

Let $A \mathrel{\triangle\!\!\!\triangle} \mathbf{p}P$. The behavior of P with A concealed, denoted by $[\![\, A \,|\, P \,]\!]$, is defined as

$$\langle B, (\mathbf{t}P \cup div \cdot \langle \mathbf{p}P \cup \overline{A}, \mathbf{t}P^{\le}\rangle) \lceil B, \mathbf{u}P \lceil B \rangle$$

where $B = \mathbf{p}P \setminus A$.

□

Concealment enjoys the following properties.

Property 5.19

Let A and B be port structures and P a sequential process such that A, B and $\mathbf{p}P$ are mutually conformant. Then

0. $[\![\, A \,|\, P \,]\!]$ is a sequential process.

1. $[\![\, A \,|\, P \,]\!] = [\![\, A \cap \mathbf{p}P \,|\, P \,]\!]$

2. $[\![\, A \,|\, [\![\, B \,|\, P \,]\!] \,]\!] = [\![\, A \cup B \,|\, P \,]\!]$

3. $[\![\, \langle \emptyset, \emptyset \rangle \,|\, P \,]\!] = P$

□

The following property is helpful in translating Tangram programs into handshake circuits.

Property 5.20

Let A be a port structure and P a permanent sequential process, such that $A \mathrel{\triangle\!\!\!\triangle} \mathbf{p}P$. Then

$$[\![\, A \,|\, P \,]\!] = P \parallel RUN \cdot (\overline{A \cap \mathbf{p}P})$$

Sequential process $[\![\, A \,|\, P \,]\!]$ is then also permanent.

□

Nondeterministic composition

This subsection generalizes nondeterministic composition of sequential processes with equal port structures to sequential processes with different, yet conformant, port structures.

Definition 5.21   (nondeterministic composition)

Let $P \triangle\!\!\!\triangle Q$. The nondeterministic composition of P and Q is denoted by $P \sqcap Q$, and defined as

$$(\mathbf{p}Q) \cdot P \sqcap (\mathbf{p}P) \cdot Q$$

□

Property 5.22

Let P and Q be conformant sequential processes.

  0. $P \sqcap Q$ is a sequential process.

  1. Nondeterministic composition is idempotent, commutative, associative, distributive, and continuous (cf. continuity of sequential composition below).

  2. $P \sqcap CHAOS \cdot \mathbf{p}P = CHAOS \cdot \mathbf{p}P$

□

Sequential composition

The sequential composition of P and Q first behaves like P and, upon successful termination of P, continues by behaving like Q. The definition of sequential composition starts with the sequential composition of sequential processes with equal port structures.

Definition 5.23   (sequential composition)

  0. Let P and Q be handshake processes with port structure A. The sequential composition of P and Q is denoted by $P ;_A Q$, and defined as

$$\langle A, \mathbf{t}P \cup (\mathbf{u}P; \mathbf{t}Q)^{\mathbf{r}}, (\mathbf{u}P; \mathbf{u}Q)^{\mathbf{r}} \rangle$$

where the sequential composition of trace sets V and W is defined by

$$V; W = \{v, w : v \in V \wedge w \in W : vw\}$$

  1. Let P and Q be handshake processes with conformant port structure. The sequential composition of P and Q is denoted by $P ; Q$, and defined as

$$(\mathbf{p}Q) \cdot P \; ;_A \; (\mathbf{p}P) \cdot Q$$

where $A = \mathbf{p}P \cup \mathbf{p}Q$.

□

Note that if $\mathbf{p}P = \mathbf{p}Q$ we have $P ;_{\mathbf{p}P} Q \; = \; P ; Q$.

Property 5.24

0. $P; Q$ is a sequential process.

1. Sequential composition is associative and distributive.

2. $skip; P = P = P; skip$

3. $stop; P = stop$

4. $P; stop = \langle \mathbf{p}P, \mathbf{t}P \sqcup \mathbf{u}P^{\mathbf{x}\,\mathbf{r}}, \emptyset \rangle$, which is clearly permanent.

□

The next property finds application in the definition of unbounded repetition.

Property 5.25

Sequential composition is continuous in both operands, that is

$$(\sqcup i : 0 \le i : P_i; Q) = (\sqcup i : 0 \le i : P_i); Q$$

and

$$(\sqcup i : 0 \le i : P; Q_i) = P; (\sqcup i : 0 \le i : Q_i)$$

We prove the latter.

Proof   Continuity is proven for the terminal traces; the proof for the quiescent traces is similar.

$\quad t \in \mathbf{u}(\sqcup i :: P; Q_i)$

$=\quad$ { definitions of $\sqcup$ and sequential composition }

$\quad t \in (\cap i :: (\mathbf{u}P; \mathbf{u}Q_i)^{\mathbf{r}})$

$=\quad$ { continuity of $\mathbf{r}$-closure (Property 3.41) }

$\quad t \in (\cap i :: (\mathbf{u}P; \mathbf{u}Q_i))^{\mathbf{r}}$

$=\quad$ { definition of $\mathbf{r}$-closure }

$\quad (\exists u : t \mathbf{\,r\,} u : u \in (\cap i :: \mathbf{u}P; \mathbf{u}Q_i))$

$=\quad$ { definitions of chain and sequential composition }

$\quad (\exists u : t \mathbf{\,r\,} u : (\forall i :: (\exists r, s : u = rs : r \in \mathbf{u}P \wedge s \in \mathbf{u}Q_i)))$

$=\quad$ { finite number of u and hence of s (cf. Property 3.41) }

$\quad (\exists u, r, s : t \mathbf{\,r\,} u \wedge u = rs \wedge r \in \mathbf{u}P : (\forall i :: (s \in \mathbf{u}Q_i)))$

$=\quad$ { definition of limit; calculus }

$\quad (\exists r, s : t \mathbf{\,r\,} rs \wedge r \in \mathbf{u}P : s \in (\cap i :: \mathbf{u}Q_i))$

$=\quad$ { definitions of sequential composition, $\mathbf{r}$-closure, and limit }

$\quad t \in (\mathbf{u}P; \mathbf{u}(\sqcup i :: Q_i))^{\mathbf{r}}$

=   { definition of sequential composition }

  $t \in \mathbf{u}(P; (\sqcup i :: Q_i))$

□

N-fold repetition

The 0-fold repetition of P behaves like *skip*. For positive N, the N-fold repetition of P behaves like P, and after successful termination of P behaves like the $(N-1)$-fold repetition of P.

Definition 5.26   (*N*-fold repetition)

Let N be a natural number. The N-fold repetition of P is denoted by $\#N[P]$, and defined as

$$
\begin{array}{lll}
\textbf{if} & N = 0 & \rightarrow \quad SKIP \cdot \mathbf{p}P \\
{[]} & N > 0 & \rightarrow \quad P; \#(N-1)[P] \\
\textbf{fi}
\end{array}
$$

□

Property 5.27

Let P be a sequential processes and let N be a natural number.

  0. $\#N[P]$ is a sequential process.

  1. N-fold repetition is continuous.

  2. $\#N[stop] = stop$, for $N > 0$.

  3. $\#N[skip] = skip$.

□

N-fold repetition is not distributive, i.e. in general we do *not* have

$$
\#N[P \sqcap Q] \;=\; \#N[P] \sqcap \#N[Q]
$$

Sequential process $\#N[P \sqcap Q]$ may choose between P and Q at *every* step of the iteration; in the case of $\#N[P] \sqcap \#N[Q]$ this choice is made only once. The latter is a refinement of the former.

Unbounded repetition

The unbounded repetition of P behaves like an unbounded sequential composition of sequential process P, schematically suggested by $P; P; P; \dots$.

Definition 5.28   (unbounded repetition)

The unbounded repetition of P is denoted by $\#[P]$ and defined as the least fixpoint of F, where F is defined by $F \cdot X = P; X$.

□

This fixpoint is the limit of the chain $(i : 0 \leq i : \#i[P]; CHAOS \cdot \mathbf{p}P)$ as explained in Section 5.1.

Property 5.29

    0. $\#[P]$ is a sequential process; it is also permanent.

    1. Unbounded repetition is continuous.

    2. $P; \#[P] = \#[P]$

    3. $\#[stop] = stop$

    4. $\#[skip] = CHAOS \cdot \emptyset$

□

It is interesting to compare these properties with Property 5.27. The last property shows that unbounded repetition of P cannot be regarded as the limit of the chain $(i : 0 \leq i : \#i[P])$. Unbounded repetition is not distributive, for the same reason as n-fold repetition.

Enclosure

The *enclosure* of a sequential process P by a passive handshake a° (assume $a^\circ \not\subseteq \mathbf{p}P$) first behaves like $STOP \cdot \mathbf{p}P$. After event a_0 it behaves like P, and if P terminates successfully, the enclosure terminates successfully with event a_1.

Definition 5.30   (enclosure)

Let a° be a port structure, such that a° is not contained in $\mathbf{p}P$. The enclosure of P by a° is denoted by $a^\circ : P$ and defined as

$$\langle a^\circ \cup \mathbf{p}P, \ \mathbf{t}(STOP \cdot \mathbf{p}P) \cup (\{a_0\}; \mathbf{t}P)^\mathbf{r}, \ (\{a_0\}; \mathbf{u}P; \{a_1\})^\mathbf{r} \rangle$$

□

Enclosure by an active port is not defined.

Property 5.31

Let P be a sequential process, and let a and b be distinct names, such that a° and b° are not contained in $\mathbf{p}P$.

    0. $a^\circ : P$ is a sequential process.

1. Enclosure is distributive and continuous.

2. $a° : skip = a°$

3. $a° : stop = STOP \cdot a°$

4. $a° : b° : P = b° : a° : P$. In particular, $a° : b° = b° : a°$.

$\square$

The last property, which may come somewhat as a surprise, is a direct consequence of the reordering in Definition 5.30.

Choice

Consider the conformant sequential processes $a°; P$ and $b°; Q$. Sequential processes of this form are called *guarded* processes. We are interested in a sequential process that behaves either like $a°; P$ or like $b°; Q$, such that the environment may choose between the two sequential processes by offering either a_0 or b_0. This is quite different from $a°; P \sqcap b°; Q$, in which the choice between the operands of $\sqcap$ is made nondeterministically.

The above choice is denoted by $[a°; P \mid b°; Q]$, and behaves like the sequential process $a°; P \sqcap b°; Q$, except that traces a_0 and b_0 are not quiescent. The choice construct can be generalized by allowing enclosures as guarded processes. Recall that an enclosure is a sequential process of the form $a° : P$. This brings us to the following definitions.

Definition 5.32   (guarded process)

A guarded process is a sequential process that can be written as $b°; P$ or as $b° : P$, for a *unique b*. Port $b°$ is called the *guard* of the guarded process.

$\square$

Recall that $b°$ is equivalent to $b°; skip$ and to $b° : skip$. The above definition of guarded processes excludes processes of the form $a° : (b° : P)$, because they can be rewritten as $b° : (a° : P)$ (cf. Property 5.31.4). Guarded processes with multiple guards are not required for the compilation of Tangram, and are excluded to simplify the definition of choice.

Definition 5.33   (choice)

Let P and Q be two conformant guarded processes, with disjoint guards p and q. If P is an enclosure we require $p \notin \mathbf{p}°P$ and similarly for Q and q. The choice between P and Q is denoted by $[P \mid Q]$, and defined as

$$\langle A, \mathbf{t}((A) \cdot P) \setminus \{q_0\} \cup \mathbf{t}((A) \cdot Q) \setminus \{p_0\}, \mathbf{u}P \cup \mathbf{u}Q \rangle$$

where $A = \mathbf{p}P \cup \mathbf{p}Q$.

$\square$

The difference with the nondeterministic composition of P and Q is rather subtle. In contrast with nondeterministic composition trace p_0 is not a quiescent trace, *unless* it is a quiescent trace of P; similarly for trace q_0 and Q.

Property 5.34

Let P and Q be two conformant guarded processes.

0. $[P \mid Q]$ is a sequential process.

1. Choice is commutative, distributive and continuous.

2. $[a^\circ : stop \mid b^\circ : stop] = STOP \cdot (a^\circ \cup b^\circ)$

3. $[a^\circ; b^\circ \mid b^\circ; a^\circ] = a^\circ \parallel b^\circ$

□

The sequential process denoted in the last property is

$$\langle a^\circ \cup b^\circ, \{\varepsilon, a_0 a_1, b_0 b_1\}, \{a_0 a_1 b_0 b_1\}^{\mathbf{r}} \cup \{b_0 b_1 a_0 a_1\}^{\mathbf{r}} \rangle$$

The choice construct can readily be generalized to provide a choice among N, $N > 0$, guarded processes.

5.3 Examples

Since handshake processes correspond to permanent sequential handshake processes, the calculus of Section 5.2 can be used to specify handshake processes.

Example 5.35

Most handshake processes of Example 3.23 are repeated below, but now represented by expressions in the handshake calculus.

0.	$STOP \cdot (a^\circ)$	$=$	$(a^\circ) \cdot stop$
1.	$RUN \cdot (a^\circ)$	$=$	$\#[a^\circ]$
2.	$CON \cdot (a^\circ, b^\bullet)$	$=$	$\#[a^\circ : b^\bullet]$
3.	$OR \cdot (a^\circ, b^\bullet, c^\bullet)$	$=$	$\#[a^\circ : (b^\bullet \sqcap c^\bullet)]$
4.	$SEQ \cdot (a^\circ, b^\bullet, c^\bullet)$	$=$	$\#[a^\circ : (b^\bullet; c^\bullet)]$
5.	$DUP \cdot (a^\circ, b^\bullet)$	$=$	$\#[a^\circ : (b^\bullet; b^\bullet)]$
6.	$REP \cdot (a^\circ, b^\bullet)$	$=$	$(a^\circ : \#[b^\bullet])$
7.	$PAR \cdot (a^\circ, b^\bullet, c^\bullet)$	$=$	$\#[a^\circ : (b^\bullet \parallel c^\bullet)]$
8.	$MIX \cdot (a^\circ, b^\circ, c^\bullet)$	$=$	$\#[[a^\circ : c^\bullet \mid b^\circ : c^\bullet]]$
9.	$PAS \cdot (a^\circ, b^\circ)$	$=$	$\#[a^\circ : b^\circ]$
10.	$JOIN \cdot (a^\circ, b^\circ, c^\bullet)$	$=$	$\#[a^\circ : b^\circ : c^\bullet]$

11. $COUNT_N \cdot (a^\circ, b^\bullet) \;=\; \#[a^\circ : \#N[b^\bullet]]$

□

In Chapter 3 we have established the above components to be *initial-when-closed*, meaning that for each closed trace t in $P^\leq$ the process $after \cdot (t, P)$ is a refinement of P itself. The property initial-when-closed can be checked syntactically, as shown by the next property.

Property 5.36

A sequential handshake process that can be written in the form $\#[a^\circ : P]$ or in the form $\#[a^\circ : P \mid b^\circ : Q]$ is permanent. The corresponding (non-sequential) handshake process is both passive and initial-when-closed.

□

Note that $(a^\circ) \cdot stop$ can also be written as $\#[a^\circ : stop]$. As a matter of fact, all handshake components required for the compilation of Tangram can be written in one of the two forms of Property 5.36.

5.4   Directed communications

With the calculus introduced so far we can only specify sequential processes with nonput ports. The handshake circuits obtained by the translation of Tangram programs also require handshake components with input and output ports, such as $VAR_{bool} \cdot (a^\circ, b^\circ)$ in Example 3.23. This section extends the calculus of the previous section to sequential handshake processes that communicate data. These extensions are introduced informally and applied to the specification of handshake components.

Declarations

The first operand of the concealment construct $[\![\; A \mid P \;]\!]$ may also contain declarations of variables. For instance, $x : \textbf{var}\ T$ declares variable x of type T. The scope of such a declaration is delineated by the enclosing bracket pair.

Input

Assume port definition $a^\circ ? T$, where T is a finite set of values, such as *bool*. The sequential process $a^\circ ? x$ has the above port structure, and responds to any input $a_0 : v$, with $v \in T$, with an acknowledgement a_1.

The x in $a^\circ ? x$ is a variable that denotes the incoming value (cf. Tangram), and may be referenced elsewhere. In the sequential composition $a^\circ ? x ; F \cdot x$ the second operand $F \cdot x$ denotes a sequential process whose behavior depends on the value of x. In the enclosure $a^\circ ? x : F \cdot x$ the acknowledgement to an incoming value through a° is postponed until after the successful termination of $F \cdot x$. Both $a^\circ ? x ; F \cdot x$ and $a^\circ ? x : F \cdot x$ are guarded processes and may therefore occur as alternatives in choice processes.

With active port $a^\bullet?T$, sequential process $a^\bullet?x$ requests an input by outputting a_0. Then it is receptive to all inputs $a_1 : v$ with $v \in T$. In the sequential composition $a^\bullet?x; F \cdot x$ the behavior of sequential process $F \cdot x$ depends on the value of x, being the most recent value input through $a^\bullet$.

Output

An example of a sequential process whose behavior depends on the value of x is the output process $a^\circ!E(x)$, where $E(x)$ is an expression in which x occurs as a free variable. The enclosure $a^\circ!E(x) : P$ is a sequential process, that behaves like P after communication a_0, and, after successful termination of P *and* successful evaluation of E, concludes with communication $a_1 : E(x)$. The value of $E(x)$ may depend on P. For instance, the terminal traces of $b^\circ!x : a^\bullet?x$ are $b_0 \, a_0 \, a_1 : v \, b_1 : v$, with v ranging over T. The active counterpart of $a^\circ!E(x)$ is $a^\bullet!E(x)$.

Guarded selection

The equivalent of guarded commands (see Chapter 2) can be introduced as well. With B a Boolean expression, **if** $B \to P$ **fi** behaves as P if B evaluates to *true*, and is left unspecified otherwise. This generalizes to selections with multiple guards in the well-known way.

Sequential process **do** $B \to P$ **od** repeatedly behaves as P, as long as B evaluates to *true*. In particular **do** *false* $\to P$ **od** behaves like $SKIP \cdot (\mathbf{p}P)$ and **do** *true* $\to P$ **od** behaves like $\#[P]$.

Examples

The handshake processes below illustrate the above extensions. Together with the handshake processes of Example 3.23 they form a complete list of all handshake components required for the compilation of Tangram programs.

Example 5.37

0. $STOP_{(?,T)} \cdot (a^\circ)$ accepts any input $a : v$, with $v \in T$, but does not respond to it:

$STOP_{(?,T)} \cdot (a^\circ)$
$=$
$STOP \cdot (a^\circ?T)$

1. $STOP_{(!,T)} \cdot (a^\circ)$ does not respond to a request for a value in T.

$STOP_{(!,T)} \cdot (a^\circ)$
$=$
$STOP \cdot (a^\circ!T)$

2. $RUN_{(?,T)} \cdot (a^\circ)$ repeatedly responds to any input through a of type T with the acknowledgement a_1:

$RUN_{(?,T)} \cdot (a^\circ)$

$=$

$RUN \cdot (a^\circ ? T)$

3. $RUN_{(!,T)} \cdot (a^\circ)$ repeatedly responds to a_0 by an output of the form $a_1 : v$, with $v \in T$, and is clearly static nondeterministic:

$RUN_{(!,T)} \cdot (a^\circ)$

$=$

$RUN \cdot (a^\circ ! T)$

4. With C a constant, $CST \cdot_C (a^\circ)$ repeatedly responds to input a_0 with output $a_1 : C$. Process $CST \cdot_C (a^\circ)$ may be regarded as a deterministic refinement of $RUN_{(!,T)} \cdot (a^\circ)$, provided that the value of C is in T.

$CST \cdot_C (a^\circ)$

$=$

$(a^\circ ! \{C\}) \cdot \#[a^\circ ! C]$

5. *Connector* $CON_{(?,T)} \cdot (a^\circ, b^\bullet)$ repeatedly passes a value of set T arriving at passive port a through active port b.

$CON_{(?,T)} \cdot (a^\circ, b^\bullet)$

$=$

$(a^\circ ? T, b^\bullet ! T) \cdot \#[\, \| \; x : \; \mathbf{var} \; T \mid a^\circ ? x : b^\bullet ! x \, \|\,]$

6. *Connector* $CON_{(!,T)} \cdot (a^\circ, b^\bullet)$ is similar to $CON_{(?,T)} \cdot (a^\circ, b^\bullet)$, except that it is "demand driven", whereas the latter is "data driven".

$CON_{(!,T)} \cdot (a^\circ, b^\bullet)$

$=$

$(a^\circ ! T, b^\bullet ? T) \cdot \#[\, \| \; x : \; \mathbf{var} \; T \mid a^\circ ! x : b^\bullet ? x \, \|\,]$

7. $UN_{(\square,T)} \cdot (a^\circ, b^\bullet)$ behaves rather similar to $CON_{(!,T)} \cdot (a^\circ, b^\bullet)$. The main difference is that the value output through a° is $\square v$, where v is the most recent value input through $b^\bullet$, and $\square$ is a unary operator. If $\square v$ is not defined, the subsequent behavior is left unspecified. The type of port a° is $\square T$.

$UN_{(\square,T)} \cdot (a^\circ, b^\bullet)$

$=$

$(a^\circ ! \square T, b^\bullet ? T) \cdot \#[\, \| \; x : \; \mathbf{var} \; T \mid a^\circ ! (\square x) : b^\bullet ? x \, \|\,]$

Examples of unary operators are '$\neg$' and '$-$'.

8. $ADAPT_{(T,U)} \cdot (a^\circ, b^\bullet)$ is a specialization of $UN_{(\square,T)} \cdot (a^\circ, b^\bullet)$. For input values in T it behaves as a connector. After reception of a value in $U \setminus T$ its subsequent behavior is left unspecified.

$ADAPT_{(T,U)} \cdot (a^\circ, b^\bullet)$
=
$(a^\circ!T, b^\bullet?U) \cdot$
#[[x : **var** $T \cup U \mid a^\circ!x : (b^\bullet?x; \text{ if } x \in T \to skip \text{ fi})$]]

9. $BIN_{(\square,U,V)} \cdot (a^\circ, b^\bullet, c^\bullet)$ is the generalization of $UN_{(\square,T)} \cdot (a^\circ, b^\bullet)$ to binary operators. The type of port a° is $U \square V$.

$BIN_{(\square,U,V)} \cdot (a^\circ, b^\bullet, c^\bullet)$
=
$(a^\circ!(U \square V), b^\bullet?U, c^\bullet?V) \cdot$
  #[[x : **var** U & y : **var** V
    $\mid a^\circ!(x \square y) : (b^\bullet?x \parallel c^\bullet?y)$
      ]
  ]

Examples of binary operators are '$\vee$', '$\wedge$', '$=$', '$<$', '$+$', '$-$', and '$*$'.

10. $MIX_{(!,T)} \cdot (a^\circ, b^\circ, c^\bullet)$ is one of the two generalizations of $MIX \cdot (a^\circ, b^\circ, c^\bullet)$ that is considered. Incoming values of type T through ports $a?T$ and $b?T$ are passed through $c!T$. The subsequent acknowledgement through $c^\bullet!T$ is routed to the origin of the last message. $MIX_{(!,T)} \cdot (a^\circ, b^\circ, c^\bullet)$ may be called a *multiplexer*.

$MIX_{(!,T)} \cdot (a^\circ, b^\circ, c^\bullet)$
=
$(a^\circ?T, b^\circ?T, c^\bullet!T) \cdot$
#[[x : **var** $T \mid [a^\circ?x : c^\bullet!x \mid b^\circ?x : c^\bullet!x]$]]

11. $MIX_{(?,T)} \cdot (a^\circ, b^\circ, c^\bullet)$ is the other generalization of $MIX \cdot (a^\circ, b^\circ, c^\bullet)$. Requests through $a^\circ!T$ and $b^\circ!T$ are passed through $c^\bullet?T$. The subsequent value input through $c^\bullet?T$ is passed through the output port where the request came from. An appropriate name for this process is *demultiplexer*.

$MIX_{(?,T)} \cdot (a^\circ, b^\circ, c^\bullet)$
=
$(a^\circ!T, b^\circ!T, c^\bullet?T) \cdot$
#[[x : **var** $T \mid [a^\circ!x : c^\bullet?x \mid b^\circ!x : c^\bullet?x]$]]

If a multiplexer is considered as the data-driven generalization of the mixer, the demultiplexer is to be considered as its demand-driven generalization.

12. $JOIN_{(?,T)} \cdot (a^\circ, b^\circ, c^\bullet)$ generalizes the $JOIN \cdot (a^\circ, b^\circ, c^\bullet)$ in a demand-driven way. Requests through a and b are joined before the request is passed through c. The incoming data through c is forked through a and b.

$JOIN_{(?,T)} \cdot (a^\circ, b^\circ, c^\bullet)$

$=$

$(a^\circ!T, b^\circ!T, c^\bullet?T) \cdot \#[\,[\![\ x :\ \textbf{var}\ T\ |\ a^\circ!x : b^\circ!x : c^\bullet?x\ ]\!]\,]$

13. $JOIN_{(!,T)}(a^\circ, b^\circ, c^\bullet)$ generalizes the $JOIN(a^\circ, b^\circ, c^\bullet)$ in a data-driven (though rather subtle) way. The incoming data through a is joined with a request through b before the value is passed through c. An acknowledgement through c leads to an acknowledgement through a and an output of the value through b.

$JOIN_{(!,T)} \cdot (a^\circ, b^\circ, c^\bullet)$

$=$

$(a^\circ?T, b^\circ!T, c^\bullet!T) \cdot \#[\,[\![\ x :\ \textbf{var}\ T\ |\ a^\circ?x : b^\circ!x : c^\bullet!x\ ]\!]\,]$

14. $TRF_T \cdot (a^\circ, b^\bullet, c^\bullet)$ is a *transferrer*. Repeatedly, after activation through a° it actively requests an input through port $b^\bullet?T$ and actively passes the message through port $c^\bullet!T$, before it acknowledges through a°. It is a key component in the translation of Tangram input, output and assignment commands.

$TRF_T \cdot (a^\circ, b^\bullet, c^\bullet)$

$=$

$(a^\circ, b^\bullet?T, c^\bullet!T) \cdot \#[a^\circ :\ [\![\ x :\ \textbf{var}\ T\ |\ b^\bullet?x ; c^\bullet!x\ ]\!]\,]$

15. The Boolean variable of Example 3.23 is generalized to a variable of arbitrary type below.

$VAR_T \cdot (a^\circ, b^\circ)$

$=$

$(a^\circ?T, b^\circ!T) \cdot [\![\ x :\ \textbf{var}\ T\ |\ \#[[a^\circ?x\ |\ b^\circ!x]]\ ]\!]$

Variable x is declared outside the unbounded repetition. This ensures that the value output with $b^\circ!x$ is the most recent value input through a°. If an output is requested before any value has been input, VAR_T may output any value from T.

16. The last three components are needed for the translation of Tangram's guarded commands. Component $IF \cdot (a^\circ, b^\bullet, c^\bullet)$ responds to an a_0 by an active input of a Boolean value through $b^\bullet?bool$. If this value equals *false*, its subsequent behavior is left unspecified. If this value is *true*, an active handshake through $c^\bullet$ follows and after a subsequent a_1 the component returns to its initial state.

$IF \cdot (a^\circ, b^\bullet, c^\bullet)$
=
$(a^\circ, b^\bullet?bool, c^\bullet) \cdot$
$\#[a^\circ : \ [\![\ x : \ \mathbf{var}\ bool\ |\ b^\bullet?x;\ \mathbf{if}\ x \to c^\bullet\ \mathbf{fi}\ ]\!]\ ]$

17. Component $DO \cdot (a^\circ, b^\bullet, c^\bullet)$ responds to an a_0 by an active input of a Boolean value through $b^\bullet?bool$. If this value equals *true*, an active $c^\bullet$ comes next, followed by another active input through $b^\bullet?bool$. This repeats until the value *false* arrives. When the value *false* arrives, the component returns to its initial state after an a_1.

$DO \cdot (a^\circ, b^\bullet, c^\bullet)$
=
$(a^\circ, b^\bullet?bool, c^\bullet) \cdot$
$\#[a^\circ : \ [\![\ x : \ \mathbf{var}\ bool\ |\ b^\bullet?x;\ \mathbf{do}\ x \to c^\bullet; b^\bullet?x\ \mathbf{od}\ ]\!]\ ]$

18. $BAR \cdot (b^\circ, c^\circ, lb^\bullet, lc^\bullet, rb^\bullet, rc^\bullet)$ is the most complex component for more than one reason. Firstly, it has as many as 6 ports, organized in three pairs (b, c), (lb, lc) and (rb, rc). Secondly, it combines two more or less independent behaviors, from which the environment can choose. Its behavior is best explained by the restricted form in which it is used in compiled Tangram programs: as a 2-phase behavior.

Phase 0 starts with a request for a Boolean output through b. This request is forked through lb and rb. The disjunction of the incoming Boolean values is then returned through b. Let x and y denote these incoming Boolean values.

Phase 1 starts with a request through c°. Depending on the values of x and y, the component responds with an active handshake through lc (if $x = true$), or with an active handshake through rc (if $y = true$). If both x and y are *true*, the choice between lc and rc is nondeterministic. If both values are *false* the subsequent behavior is left unspecified.

$BAR \cdot (b^\circ, c^\circ, lb^\bullet, lc^\bullet, rb^\bullet, rc^\bullet)$
=
$(b^\circ!bool, c^\circ, lb^\bullet?bool, lc^\bullet, rb^\bullet?bool, rc^\bullet) \cdot$
$\ \ [\![\quad x, y : \ \mathbf{var}\ bool$
$\ \ |\quad \#[\quad [b^\circ!(x \vee y) \quad : (lb^\bullet?x\ ||\ rb^\bullet?y)$
$\ \ \qquad\qquad |\ c^\circ \qquad\qquad : \mathbf{if}\ x \to lc^\bullet\ []\ y \to rc^\bullet\ \mathbf{fi}$
$\ \ \qquad\qquad]$
$\ \ \qquad]$
$\ \ ]\!]$

□

Chapter 6

Tangram

6.0 Introduction

Tangram is a VLSI-programming language based on CSP, and has much in common with the programming language OCCAM [INM89] (see Section 2.7 for some of the differences). The main construct of Tangram is the *command*. Commands are either primitive commands, such as $a?x$ and $x := x + 1$, or composite commands, such as $R; S$ and $R \parallel S$, where R and S are commands themselves.

Execution of a command may result in a number of communications with the environment through external ports. Another form of interaction with the environment is the reading from and writing into external variables. A Tangram *program* is a command without external variables, prefixed by an explicit definition of its external ports.

Not all compositions of commands are valid in Tangram. For instance, in a sequential composition the two constituent commands must agree on the input/output direction of their common ports. Also, two commands composed in parallel may not write concurrently into a common variable. Similarly, concurrent reading from and writing into a common variable is not allowed. Section 6.1 defines the syntax of Tangram, including these composition rules. The meaning of each command is described informally.

For a subset of the Tangram commands the *handshake-process* denotations are given in Section 6.3. This subset is referred to as *Core Tangram*.

6.1 Tangram

The main syntactic constructs of Tangram are program, command, guarded-command set, and expression. With each construct we associate a so-called alphabet structure: a set of typed ports and variables.

Alphabet structures

Let *Val* denote the set of all values. *Val* includes the Boolean values *bool*, *bool* = {*false*, *true*} , and the integer numbers. *Val* also contains the special *null* value ~. A *type* is a finite subset of *Val*. The set of all types is denoted by $\mathcal{P} \cdot Val$, viz. the power set of *Val*. Ports and variables are typed. The type information of ports and variables is recorded in an *alphabet structure*.

Definition 6.0   (alphabet structure)

0. An alphabet structure A is a 5-tuple $\langle \mathbf{p?}A, \mathbf{p!}A, \mathbf{v?}A, \mathbf{v!}A, \tau_A \rangle$, where $\mathbf{p?}A$, $\mathbf{p!}A$, $\mathbf{v?}A$, $\mathbf{v!}A$ are sets of names.

1. $\mathbf{p?}A$ is the set of *input ports*, and $\mathbf{p!}A$ the set of *output ports*. $\mathbf{p?}A$ and $\mathbf{p!}A$ must be disjoint; their union is denoted by $\mathbf{p}A$.

2. $\mathbf{v?}A$ is the set of *read ports* and $\mathbf{v!}A$ the set of *write ports*. Sets $\mathbf{v?}A$ and $\mathbf{v!}A$ need not be disjoint, because a process may read from and write into the same variable. The union of the two sets is denoted by $\mathbf{v}A$.

3. $\mathbf{p}A$ and $\mathbf{v}A$ must be disjoint. The set of all ports, i.e. the union of $\mathbf{p}A$ and $\mathbf{v}A$, is denoted by $\mathbf{c}A$.

4. τ_A is the *type function* of alphabet structure A:

$$\tau_A : \mathbf{c}A \rightarrow \mathcal{P} \cdot Val$$

   It assigns a type to each name in $\mathbf{c}A$.

5. The empty alphabet structure $\langle \emptyset, \emptyset, \emptyset, \emptyset, \emptyset \rangle$ is abbreviated to $\emptyset$.

□

Symbols $\mathbf{p?}$, $\mathbf{p!}$, $\mathbf{p}$, $\mathbf{v?}$, $\mathbf{v!}$, $\mathbf{v}$ and $\mathbf{c}$ are considered as operators on alphabet structures. A concise notation for alphabet structures is based on so-called *port definitions*. A port definition may have one of the four forms below.

Definition 6.1   (port definition)

Let a and x be names and let T be a finite subset of *Val*.

0. $a\sim = \langle \{a\}, \emptyset, \emptyset, \emptyset, \{(a, \{\sim\})\} \rangle$, a synchronization port.

1. $a?T = \langle \{a\}, \emptyset, \emptyset, \emptyset, \{(a, T)\} \rangle$, an input port of type T.

2. $a!T = \langle \emptyset, \{a\}, \emptyset, \emptyset, \{(a, T)\} \rangle$, an output port of type T.

3. $x : T = \langle \emptyset, \emptyset, \{x\}, \{x\}, \{(x, T)\} \rangle$, a variable of type T.

□

Without loss of generality we may treat a synchronization port as an input port of type $\{\sim\}$ in 6.1.1. In the definition of connectable alphabet structures below it becomes clear that treating synchronization ports a output ports would have been restrictive.

The following definition introduces a few notions that are useful when composing Tangram commands and expressions. For the remainder of this chapter, let A and B be alphabet structures.

Definition 6.2   **(relations and operations on alphabet structures)**

0. A and B are *type compatible* if common names are either ports or variables in both alphabet structures, and if these common names are of the same type, i.e. if

$$(\mathbf{p}A \cap \mathbf{v}B = \emptyset) \wedge (\mathbf{p}B \cap \mathbf{v}A = \emptyset)$$
$$\wedge \quad (\forall a : a \in \mathbf{c}A \cap \mathbf{c}B : \tau_A \cdot a = \tau_B \cdot a)$$

1. A and B are *conformant*, denoted by $A \bigtriangleup\!\!\bigtriangleup B$, if they are type compatible and if their common ports agree in direction:

$$A \bigtriangleup\!\!\bigtriangleup B = \quad A \text{ and } B \text{ are type compatible}$$
$$\wedge \quad (\mathbf{p?}A \cap \mathbf{p!}B = \emptyset) \wedge (\mathbf{p?}B \cap \mathbf{p!}A = \emptyset)$$

2. The *conformant union* of two conformant alphabet structures A and B is denoted by $A \cup_{\bigtriangleup\!\!\bigtriangleup} B$, and is defined as the componentwise union of A and B.

3. The *conformant difference* of two conformant alphabet structures A and B is denoted by $A \setminus_{\bigtriangleup\!\!\bigtriangleup} B$, and is defined as the componentwise set difference of A and B.

4. A and B are *connectable*, denoted by $A \bowtie B$, if they are type compatible, have no common output ports, and variables with write access in one structure do not occur in the other structure:

$$A \bowtie B = \quad A \text{ and } B \text{ are type compatible}$$
$$\wedge \quad (\mathbf{p!}A \cap \mathbf{p!}B = \emptyset) \wedge (\mathbf{v}A \cap \mathbf{v!}B = \emptyset) \wedge (\mathbf{v!}A \cap \mathbf{v}B = \emptyset)$$

5. The *connectable union* of two conformant alphabet structures A and B is denoted by $A \cup_{\bowtie} B$, and is defined as the componentwise union of A and B, *except* for $\mathbf{p?}(A \cup_{\bowtie} B)$:

$$\mathbf{p?}(A \cup_{\bowtie} B) = (\mathbf{p?}A \cup \mathbf{p?}B) \setminus (\mathbf{p!}A \cup \mathbf{p!}B)$$

i.e. the output ports dominate.

6. Let D denote a list of port definitions that define mutually conformant alphabet structures. Then D defines the alphabet structure formed by the conformant union of the alphabet structures of the individual port definitions. This alphabet structure is denoted by $\mathbf{A}D$.

$\square$

Alphabet structures will be defined for Tangram programs, commands, guarded-command sets and expressions. In many instances, these alphabet structures are expressed in terms of the alphabet structures of the constituent constructs, with an associated composition rule.

Programs

Let S be a command and let D be a list of port definitions. Then the following table defines valid Tangram programs. (Let $\mathbf{A}S$ denote the alphabet structure of command S.)

construct	alphabet structure	rule
$(D) \cdot S$	$\mathbf{A}D$	$\mathbf{A}S \subseteq \mathbf{A}D \wedge \mathbf{v}\mathbf{A}S = \emptyset$

The (composition) rule states that S has no external variables, and that all external ports must be defined in D. The behavior of program $(D) \cdot S$ is that of command S. The program does not participate in communications though ports in $\mathbf{A}D \setminus \mathbf{A}S$.

Primitive commands

The primitive commands of Tangram are listed in the table below. Let a be declared[0] as a port of type U, let x be declared as a variable of type V, and let E be an expression with alphabet structure $\mathbf{A}E$.

construct	alphabet structure	rule
stop	$\emptyset$	
skip	$\emptyset$	
a	$a\sim$	
$a?x$	$a?U \cup_{\triangle\triangle} \langle \emptyset, \emptyset, \emptyset, \{x\}, \{(x,V)\} \rangle$	$a \neq x$
$a!E$	$a!U \cup_{\triangle\triangle} \mathbf{A}E$	$a \notin \mathbf{v}?\mathbf{A}E$
$x := E$	$\langle \emptyset, \emptyset, \emptyset, \{x\}, \{(x,V)\} \rangle \cup_{\triangle\triangle} \mathbf{A}E$	

- *stop* does not engage in any action; it corresponds to an unconditional deadlock.

- *skip* does not engage in any action either, but it does terminate successfully.

- a is a *synchronization command*. The execution of a amounts to a synchronization action through port a.

- $a?x$ is an *input command*. The execution of $a?x$ involves the reception of a value through port a and the subsequent storage of that value in variable x. If the received value is not in V the effect of $a?x$ is left unspecified.

- $a!E$ is an *output command*. The execution of $a!E$ starts with the evaluation of E. If this evaluation terminates and the result is in U, this value is sent through a as soon as the environment is ready to receive it. Otherwise the behavior of $a!E$ is left unspecified: it may for instance result in deadlock, or in sending an unspecified value ($\in U$) through a.

- $x := E$ is an assignment command. If the evaluation of E terminates and the result value is in V, the execution of $x := E$ assigns the result value of this evaluation to x. Otherwise the behavior of $x := E$ is left unspecified.

---

[0]Declarations are discussed with the block command.

Composite commands

All composite commands, except the selection and repetition commands, are listed in the table below. Let R and S be commands, N a natural number, and let D be a list of port definitions.

construct	alphabet structure	rule
$R \sqcap S$	$AR \cup_{\wedge\wedge} AS$	$AR \wedge\wedge AS$
$R; S$	$AR \cup_{\wedge\wedge} AS$	$AR \wedge\wedge AS$
$\#N[S]$	AS	
$\#[S]$	AS	
$R \parallel S$	$AR \cup_{\bowtie} AS$	$AR \bowtie AS$
$[\![\, D \mid S \,]\!]$	$AS \setminus_{\wedge\wedge} AD$	$AD \wedge\wedge AS$
$(D) \cdot S$	$AD \cup_{\wedge\wedge} AS$	$AD \wedge\wedge AS$

- $R \sqcap S$ is the *nondeterministic composition* of R and S. This composition behaves either like R or like S, where the selection between them is nondeterministic. This command is included mainly for theoretical interest, since the programmer could use the command R or the command S instead.

- $R; S$ is the *sequential composition* of R and S. It first behaves like R and, when R terminates successfully, continues by behaving like S. If R does not terminate successfully, neither does $R; S$.

- $\#N[S]$ is the *N-fold repetition* of S. Command $\#0[S]$ behaves like *skip* (but has a different alphabet structure), and for $N > 0$ the behavior of $\#N[S]$ is that of $S; \#(N-1)[S]$.

- $\#[S]$ is the *unbounded repetition* of S. It never terminates successfully.

- $R \parallel S$ is the *parallel composition* of R and S. Note that neither R nor S is allowed to have write access to common variables. Also, R and S may not share output ports. However, R and S may share input ports and variables with read access.

  The behavior of this composition must agree with the behavior of both R and S. Its execution involves the parallel execution of both R and S. Communications on common ports must occur simultaneously in R and S. The synchronized execution of $a!E$ in one process and $a?x$ in the other has also the effect of $x := E$, provided that the value of E is in the type of a.

- $[\![\, D \mid S \,]\!]$ is a *block (command)*. A port definition in D has two roles in this construct. Firstly, the type function of the alphabet structure of D applies to the ports of S. Secondly, the names declared in D are hidden (concealed) from the environment of the block. In other words, D declares port and variable names, whose scope is bound by the enclosing scope brackets. The behavior of $[\![\, D \mid S \,]\!]$ is that of S, with all interaction on ports and variables declared in D concealed from the environment.

- $(D) \cdot S$ extends the alphabet structure of S by the port definitions of D. $(D) \cdot S$ is not prepared to engage in any communication through the ports $AD \setminus_{\wedge\wedge} AS$; otherwise it behaves like S.

Of the binary command operators, the semicolon binds the strongest, followed by '||' and then '⊓'. As usual, the bracket pair '(' and ')' may be used to overrule this priority rule.

Guarded commands

The selection and repetition commands are listed in the table below. They introduce so-called *guarded-command sets* [Dij75], a third syntactic category next to programs and commands. Let B be a Boolean expression, S a command, and let G and H be guarded-command sets.

construct	alphabet structure	rule
if G **fi**	AG	
do G **od**	AG	
$B \to S$	$AB \cup_\text{⅍} AS$	$AB \mathbin{\text{⅍}} AS$
$G \,[\!]\, H$	$AG \cup_\text{⅍} AH$	$AG \mathbin{\text{⅍}} AH$

- The execution of a selection command with a guarded-command set G depends on the value of $BB \cdot G$, the disjunction of the guards of G:

$$BB \cdot \emptyset \qquad\qquad = \textit{false}$$
$$BB \cdot (B \to S) = \text{ value of } B$$
$$BB \cdot (G \,[\!]\, H) \;\; = \;\; BB \cdot G \vee BB \cdot H$$

If $BB \cdot G$ evaluates to *false*, the behavior of the selection command is left unspecified: for instance, it may stop. Otherwise, the selection command behaves like one of the commands of the guarded-command set for which the guard evaluates to *true*.

- **do** G **od** is Tangram's guarded repetition command. As long as $BB \cdot G$ evaluates to *true*, one of the commands for which the guard evaluates to *true* is selected for execution. When $BB \cdot G$ evaluates to *false*, **do** G **od** terminates successfully. Accordingly, **do od** is equivalent to *skip*.

Expressions

Expressions form a fourth syntactic category in Tangram. They occur in assignments, output commands and guards. The four forms of expression are listed in the table below. Let E and F be expressions, x a variable declared of type V, and let C be a constant.

construct	alphabet structure	rule
C	$\emptyset$	
x	$\langle \emptyset, \emptyset, \{x\}, \emptyset, \{(x, V)\}\rangle$	
$\square E$	AE	
$E \square F$	$AE \cup_\text{⅍} AF$	$AE \mathbin{\text{⅍}} AF$

- The value of expression C is simply the value of constant C; its type is $\{C\}$. The evaluation of expression C always terminates successfully.

- If x is declared as a variable, then x is also an expression with type V. The value of x is the value of the variable. The initial value of x is in V, but is otherwise unspecified. A program may therefore start with $b!x$, as was the case with the shift registers of Section 1.2. Successful termination is guaranteed.

- $\square E$ is an expression constructed from expression E and a unary operator '$\square$'. The type of $\square E$ is the set of values obtained by applying $\square$ to all elements of the type of E. The evaluation of $\square E$ terminates successfully if that of E does *and* the operator '$\square$' is defined for the value of E. If the evaluation of E terminates successfully the value of $\square E$ is obtained by applying $\square$ to the value of E.

- $E \square F$ is the natural generalization of $\square E$ to binary operators.

6.2   Tangram semantics

In Chapter 7 we shall develop a mapping from Tangram programs to handshake circuits. Recall that the (external) behavior of such a handshake circuit has been defined as the handshake process obtained by the parallel composition of its constituent handshake components (cf. Chapter 4). In order to relate a compiled handshake circuit to the original Tangram program, a handshake-process denotation of that Tangram program is required. Given such a denotation, it is sensible to require that the external behavior of the compiled handshake circuit is a refinement of that handshake-process denotation. In this section we investigate the semantics of Tangram in terms of (sequential) handshake processes.

There are two viable approaches to obtain a handshake-process denotation of a Tangram program:

0. the *direct approach* in which a sequential handshake processes is associated with each Tangram command;

1. the *indirect approach* comprising a denotation in terms of an existing process model (such as the well-known synchronous failures/divergences model of CSP) and a mapping from that model to handshake processes.

The direct approach is elaborated next. The indirect approach is discussed in Appendix B.

Direct approach

We want to associate a sequential handshake process with each Tangram command. An issue with far-reaching consequences is the choice between a passive or an active implementation for each Tangram port. It is clear that read and write accesses to external variables must be through active ports (cf. *VAR* in Example 3.23). Also, connectability requirements in the case of parallel composition have to be considered in the choice between passive or active port implementations. Note, for example, that a Tangram command without output ports is connectable to itself, which is obviously not true for a (sequential) handshake process. Another complication is that broadcast in Tangram (i.e. common ports are not concealed with parallel composition) has no counterpart in sequential handshake processes.

We shall ignore such complications for a while and first consider two simple strategies:

- *directed* mappings, viz. inputs passive and outputs active, or vice versa;

- *uniform* mappings, viz. the *all-passive* mapping (all ports implemented passively) or the *all-active* mapping (all ports implemented actively).

Both strategies are viable. Directed mappings have the advantage that directed point-to-point channels do not give rise to connectability violations. However, a provision has to be made for undirected channels and broadcast in Tangram. The directed mapping "inputs active and outputs passive" results in simpler and cheaper circuits than the other directed mapping [Mar89].

A uniform mapping leads to a simple translation strategy, as is shown in Chapter 7. After some simple local optimizations (cf. Section 8.1) circuits are obtained that are comparable in cost and performance to the circuits obtained by the directed mappings. In the sequel we shall consider uniform mappings only.

For both the all-passive and the all-active mappings the notions of conformance of (Tangram) alphabet structures and conformance of (handshake) port structures fully agree. However, also for both choices, parallel composition of sequential handshake processes requires redefinition, since connectability is satisfied only in trivial cases.

Consider connectable Tangram commands S and T, and let the corresponding compiled handshake circuits be denoted by $C \cdot S$ and $C \cdot T$. In general, these handshake circuits cannot be connected to form a larger handshake circuit: some form of "glue" handshake component is needed. We first compare the all-passive and the all-active mappings:

- All-passive tends to result in expensive handshake circuits: here we pay the price for receptiveness, especially for passive input ports (see also Section 8.2). More importantly, glue components that synchronize passive handshakes cannot be realized, because there is no way to enforce synchronization between two passive handshakes.

- All-active is relatively straightforward, and cheap. Moreover, passive glue can be realized: e.g. a passivator synchronizes two active handshakes. Moreover, with a *JOIN* as glue component, the common ports of a parallel composition remain accessible to the environment, thus providing the equivalent of broadcast. All-active is also consistent with the requirement for active read/write access to external variables. However, the all-active mapping does not allow us to lift the choice construct from the sequential handshake-process calculus to Tangram.

The all-active approach is clearly favored by the above analysis, and is therefore adopted for the semantics of Tangram. For Core Tangram such a denotation is presented in the next subsection. We expect that this approach can be extended to full Tangram. The price we pay is that a choice construct in Tangram is not accommodated, and that separately compiled programs cannot be connected directly.

6.3   Core Tangram

Core Tangram is obtained by reducing *Val* to $\{\sim\}$, and by subsequent weeding out of all constructs that have become meaningless or redundant. The resulting language is then defined in terms of sequential handshake processes. With ~ as the only value, the Tangram distinction between input and output disappears. Also, the concept of storage is no longer meaningful. Alphabet structures in Core Tangram have the form:

$$\langle \mathbf{p}A, \emptyset, \emptyset, \emptyset, \{a : a \in \mathbf{p}A : (a, \{\sim\})\}\rangle$$

Consequently, an alphabet structure does not contain any more information than the set of port names. Also, the notions type compatibility, conformance and connectability of alphabet structures become void: all alphabet structures are both conformant and connectable. For the remainder of this section alphabet structures contain input ports only, all of type $\{\sim\}$. Note also that the syntactic categories *expression* and *guarded-command set* are meaningless when $Val = \{\sim\}$.

Definition 6.3 **(port structure of an alphabet structure)**

Let A be a alphabet structure of the form $\langle \mathbf{p}?A, \emptyset, \emptyset, \emptyset, \{a : a \in \mathbf{p}A : (a, \{\sim\})\}\rangle$. The *port structure* of A, denoted by $\mathcal{H} \cdot A$, is defined as

$$(\cup a : a \in \mathbf{p}?A : a^\bullet)$$

Let D be a list of port definitions. The handshake expansion of D is that of $\mathbf{A}D$.

□

Clearly, $(\mathcal{H} \cdot A)^\circ = \emptyset$. The next definition gives the sequential handshake-process denotations for Core Tangram commands.

Definition 6.4 **(Core Tangram commands)**

Let a be a name, D a list of port definitions, N a natural number, and S and T Core Tangram commands. The ten commands of Core Tangram and their sequential handshake-processes denotations are enumerated below.

0. $\mathcal{H} \cdot skip = skip$

1. $\mathcal{H} \cdot stop = stop$

2. $\mathcal{H} \cdot a = a^\bullet$

3. $\mathcal{H} \cdot ((D) \cdot S) = (\mathcal{H} \cdot D) \cdot (\mathcal{H} \cdot S)$

4. $\mathcal{H} \cdot (S \sqcap T) = \mathcal{H} \cdot S \sqcap \mathcal{H} \cdot T$

5. $\mathcal{H} \cdot (S; T) = \mathcal{H} \cdot S ; \mathcal{H} \cdot T$

6. $\mathcal{H} \cdot (\#N[S]) = \#N[\mathcal{H} \cdot S]$

7. $\mathcal{H} \cdot (\#[S]) = \#[\mathcal{H} \cdot S]$

8. $\mathcal{H} \cdot (S \parallel T) = \mathcal{H} \cdot S \parallel \mathcal{H} \cdot T$, provided $\mathbf{A}S \cap \mathbf{A}T = \emptyset_A$.
   A general parallel composition is defined below.

9. $\mathcal{H} \cdot [\![D \, | \, S]\!] = [\![\mathcal{H} \cdot D \, | \, \mathcal{H} \cdot S]\!]$

□

General parallel composition in Core Tangram in the above context requires an alternative form of parallel composition of sequential handshake processes. This alternative must deal with common active ports and broadcast. Unlike the calculus for sequential handshake processes, Tangram separates concealment and parallel composition. A consequence of the latter is that we do not need to worry about divergences in the definition of parallel composition in Tangram. It is presumably possible to base the definition of this form of parallel composition on the existing definition by introducing glue handshake processes. (For permanent processes this is shown in Chapter 7.) However, this seems to result in a relatively ugly definition, and the successful termination aspect is hard to deal with. A simpler and more direct alternative is developed next.

Consider sequential handshake processes P and Q. Let a be a common (active) port of P and Q, and let trace t satisfy $t \lceil \mathbf{p}P \in \mathbf{t}P^{\leq}$ and similarly for Q: trace t may be observed when P and Q operate in parallel. Assume furthermore that output a_0 would lead P subsequently into a quiescent state (i.e. $ta_0 \in \mathbf{t}P$), but that Q is not prepared to output a_0 (i.e. $ta_0 \notin \mathbf{t}Q^{\leq}$). Appearantly, P and Q are not ready to synchronize with a handshake along a after t, and should t be a quiescent trace of the parallel composition of P and Q. This shows that the weave of P and Q is insufficient to describe the effect of parallel composition. A similar complication for the synchronization of input events does not occur, because we only consider receptive handshake processes.

The following definition of parallel composition is based on the observation that the inability of one process to participate in a common output forces the composite into a quiescent state.

Definition 6.5   (parallel composition in Core Tangram)

Let S and T be connectable Tangram commands. Let $P = \mathcal{H} \cdot S$ and $Q = \mathcal{H} \cdot T$.

0. $\mathcal{H} \cdot (S \parallel T) = \mathcal{H} \cdot S \overset{\bullet\bullet}{\parallel} \mathcal{H} \cdot T$

1. where $P \overset{\bullet\bullet}{\parallel} Q$ denotes the parallel composition of all-active processes P and Q, defined as

$$\langle \mathbf{p}P \cup \mathbf{p}Q, \mathbf{t}P^{\mathbf{S}} \; \mathbf{w} \; \mathbf{t}Q \; \cup \; \mathbf{t}P \; \mathbf{w} \; \mathbf{t}Q^{\mathbf{S}}, \mathbf{u}P \; \mathbf{w} \; \mathbf{u}Q \rangle$$

where weaving of trace sets is used as in Definition 4.14.

2. where $P^{\mathbf{S}}$ is the s-*closure* of P, based on the preorder s on handshake traces:

$$s \; \mathbf{s} \; t = (\exists u : u \in (\mathbf{o}P)^* : su = t)$$

s is a prefix of t that can be extended to t with outputs only.

□

Now that we have defined the parallel composition of connectable Tangram commands, we can complete the definition of the semantics of Core Tangram.

Definition 6.6   (Core Tangram program)

A Core Tangram program is an extension command of the form $(D) \cdot S$, such that $\mathbf{A}S \subseteq \mathbf{A}D$.

□

In Chapter 7 we also use the "repeatable go" of $\mathcal{H} \cdot T$.

Definition 6.7   (repeatable go)

Let P be a sequential handshake process. The *repeatable go* of P, denoted by $\rhd^* \cdot P$, is the sequential handshake process

$$\#[\, \rhd^\circ : P]$$

where port name $\rhd$ is pronounced as "go".

□

Consider $\rhd^* \cdot \mathcal{H} \cdot T$. The environment may start the execution of T by sending a $\rhd_0$. After T terminates successfully $\rhd^* \cdot \mathcal{H} \cdot T$ replies with a $\rhd_1$. After event $\rhd_1$ the handshake process is ready for another execution of T. Note also that $\rhd^* \cdot \mathcal{H} \cdot T$ is passive and initial-when-closed.

Function $\mathcal{H}$ defines a semantics for Tangram. We shall refer to this semantics as *handshake semantics* of Tangram. Extending $\mathcal{H}$ to full Tangram relies on the extension of the calculus in Chapter 5. In Chapter 7 we assume that $\mathcal{H}$ has been extended to cover all Tangram.

Chapter 7

Tangram → handshake circuits

7.0 Introduction

The topic of this chapter is the translation of Tangram programs into handshake circuits. Let T be a Tangram program. In Chapter 6 we have defined the meaning of T as the handshake process $\mathcal{H} \cdot T$. The translation to handshake circuits is presented as a mathematical function $\mathcal{C}$, from the set of Tangram programs to the set of handshake circuits. Thus, $\mathcal{C} \cdot T$ is a handshake circuit, and handshake process $\| \cdot \mathcal{C} \cdot T$ is the behavior of that circuit. Function $\mathcal{C}$ is designed such that

$$\triangleright^* \cdot \mathcal{H} \cdot T \ = \ \| \cdot \mathcal{C} \cdot T$$

where $\triangleright^* \cdot P$ was defined as $\#[\ \triangleright^\circ : P]$ (see Definition 6.7). That is, the translation preserves all the nondeterminism of the program. From a practical viewpoint it is sufficient to realize

$$\triangleright^* \cdot \mathcal{H} \cdot T \ \sqsubseteq \ \| \cdot \mathcal{C} \cdot T$$

in which the behavior of the handshake circuit is a refinement of the handshake behavior of the Tangram program. It may be expected that this relaxed form results in cheaper handshake circuits. The advantage of defining the most nondeterministic handshake circuit of T is that alternative translation functions that synthesize more deterministic circuits can readily be derived from it. Some of these alternatives will be indicated.

Also, we have chosen to translate a Tangram program into the handshake circuit with the most internal parallelism. In particular, all guards of a guarded command are evaluated in parallel, as are the two subexpressions of a binary operation. In general this leads to the fastest implementation, but not necessarily the most area-efficient one. If the VLSI programmer wishes a more sequential handshake circuit he can specify such at the Tangram level. For example, guarded selection

$$\textbf{if} \ B \ \rightarrow \ S$$
$$[\!]\ G$$
$$\textbf{fi}$$

with guarded command $B \rightarrow S$ and guarded command set G can be rewritten into the slightly more deterministic

$$\textbf{if} \ B \ \rightarrow \ S$$
$$[\!]\ \neg B \ \rightarrow \ \textbf{if} \ G \ \textbf{fi}$$
$$\textbf{fi}$$

This transformation also makes it possible to share resources in the evaluation of B and the guards in G. A sequential evaluation of the guards would give less of such freedom to the VLSI programmer.

The translation function $\mathcal{C}$ has been described briefly and incompletely in [vBKR⁺91]. A predecessor of the translation method [vBRS88] is organized quite differently, but yields essentially the same handshake circuits. Similar syntax-directed translation methods have been presented in [BM88, BS89, Bru91, Bro90, WBB91]. A major difference, however, is that these methods translate directly into some form of asynchronous gate-level circuits.

The translation of Tangram programs into handshake circuits is *syntax directed*, that is, the compilation function $\mathcal{C}$ is structured according to the syntax of Tangram. This technique is conveniently introduced by means of an example in which we apply $\mathcal{C}$ to *command T*. This example is also used to explain a graphical representation of the compilation function.

The concentric circles enclosing T denote the application of function $\mathcal{C}$ to the Tangram command T. The peripheral open circle represents the passive port $\triangleright$ and the peripheral filled circles represent the active ports of the compiled circuit. Now, suppose that T is of the form $R \, ; S$, such that the alphabet structures of R and S are disjoint. Syntax-directed translation suggests constructing the handshake circuit for T from the two handshake circuits obtained by the translation of R and S. These subcircuits behave like $\#[l \triangleright^\circ : \mathcal{H} \cdot R]$ and $\#[r \triangleright^\circ : \mathcal{H} \cdot S]$ respectively (with activation ports $l \triangleright$ and $r \triangleright$). The sequential activation of these two circuits can be enforced by connecting them to a sequencer as in

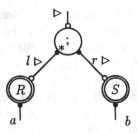

After the circuit is activated through $\triangleright$, by $\triangleright_0$, the sequencer activates the circuit corresponding to R by $l \triangleright_0$. Successful termination of R is acknowledged by $l \triangleright_1$, to which the sequencer responds with $r \triangleright_0$. If S also terminates successfully it indicates so by $r \triangleright_1$, and the execution of $R \, ; S$ is completed by $\triangleright_1$. Then the circuit is in its initial state, available for another execution of $R \, ; S$.

When R and S have ports in common, the translation of $R \, ; S$ is only slightly more complicated. Given the disjoint nature of the compiled subcircuits, a "glue" component is required to give both R and S access to a single external port. A mixer for each common port, together with proper renaming of the ports involved, results in the desired handshake circuit. In the circuit below, it is assumed that command R has ports a and b and that command S has ports b and c.

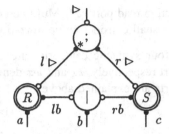

The general translation of Tangram commands of the form $R \; ; S$ is described later. The significance of the approach sketched above is that the compilation function can now be applied recursively to R and S *independently*. The required port renaming will be made more precise later.

Section 7.1 presents the translation of Tangram programs in a semiformal manner. For each Tangram production rule (cf. Section 6.1) a corresponding compilation rule is defined, supported by a graphical version of it and an operational interpretation. The required handshake components have been introduced in Examples 3.23, 5.35, and 5.37.

The aim of Section 7.2 is to formalize the discussed equivalence between Tangram programs and the corresponding handshake circuits in the Compilation Theorem. The scope of the Compilation Theorem is restricted to Core Tangram, as a consequence of similar restrictions on $\mathcal{H}$ and the handshake calculus in Section 5.2.

7.1 The compilation function

The translation of Tangram into handshake circuits is defined by means of compilation function $\mathcal{C}$. The syntax-directed organization of $\mathcal{C}$ makes it necessary to include all syntactic categories of Tangram in the domain of $\mathcal{C}$, viz. program, command, guarded-command set, and expression. The application of $\mathcal{C}$ to an element of each of these categories results in a handshake circuit. The port structures and behaviors of the handshake circuits corresponding to these syntactic categories are introduced informally below.

- Let S be a Tangram command. The port structure of $\mathcal{C} \cdot S$ consists of the passive activation port $\triangleright^\circ$ and an active port corresponding to each port of alphabet structure AS. A handshake through $\triangleright^\circ$ results in the execution of S, according to the handshake semantics of Tangram discussed in Chapter 6.

- Let T be a Tangram program. The port structure and behavior are those of *command T*.

- Let G be a non-empty guarded-command set in Tangram. The handshake circuit $\mathcal{C} \cdot G$ has, in addition to the handshake ports that stem from its alphabet structure, two passive ports, viz. b° and $\triangleright^\circ$. Port b° is a Boolean output port through which the environment may collect the *disjunction of the guards*. Port $\triangleright^\circ$ is the activation port through which the appropriate guarded command is selected for execution.

- Let E be a Tangram expression. The handshake circuit $\mathcal{C} \cdot E$ has a passive output port e° through which the value of E is output. For each variable x that occurs in E the circuit $C \cdot E$ has a single active read port $rx^\bullet$. Multiple occurrences of x share the same read port. (In Chapter 8 we shall consider an optimization.)

The handshake circuits for the four syntactic categories are depicted below. Here i and o denote an input and an output port respectively, rx and wx denote the read port and write port of a variable x, and the other ports are explained above.

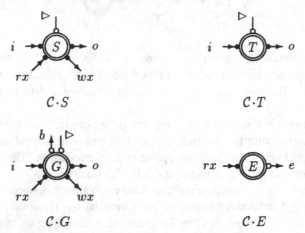

In the presentation of the compilation function C the grouping of syntactic constructs of Chapter 6 is followed. The order of these groups is slightly different for presentational purposes. Before defining C for all of Tangram's production rules, the technical issue of renaming of ports must be dealt with.

Renaming

The translation of composite Tangram commands, such as $R \, ; S$, results in a handshake circuit consisting of the subcircuits $C \cdot R$ and $C \cdot S$, and some "glue" circuitry. Part of this glue circuitry is required to deal with ports common to both $C \cdot R$ and $C \cdot S$. The introduction of glue components makes it necessary to introduce new names for specifying the interconnections. This requires a systematic way of renaming the activation ports and the common ports of R and S. The names introduced by such a renaming must not clash with existing names. A simple and effective renaming that avoids clashes is to modify *all* names in R and S by prefixing the name with a fixed character string.

Definition 7.0   (renaming)

0. Let n be a name. $\underline{l} \cdot n$ is the $\underline{l}$-renaming of n and equals ln, i.e. the character string n prefixed with the letter l.

1. Let A be an alphabet structure. $\underline{l} \cdot A$ is the alphabet structure A with all port and variable names $\underline{l}$-renamed.

2. Let T be a Tangram command. $\underline{l} \cdot T$ is the command T with all occurrences of port and variable names $\underline{l}$-renamed.

3. Let P be a handshake component. $l \cdot P$ is the handshake component P with all occurrences of symbol names l-renamed. A similar renaming also applies to handshake circuits.

4. The r-renaming is defined similarly.

□

The following properties of renaming are frequently used.

Property 7.1

l- and r- renaming commute with

0. Tangram operators and $\mathcal{H}$ (when applied to commands),

1. parallel composition (when applied to handshake processes), and

2. $\cup$ (when applied to handshake circuits).

□

Furthermore, $\mathcal{C}$ is designed to commute with renaming as well.

Tangram program

The translation of Tangram program $(B) \cdot S$ yields the same handshake circuit as the translation of the extension command $(B) \cdot S$, which is treated next.

Extension and concealment

Extension

The extension of a command S with an alphabet structure B behaves like S. The ports of B that were not already part of S are simply connected to *STOP* components (cf. Property 5.17).

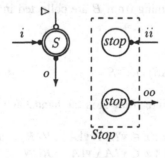

$$\mathcal{C} \cdot ((B) \cdot S)$$

The definition of this compilation rule is somewhat streamlined by introducing a *Stop* term.

Definition 7.2

0. $C \cdot ((B) \cdot S) = Stop \cdot (B \setminus \mathbf{a}S) \cup C \cdot S$

1. Let A be an alphabet structure. $Stop \cdot A$ is the handshake circuit

$$\{c : c \in \mathbf{c}?A \quad : STOP_{(!,\tau_c)} \cdot (c^\bullet)\}$$
$$\cup \ \{c : c \in \mathbf{c}!A \quad : STOP_{(!,\tau_c)} \cdot (c^\bullet)\}$$

$\square$

Concealment

In the translation of $[\![B \mid S]\!]$, ports and variables of B have to be treated differently. Ports can simply be connected to appropriate *RUN* components (cf. Property 5.20). Variables to which S has both read and write access are implemented by *VAR* components of the appropriate type. Variables to which S has either read or write access are connected to appropriate *RUN* components as well, in order to avoid dangling write or read ports of *VAR* components.

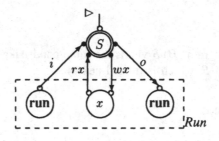

$$C \cdot [\![B \mid S]\!]$$

The handshake components stemming from B are collected into a *Run* term.

Definition 7.3

0. $C \cdot [\![B \mid S]\!] = Run \cdot (B \cap \mathbf{A}S) \cup C \cdot S$

1. Let A be an alphabet structure. $Run \cdot A$ is the handshake circuit

$$\{x : x \in \mathbf{v}?A \cap \mathbf{v}!A \quad : VAR_{\tau_x} \cdot (wx^\circ, rx^\circ)\}$$
$$\cup \ \{x : x \in \mathbf{v}?A \setminus \mathbf{v}!A \quad : RUN_{(!,\tau_x)} \cdot (wx^\circ)\}$$
$$\cup \ \{x : x \in \mathbf{v}!A \setminus \mathbf{v}?A \quad : RUN_{(?,\tau_x)} \cdot (rx^\circ)\}$$
$$\cup \ \{c : c \in \mathbf{p}?A \quad\quad\quad : RUN_{(!,\tau_c)} \cdot (c^\circ)\}$$
$$\cup \ \{c : c \in \mathbf{p}!A \quad\quad\quad : RUN_{(?,\tau_c)} \cdot (c^\circ)\}$$

$\square$

Composite commands

Sequential composition

The translation of Tangram commands of the form $R \mathrel{;} S$ is depicted by

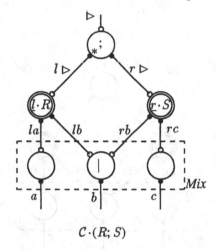

$$\mathcal{C}\cdot(R; S)$$

It contains the handshake subcircuits $\underline{l}\cdot \mathcal{C}\cdot R$ and $\underline{r}\cdot \mathcal{C}\cdot S$ (in the circuit diagram we have used the commutativity of renaming and application of $\mathcal{C}$).

The subcircuit contained in the dashed box is called a *Mix* term, and contains appropriate *MIX* components for ports common to R and S, and *CON* components for other ports in R and S. These connectors are a byproduct of the renaming of *all* ports of R and S. The introduction of the connectors can be avoided, by using a more complex renaming scheme.

Definition 7.4

0. $\mathcal{C}\cdot(R; S) = \quad \{SEQ\cdot(\triangleright^\circ, l\triangleright^\bullet, r\triangleright^\bullet)\} \;\cup\; Mix\cdot(AR, AS)$
$$\cup\; \underline{l}\cdot \mathcal{C}\cdot R \;\cup\; \underline{r}\cdot \mathcal{C}\cdot S$$

1. Let A and B be conformant alphabet structures. $Mix\cdot(A, B)$ is the handshake circuit

$$Con_l \cdot (A \setminus B) \;\cup\; Con_r \cdot (B \setminus A)$$
$$\cup\; \{c : c \in \mathbf{c?}A \cap \mathbf{c?}B : MIX_{(?,\tau_c)}\cdot(lc^\circ, rc^\circ, c^\bullet)\}$$
$$\cup\; \{c : c \in \mathbf{c!}A \cap \mathbf{c!}B : MIX_{(!,\tau_c)}\cdot(lc^\circ, rc^\circ, c^\bullet)\}$$

2. Let A be an alphabet structure. *Con* term $Con_l \cdot A$ is the handshake circuit

$$\{c : c \in \mathbf{c?}A \;\; : CON_{(?,\tau_c)}\cdot(lc^\circ, c^\bullet)\}$$
$$\cup\; \{c : c \in \mathbf{c!}A \;\; : CON_{(!,\tau_c)}\cdot(lc^\circ, c^\bullet)\}$$

Similarly for $Con_r \cdot A$.

$\square$

Nondeterministic choice

The translation for Tangram commands of the form $R \sqcap S$ closely resembles that of sequential commands. Since R and S are never activated concurrently, a *Mix* term takes care of the common ports.

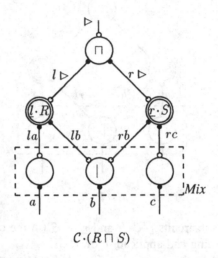

$$C \cdot (R \sqcap S)$$

Definition 7.5

$$C \cdot (R \sqcap S) = \quad \{ OR \cdot (\rhd^\circ, l \rhd^\bullet, r \rhd^\bullet) \} \ \cup \ Mix \cdot (\mathbf{A}R, \mathbf{A}S)$$
$$\cup \ \underline{l} \cdot C \cdot R \ \cup \ \underline{r} \cdot C \cdot S$$

□

The *OR* component nondeterministically selects between the activation of the subcircuits $\underline{l} \cdot C \cdot R$ and $\underline{r} \cdot C \cdot S$. An alternative compilation rule, which reduces nondeterminism and avoids the costly *Mix* term, is

$$C \cdot (R \sqcap S) \ = \ C \cdot R$$

Parallel composition

The compilation of commands of the form $R \parallel S$ is a little more complicated, because accesses to common ports and to common variables have to be treated differently. Communications through common ports have to be synchronized by *JOIN* components. Read access to common variables must be mixed by a *MIX* component. Recall that parallel commands do not have write access to common variables. In the circuit diagram below, i and o are common ports and rx provides read access to common variable x.

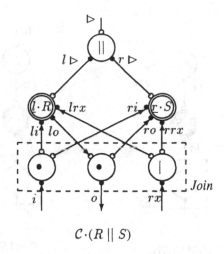

$$\mathcal{C}\cdot(R \parallel S)$$

The required "glue" for parallel composition is collected into a *Join* term.

Definition 7.6

0. $\mathcal{C}\cdot(R \parallel S) = \quad \{PAR\cdot(\triangleright^\circ, l\triangleright^\bullet, r\triangleright^\bullet)\} \cup Join\cdot(\mathbf{A}R, \mathbf{A}S)$
$\qquad\qquad\qquad \cup \;\; \underline{l}\cdot\mathcal{C}\cdot R \;\cup\; \underline{r}\cdot\mathcal{C}\cdot S$

1. Let A and B be connectable alphabet structures. $Join\cdot(A, B)$ is the handshake circuit

$$Con_l \cdot(A \setminus B) \cup Con_r \cdot(B \setminus A)$$
$$\cup \;\; \{x : x \in \mathbf{v?}A \cap \mathbf{v?}B : MIX_{(?,\tau_c)}\cdot(lrx^\circ, rrx^\circ, rx^\bullet)\}$$
$$\cup \;\; \{c : c \in \mathbf{p?}A \cap \mathbf{p?}B : JOIN_{(?,\tau_c)}\cdot(lc^\circ, rc^\circ, c^\bullet)\}$$
$$\cup \;\; \{c : c \in \mathbf{p!}A \cap \mathbf{p?}B : JOIN_{(!,\tau_c)}\cdot(lc^\circ, rc^\circ, c^\bullet)\}$$
$$\cup \;\; \{c : c \in \mathbf{p?}A \cap \mathbf{p!}B : JOIN_{(!,\tau_c)}\cdot(rc^\circ, lc^\circ, c^\bullet)\}$$

□

Repetition

The two forms of repetition in Tangram are easily included in the definition of $\mathcal{C}$. A *Con* term makes the renaming of the repeated command consistent with earlier commands.

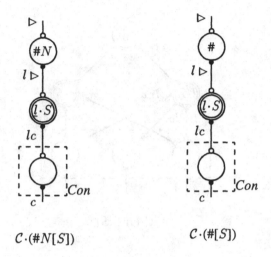

$$\mathcal{C}\cdot(\#N[S])$$ $$\mathcal{C}\cdot(\#[S])$$

Definition 7.7

   0. $\mathcal{C}\cdot(\#N[S]) = \{COUNT_N\cdot(\triangleright^\circ, l\triangleright^\bullet)\} \ \cup \ Con_l \cdot \mathbf{A}S \ \cup \ \underline{l}\cdot\mathcal{C}\cdot S$

   1. $\mathcal{C}\cdot(\#[S]) = \{REP\cdot(\triangleright^\circ, l\triangleright^\bullet)\} \ \cup \ Con_l \cdot \mathbf{A}S \ \cup \ \underline{l}\cdot\mathcal{C}\cdot S$

☐

Guarded commands

Selection

Each selection or guarded repetition contains a set of guarded commands. Let G be a guarded-command set. Given $\mathcal{C}\cdot G$ the translation of a selection command is depicted by

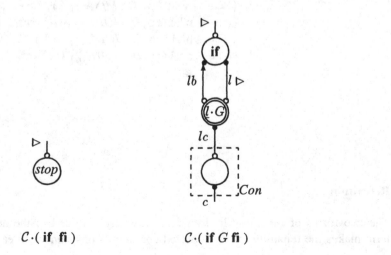

$$\mathcal{C}\cdot(\text{ if fi })$$ $$\mathcal{C}\cdot(\text{ if } G \text{ fi })$$

After activation through $\triangleright°$, the **if** component collects the disjunction of the guards through $lb°$, as computed by $l\,C\cdot G$. If this value is *true*, the subcircuit $l\,C\cdot G$ is activated through $l\,\triangleright$; if *false* the subsequent behavior of circuit is left unspecified.

Definition 7.8

   0. $C\cdot(\textbf{if fi}) = \{STOP\cdot(\triangleright°)\}$

   1. $C\cdot(\textbf{if } G \textbf{ fi}) = \{IF\cdot(\triangleright°, lb°, l\,\triangleright°)\}\ \cup\ Con_l \cdot AG\ \cup\ \underline{l}\cdot C\cdot G$

□

Note that the inclusion in Tangram's guarded commands of a default guard "otherwise" can be implemented straightforwardly by modifying the **if** component. An additional "otherwise" activation port is selected for handshaking if the value *false* is received through b.

Guarded-command set

A singleton guarded-command set has the form $B \to S$. The corresponding handshake circuit consists of subcircuits $\underline{l}\cdot C\cdot B$ and $\underline{r}\cdot C\cdot S$. The guard B and the command S may have read-access to common variables. Hence, renaming and a *Mix* term are required. Both connectors are also a consequence of renaming.

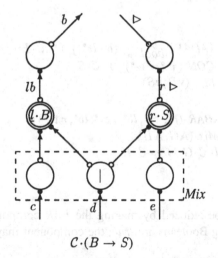

$$C\cdot(B \to S)$$

A guarded-command set with at least two elements can be decomposed into two non-empty guarded-command sets. In Tangram such a set is denoted by connecting the component sets with a ' [] '. The circuit $C\cdot(G \text{ [] } H)$ contains the subcircuits $\underline{l}\cdot\ C\cdot G$ and $\underline{r}\cdot\ C\cdot H$. A *BAR* component implements the Tangram ' [] '. Common ports and variables of guarded-command sets G and H are accessed through a *Mix* term.

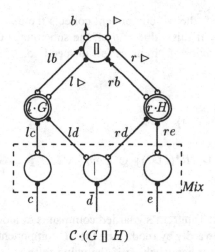

$$\mathcal{C}\cdot(G \; [] \; H)$$

The operation of the circuit $\mathcal{C}\cdot(G \; [] \; H)$ can be understood as follows. Firstly, the environment requests a value through $b°$. This request is passed on to the subcircuits $\underline{l}\cdot \mathcal{C}\cdot G$ and $\underline{r}\cdot \mathcal{C}\cdot H$, and the disjunction of the Booleans that arrive through lb and rb is then output through $b°$.

If this value is *true*, the circuit is ready for the second phase, which starts with $\triangleright_0°$. The *BAR* component nondeterministically selects either $l \triangleright^{\bullet}$ or $r \triangleright^{\bullet}$, *provided* that a *true* value arrived through the corresponding Boolean port in the first phase. After termination of the selected guarded-command subset, the second phase is completed with $\triangleright_1°$.

Definition 7.9

0. $\mathcal{C}\cdot(B \to S) = \quad \{ADAPT_{(bool, \tau_B)}\cdot(b°, lb^{\bullet})\} \; \cup \; \mathcal{C}\cdot B$
    $\qquad\qquad\qquad \cup \;\; CON\cdot(\triangleright°, r \triangleright^{\bullet}) \; \cup \; \mathcal{C}\cdot S$
    $\qquad\qquad\qquad \cup \;\; Mix\cdot(\mathbf{v}B, \mathbf{v}S)$

1. $\mathcal{C}\cdot(G \; [] \; H) = \quad \{BAR\cdot(b°, \; \triangleright°, lb^{\bullet}, l \triangleright^{\bullet}, lb^{\bullet}, r \triangleright^{\bullet})\}$
    $\qquad\qquad\qquad \cup \;\; Mix\cdot(\mathbf{A}G, \mathbf{A}H)$
    $\qquad\qquad\qquad \cup \;\; \underline{l}\cdot \mathcal{C}\cdot G \; \cup \; \underline{r}\cdot \mathcal{C}\cdot H$

□

Nondeterminism can be reduced by making the *BAR* component more deterministic. For instance, if both incoming Booleans are *true*, the component may favor $l \triangleright^{\bullet}$ after reactivation through $\triangleright°$.

Guarded repetition

The handshake circuit for a guarded repetition closely resembles that of a selection command. The behavior of **do od** equals that of *skip*, which is simply implemented by a *RUN* component. If there is at least one guarded command, the resulting handshake circuit becomes:

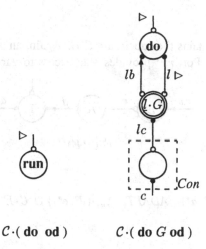

$$\mathcal{C}\cdot(\text{ do od })\qquad\qquad \mathcal{C}\cdot(\text{ do } G \text{ od })$$

After activation through $\triangleright°$, the **do** component inputs a Boolean through $lb^\bullet$ and, if *true*, handshakes through $l \triangleright^\bullet$. This is repeated until *false* arrives. Then the **do** component returns in its initial state after a $\triangleright°_1$.

Definition 7.10

0. $\mathcal{C}\cdot(\text{ do od }) = \{RUN\cdot(\triangleright°)\}$

1. $\mathcal{C}\cdot(\text{ do } G \text{ od }) = \{DO\cdot(\triangleright°, lb^\bullet, l \triangleright^\bullet)\} \cup Con_l \cdot AG \cup \underset{\cdot}{l}\cdot \mathcal{C}\cdot G$

$\square$

Primitive commands

Input

The circuit of $\mathcal{C}\cdot(a?x)$ is depicted by

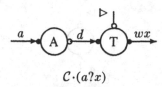

$$\mathcal{C}\cdot(a?x)$$

The adapter takes care of a possible mismatch between the types of a and x.

Definition 7.11

$$\mathcal{C}\cdot(a?x) = \{TRF_{\tau_x}\cdot(\triangleright°, d^\bullet, wx^\bullet)\, ,\ ADAPT_{(\tau_x,\tau_a)}\cdot(d°, a^\bullet)\}$$

$\square$

Output

The circuit of $C\cdot(a!E)$ contains the subcircuit $C\cdot E$. Again, an adapter is introduced to resolve possible type mismatches. Port $rx^\bullet$ provides read access to variable x.

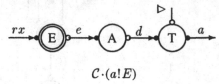

$$C\cdot(a!E)$$

Definition 7.12

$$C\cdot(a!E) = \{TRF_{\tau_a}\cdot(\triangleright^\circ, d^\bullet, a^\bullet)\,,\; ADAPT_{(\tau_a,\tau_E)}\cdot(d^\circ, e^\bullet)\} \cup C\cdot E$$

□

Assignment

The translation of the assignment is very similar to that of the output command.

$$C\cdot(x := E)$$

Definition 7.13

$$C\cdot(x := E) = \{TRF_{\tau_x}\cdot(\triangleright^\circ, d^\bullet, wx^\bullet)\,,\; ADAPT_{(\tau_x,\tau_E)}\cdot(d^\circ, e^\bullet)\} \cup C\cdot E$$

□

Synchronization

The synchronization command a is implemented by connecting the activation port $\triangleright^\circ$ to port $a^\bullet$.

$$C\cdot a$$

Definition 7.14

$$C\cdot a = \{CON\cdot(\triangleright^\circ, a^\bullet)\}$$

□

Skip and stop

The translations of *skip* and *stop* are self-evident.

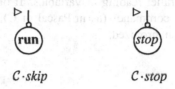

$$C \cdot skip \qquad\qquad C \cdot stop$$

Definition 7.15

0. $C \cdot skip = \{RUN \cdot (\triangleright^\circ)\}$

1. $C \cdot stop = \{STOP \cdot (\triangleright^\circ)\}$

□

Expressions

Expressions form the last syntactic category which we still have to consider for compilation to handshake circuits.

Binary operators

The circuit $C \cdot (D \square E)$ contains the subcircuits $C \cdot D$ and $C \cdot E$, appropriately renamed. If D and E both refer to the same variable, say x, a *JOIN* component can be used to combine the read accesses to x. A *Join* term is then needed to allow for an overlap $v?D$ and $v?E$.

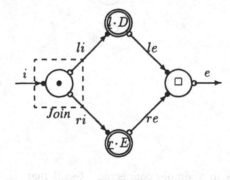

$$C \cdot (D \square E)$$

Definition 7.16

$$C \cdot (D \square E) = \quad \{BIN_{(\square, \tau_D, \tau_E)} \cdot (e^\circ, le^\bullet, re^\bullet)\} \;\cup\; Join \cdot (\mathbf{A}D, \mathbf{A}E)$$
$$\cup\;\; \underline{l} \cdot C \cdot D \;\cup\; \underline{r} \cdot C \cdot E$$

□

Note that a *Mix* term would do the job as well. Whereas a *Join* term enforces synchronization of accesses to common variables, the *Mix* term enforces sequentialization. Cost and performance considerations favor the *Join* term in most cases. Note also that the introduction of the *Join* term takes advantage of the parallel reading of variables. If one would extend Tangram with functions containing sequential commands (as in Pascal or C), the danger of deadlock would arise when read accesses are synchronized.

Unary operators

Expressions of the form $\Box E$ are translated similarly.

$$\mathcal{C}\cdot(\Box E)$$

The *Join* term reduces to a *Con* term.

Definition 7.17

$$\mathcal{C}\cdot(\Box E) = \{UN_{(\Box,\tau_E)}\cdot(e^\circ, le^\bullet)\} \;\cup\; Con_l \cdot AE \;\cup\; \underline{l}\cdot \mathcal{C}\cdot E$$

$\Box$

Constants

The handshake circuit for a constant expression is self-evident.

$$\mathcal{C}\cdot C$$

Definition 7.18

$$\mathcal{C}\cdot C = \{CST\cdot_C(e^\circ)\}$$

$\Box$

Variables

The expression x translates to a simple connector. Recall that the declaration of variable x yields a *VAR* component with read port rx°.

$$\mathcal{C}\cdot x$$

Definition 7.19

$$\mathcal{C} \cdot x = \{CON_{(?, \tau_x)} \cdot (e^\circ, rx^\bullet)\}$$

□

This concludes the translation of Tangram commands into handshake circuits. Examples of compiled handshake circuits can be found in Chapters 1 and 2. The circuits of Figures 1.2, 1.3, 1.4, and 2.0 can be obtained by applying $\mathcal{C}$ to the corresponding Tangram programs or commands. The circuits of Figures 1.5, 1.6, 2.2, 2.6, and 2.7 can be obtained by compilation and subsequent minor optimizations at the handshake-circuit level (cf. Chapter 9). The circuits of Figure 2.9, 2.10, and 2.11 require non-trivial extensions of $\mathcal{C}$.

7.2 The compilation theorem

In this section we analyze the most important property of function $\mathcal{C}$, specifically that it yields handshake circuits that are *equivalent* to the corresponding Tangram programs in a precise sense. This analysis is restricted to Core Tangram. Recall that in Core Tangram all alphabet structures are of the form $\langle \mathbf{p}?A, \emptyset, \emptyset, \emptyset, \{\sim\} \rangle$. For convenience we shall write $\mathbf{a}S$ to denote $\mathbf{p}?AS$, where S is a Core Tangram command. Note that $\mathbf{a}S$ is a set of names.

The compilation function for Core Tangram is presented below in a self-contained form. Function $\mathcal{C}$ is consistent with the more general compilation function of the previous section.

Definition 7.20

The compilation function $\mathcal{C}$ for Core Tangram is defined by:

0. $\mathcal{C} \cdot skip$ $= \{RUN \cdot (\triangleright^\circ)\}$

1. $\mathcal{C} \cdot stop$ $= \{STOP \cdot (\triangleright^\circ)\}$

2. $\mathcal{C} \cdot a$ $= \{CON \cdot (\triangleright^\circ, a^\bullet)\}$

3. $\mathcal{C} \cdot (R; S)$ $= \quad \{SEQ \cdot (\triangleright^\circ, l \triangleright^\bullet, r \triangleright^\bullet)\} \cup Mix \cdot (\mathbf{a}R, \mathbf{a}S)$
       $\cup \ \underline{l} \cdot \mathcal{C} \cdot R \cup \underline{r} \cdot \mathcal{C} \cdot S$

4. $\mathcal{C} \cdot (R \sqcap S)$ $= \quad \{OR \cdot (\triangleright^\circ, l \triangleright^\bullet, r \triangleright^\bullet)\} \cup Mix \cdot (\mathbf{a}R, \mathbf{a}S)$
       $\cup \ \underline{l} \cdot \mathcal{C} \cdot R \cup \underline{r} \cdot \mathcal{C} \cdot S$

5. $\mathcal{C} \cdot (\#N[S])$ $= \{COUNT_N \cdot (\triangleright^\circ, l \triangleright^\bullet)\} \cup Con_l \cdot \mathbf{a}S \cup \underline{l} \cdot \mathcal{C} \cdot S$

6. $\mathcal{C} \cdot (\#[S])$ $= \{REP \cdot (\triangleright^\circ, l \triangleright^\bullet)\} \cup Con_l \cdot \mathbf{a}S \cup \underline{l} \cdot \mathcal{C} \cdot S$

7. $\mathcal{C} \cdot (R \parallel S)$ $= \quad \{PAR \cdot (\triangleright^\circ, l \triangleright^\bullet, r \triangleright^\bullet)\} \cup Join \cdot (\mathbf{p}R, \mathbf{p}S)$
       $\cup \ \underline{l} \cdot \mathcal{C} \cdot R \cup \underline{r} \cdot \mathcal{C} \cdot S$

8. $\mathcal{C} \cdot (\llbracket B \mid S \rrbracket)$ $= Run \cdot (B \cap \mathbf{a}S) \cup \mathcal{C} \cdot S$

9. $\mathcal{C} \cdot ((B) \cdot S)$ $= Stop \cdot (B \setminus \mathbf{a}S) \cup \mathcal{C} \cdot S$

where (in alphabetic order):

10. $CON \cdot (a°, b•)$ $= \#[a° : b•]$

11. $COUNT_N \cdot (a°, b•) = \#[a° : \#N[b•]]$

12. $JOIN \cdot (a°, b°, c•)$ $= \#[a° : b° : c•]$

13. $MIX \cdot (a°, b°, c•)$ $= \#[[a° : c• \mid b° : c•]]$

14. $OR \cdot (a°, b•, c•)$ $= \#[a° : (b• \sqcap c•)]$

15. $PAR \cdot (a°, b•, c•)$ $= \#[a° : (b• \parallel c•)]$

16. $REP \cdot (a°, b•)$ $= (a° : \#[b•])$

17. $RUN \cdot (a°)$ $= \#[a°]$

18. $SEQ \cdot (a°, b•, c•)$ $= \#[a° : (b•; c•)]$

19. $STOP \cdot (a°)$ $= (a°) \cdot stop$

and:

20. $Run \cdot A$ $= \{a : a \in A : RUN \cdot (a°)\}$

21. $Stop \cdot A$ $= \{a : a \in A : STOP \cdot (a°)\}$

22. $Con_l \cdot A$ $= \{a : a \in A : CON \cdot (la°, a•)\}$

23. $Mix \cdot (A, B)$ $=$ $Con_l \cdot (A \setminus B) \cup Con_r \cdot (B \setminus A)$
         $\cup \; \{a : a \in A \cap B : MIX \cdot (la°, ra°, a•)\}$

24. $Join \cdot (A, B)$ $=$ $Con_l \cdot (A \setminus B) \cup Con_r \cdot (B \setminus A)$
         $\cup \; \{a : a \in A \cap B : JOIN \cdot (la°, ra°, a•)\}$

□

One of the central theorems of this monograph is the compilation theorem.

Theorem 7.21 (compilation theorem)

Let T be a Core Tangram program. Then

$$\triangleright^* \cdot \mathcal{H} \cdot T \;\; = \;\; \parallel \cdot \mathcal{C} \cdot T$$

Proof by structural induction over Core Tangram later in this section.

□

The proof of the compilation theorem requires a little more ground work to be done.

Separation properties

The presented syntax-directed translation method is one of recursive decomposition. The circuit for a composite command is decomposed into circuits for the subcommands and some additional circuitry that is specific to the command operator and to the port alphabets of the subcommands. One could say that this additional circuitry is *separated* from the circuits of the subcommands during such a decomposition step. A systematic analysis of this form of separation is studied next.

The formulation of separation properties is based on so-called σ-functions. A σ-function is a function from sequential processes to sequential processes of a restricted form.

Definition 7.22 **(σ-function)**

Let a be a name, N a natural number, B a port structure, and P a sequential handshake process.

0. Let X be a sequential handshake process. Then the following expressions define σ-functions:

    (a) $(B) \cdot X$

    (b) $P \sqcap X$

    (c) $X; P$

    (d) $P; X$

    (e) $\#[X]$

    (f) $\#N[X]$

    (g) $P \parallel X$

    (h) $a° : X$

    Furthermore, a composition of σ-functions is also a σ-function.

1. σ-function F is said to *interfere* with port structure A if there is a port a, $a \in A$, for which $F \cdot a°$ or $F \cdot a^\bullet$ is undefined.

2. σ-function F is *permanent* if its image consists exclusively of permanent sequential processes.

□

Function $\triangleright^*$ is an example of a σ-function. In general, a σ-function is partial. For instance, function F, $F \cdot X = X; P$, is defined only if X is conformant with P. The definition of σ-functions can be extended to include the complete handshake calculus. Such extensions are not relevant to our current purposes.

Property 7.23 (separation)

0. *Command separation.* Let P be a sequential process and let F be a permanent σ-function, such that F does *not* interfere with $\mathbf{p}P$ or a°. Then

$$F \cdot P = F \cdot a^{\bullet} \;\; \| \;\; \#[a^{\circ} : P]$$

The non-interference requirement on F guarantees that $F \cdot a^{\bullet}$ and $\#[a^{\circ} : P]$ are connectable. This separation property is similar in intent to the "decomposition rule" of [Mar89].

1. *Con separation.* Let P be a sequential process such that $\mathbf{p}^{\circ}P = \emptyset$, and let $a \in \mathbf{p}^{\bullet}P$. Furthermore, let F be a σ-function, such that F does not interfere with $\mathbf{p}P$ or la. Then

$$F \cdot P = F \cdot (a := la) \cdot P \;\; \| \;\; CON \cdot (la^{\circ}, a^{\bullet})$$

where $(a := la) \cdot P$ denotes the sequential process P with all occurrences of symbols of port a l-renamed. Consequently,

$$F \cdot P = F \cdot \underline{l} \cdot P \;\; \| \;\; Con_l \cdot \mathbf{p}P$$

Again, non-interference of F with $\mathbf{p}P$ or la assures connectability.

2. *Mix separation.* Let P and Q be conformant sequential processes with $\mathbf{p}^{\circ}P = \mathbf{p}^{\circ}Q = \emptyset$, and let $a \in \mathbf{p}^{\bullet}P \cap \mathbf{p}^{\bullet}Q$. Furthermore, let F be a σ-function, such that F does not interfere with $\mathbf{p}P$, $\mathbf{p}Q$, la, or ra (to assure connectability in the decomposition below). Then

$$F \cdot (P; Q) = F \cdot ((a := la) \cdot P; (a := ra) \cdot Q) \;\; \| \;\; MIX \cdot (la^{\circ}, ra^{\circ}, a^{\bullet})$$

Consequently,

$$F \cdot (P; Q) = F \cdot (\underline{l} \cdot P; \underline{r} \cdot Q) \;\; \| \;\; Mix \cdot (\mathbf{p}P, \mathbf{p}Q)$$

3. A similar *Mix* separation exists for $F \cdot (P \sqcap Q)$.

4. *Join separation.* Let P and Q be sequential processes with $\mathbf{p}^{\circ}P = \mathbf{p}^{\circ}Q = \emptyset$ and let $a \in \mathbf{p}^{\bullet}P \cap \mathbf{p}^{\bullet}Q$. Furthermore, let F be a σ-function, such that F does not interfere with $\mathbf{p}P$, $\mathbf{p}Q$, la or ra (to assure connectability in the decomposition below). Then

$$F \cdot (P \overset{\bullet\bullet}{\|} Q) = F \cdot ((a := la) \cdot P \overset{\bullet\bullet}{\|} (a := ra) \cdot Q) \;\; \| \;\; JOIN \cdot (la^{\circ}, ra^{\circ}, a^{\bullet})$$

Consequently,

$$F \cdot (P \overset{\bullet\bullet}{\|} Q) = F \cdot (\underline{l} \cdot P \overset{\bullet\bullet}{\|} \underline{r} \cdot Q) \;\; \| \;\; Join \cdot (\mathbf{p}P, \mathbf{p}Q)$$

Since $\underline{l} \cdot P$ and $\underline{r} \cdot Q$ are obviously connectable, the $\overset{\bullet\bullet}{\|}$ in the last process expression may be replaced by $\|$.

□

The separation properties can be used to prove most of the parallel compositions in Example 4.18.

Example 7.24

Consider σ-function F defined by $F \cdot X = \#[a^\circ : \#2[X]]$. Clearly, a handshake through a° has the effect of executing X twice. Note that $F \cdot b^\bullet = DUP \cdot (a^\circ, b^\bullet)$, the duplicator of Example 3.23. Using the above separation properties, we obtain the following decomposition of $F \cdot P$:

$\quad F \cdot P$

$=\quad\{$ Separation property 0 $\}$

$\quad F \cdot b^\bullet \;\|\; \#[b^\circ : P]$

$=\quad\{$ definition of F $\}$

$\quad \#[a^\circ : \#2[b^\bullet]] \;\|\; \#[b^\circ : P]$

$=\quad\{$ definition of bounded repetition $\}$

$\quad \#[a^\circ : (b^\bullet; b^\bullet)] \;\|\; \#[b^\circ : P]$

$=\quad\{$ Separation property 2; definition of SEQ $\}$

$\quad SEQ \cdot (a^\circ, lb^\bullet, rb^\bullet) \;\|\; MIX \cdot (lb^\circ, rb^\circ, b^\bullet) \;\|\; \#[b^\circ : P]$

$\square$

Proof of the compilation theorem

The proof of the compilation theorem is by structural induction over Core Tangram, and follows the command order of Definition 7.20. The proofs for the three primitive commands *skip*, *stop* and $a^\bullet$ are skipped. The syntactic category *program* is not treated separately, since a program is a just an extension command.

Most proof cases refer to one or more separation properties. Of course, it is then a part of the proof obligations to verify that a proper σ-function is involved. In particular, the non-interference of the σ-function with its argument or with the freshly introduced ports must be checked. From the simplicity of the applied renaming scheme, non-interference can be easily established, and hence the connectability of the subcircuits introduced by the separation step is guaranteed.

Case   command $S; T$:

$\quad \triangleright^* \cdot \mathcal{H} \cdot (S; T)$

$=\quad\{$ $\mathcal{H}$ distributes over ; $\}$

$\quad \triangleright^* \cdot (\mathcal{H} \cdot S \,;\, \mathcal{H} \cdot T)$

$=\quad\{$ *Mix* separation $\}$

$\quad \triangleright^* \cdot (\underline{l} \cdot \mathcal{H} \cdot S \,;\, \underline{r} \cdot \mathcal{H} \cdot T) \;\|\; Mix \cdot (\mathbf{a}S, \mathbf{a}T)$

=   { command separation (twice) }

$\rhd^* \cdot (l \rhd^\bullet; r \rhd^\bullet) \;\|\; \underline{l} \cdot \rhd^* \cdot \mathcal{H} \cdot S \;\|\; \underline{r} \cdot \rhd^* \cdot \mathcal{H} \cdot T \;\|\; Mix \cdot (\mathbf{a}S, \mathbf{a}T)$

=   { induction hypothesis }

$\rhd^* \cdot (l \rhd^\bullet; r \rhd^\bullet) \;\|\; (\underline{l} \,\|\, \cdot \mathcal{C} \cdot S) \;\|\; (\underline{r} \,\|\, \cdot \mathcal{C} \cdot T) \;\|\; Mix \cdot (\mathbf{a}S, \mathbf{a}T)$

=   { rewrite; definition of *SEQ* }

$\| \cdot (\{ SEQ \cdot (\rhd^\circ, l \rhd^\bullet, r \rhd^\bullet) \} \;\cup\; Mix \cdot (\mathbf{a}R, \mathbf{a}S) \;\cup\; \underline{l} \cdot \mathcal{C} \cdot S \;\cup\; \underline{r} \cdot \mathcal{C} \cdot T)$

=   { definition of $\mathcal{C}$ }

$\| \cdot \mathcal{C} \cdot (S; T)$

Case   command $S \sqcap T$: similar to command $S; T$.

Case   command #[S] :

$\rhd^* \cdot \mathcal{H} \cdot (\#[S])$

=   { $\mathcal{H}$ commutes with # }

$\rhd^* \cdot \#[\mathcal{H} \cdot S]$

=   { *Con* separation }

$\rhd^* \cdot \#[\underline{l} \cdot \mathcal{H} \cdot S] \;\|\; Con_l \cdot \mathbf{a}S$

=   { command separation }

$\rhd^* \cdot \#[l \rhd^\bullet] \;\|\; \underline{l} \cdot \rhd^* \cdot \mathcal{H} \cdot S \;\|\; Con_l \cdot \mathbf{a}S$

=   { induction hypothesis }

$\rhd^* \cdot \#[l \rhd^\bullet] \;\|\; (\underline{l} \,\|\, \cdot \mathcal{C} \cdot S) \;\|\; Con_l \cdot \mathbf{a}S$

=   { rewrite; definition of *REP* }

$\| \cdot (\{ REP \cdot (\rhd^\circ, l \rhd^\bullet) \} \;\cup\; Con_l \cdot \mathbf{a}R \;\cup\; \underline{l} \cdot \mathcal{C} \cdot S)$

=   { definition of $\mathcal{C}$ }

$\| \cdot \mathcal{C} \cdot (\#[S])$

Case   command $R = \#N[S]$: similar to command #[S].

Case   command $S \,\|\, T$:

$\rhd^* \cdot \mathcal{H} \cdot (S \,\|\, T)$

=   { $\mathcal{H}$ distributes over $\|$ }

$\rhd^* \cdot (\mathcal{H} \cdot S \;\overset{\bullet\bullet}{\|}\; \mathcal{H} \cdot T)$

=   { *Join* separation }

$\rhd^* \cdot (\underline{l} \cdot \mathcal{H} \cdot S \;\|\; \underline{r} \cdot \mathcal{H} \cdot T) \;\|\; Join \cdot (\mathbf{a}S, \mathbf{a}T)$

=   { command separation (twice) }

$\triangleright^* \cdot (l \triangleright^\bullet \parallel r \triangleright^\bullet) \parallel \underline{l} \cdot \triangleright^* \cdot \mathcal{H} \cdot S \parallel \underline{r} \cdot \triangleright^* \cdot \mathcal{H} \cdot T \parallel Join \cdot (\mathbf{a}S, \mathbf{a}T)$

=   { induction hypothesis }

$\triangleright^* \cdot (l \triangleright^\bullet \parallel r \triangleright^\bullet) \parallel (\underline{l} \parallel \cdot \mathcal{C} \cdot S) \parallel (\underline{r} \parallel \cdot \mathcal{C} \cdot T) \parallel Join \cdot (\mathbf{a}S, \mathbf{a}T)$

=   { rewrite; definition of *PAR* }

$\parallel \cdot (\{ PAR \cdot (\triangleright^\circ, l \triangleright^\bullet, r \triangleright^\bullet) \} \cup Join \cdot (\mathbf{a}R, \mathbf{a}S) \cup \underline{l} \cdot \mathcal{C} \cdot S \cup \underline{r} \cdot \mathcal{C} \cdot T)$

=   { definition of $\mathcal{C}$ }

$\parallel \cdot \mathcal{C} \cdot (S \parallel T)$

Case   command $[\![\, B \mid S \,]\!]$:

$\triangleright^* \cdot \mathcal{H} \cdot [\![\, B \mid S \,]\!]$

=   { property of concealment }

$\triangleright^* \cdot \mathcal{H} \cdot [\![\, B \cap \mathbf{a}S \mid S \,]\!]$

=   { $\mathcal{H}$ "distributes over" concealment }

$\triangleright^* \cdot [\![\, \mathcal{H} \cdot (B \cap \mathbf{a}S) \mid \mathcal{H} \cdot S \,]\!]$

=   { concealment commutes with enclosure and repetition }

$[\![\, \mathcal{H} \cdot (B \cap \mathbf{a}S) \mid \triangleright^* \cdot \mathcal{H} \cdot S \,]\!]$

=   { property 5.20 of non-terminating processes }

$\triangleright^* \cdot \mathcal{H} \cdot S \parallel RUN \cdot \overline{\mathcal{H} \cdot (B \cap \mathbf{a}S)}$

=   { induction hypothesis }

$\parallel \cdot \mathcal{C} \cdot S \parallel RUN \cdot \overline{\mathcal{H} \cdot (B \cap \mathbf{a}S)}$

=   { rewrite; definition of *Run* }

$\parallel \cdot (\mathcal{C} \cdot S \cup Run \cdot \overline{\mathcal{H} \cdot (B \cap \mathbf{a}S)})$

=   { definition of $\mathcal{C}$ }

$\parallel \cdot \mathcal{C} \cdot [\![\, B \mid S \,]\!]$

Case   command $(B) \cdot S$: similar to command $[\![\, B \mid S \,]\!]$.

$\square$

Chapter 8

Handshake circuits → VLSI circuits

8.0 Introduction

Handshake circuits are proposed as an intermediary between communicating processes (Tangram programs) and VLSI circuits. Chapter 7 describes the translation of Tangram programs into handshake circuits. This chapter is concerned with the realization of handshake circuits as *efficient* and *testable* VLSI circuits. First we observe that the fine-grained parallelism available in VLSI circuits matches the fine-grained concurrency in handshake circuits nicely. The mapping of handshake circuits to VLSI circuits can therefore be relatively direct.

A rather naive mapping is suggested by the following correspondence:

0. a channel corresponds to a set of wires, one per symbol;

1. an event with name a corresponds to a voltage transition along wire a;

2. each handshake component corresponds to a VLSI circuit that satisfies the specification at the transition level.

There is no doubt that the above mapping can result in functional circuits. In general, however, the resulting circuits will be prohibitive in size, poor in performance, probably hard to initialize, and impractical to test for fabrication faults. Concerns for circuit size, performance, initialization and testability are therefore recurring themes in this chapter.

A full treatment of all relevant VLSI-realization issues is beyond the scope of this monograph. Issues that directly relate to (properties of) handshake circuits have been selected for a relatively precise treatment; other topics are sketched more briefly. This chapter discusses:

- *peephole* optimization: the replacement of subcircuits by cheaper ones;

- relaxation of the receptiveness requirement of handshake processes;

- handshake signaling between handshake components;

- decomposition into VLSI operators and (isochronic) forks;

- initialization of the resulting VLSI circuits;

- fabrication testing of the VLSI circuit.

147

8.1   Peephole optimization

An obvious method of optimization of handshake circuits is replacement of subcircuits by cheaper subcircuits on the basis of "equals for equals". Example 4.18 lists a number of pairs of circuits with equal behavior. Substitution of one member of the pair for the other does not affect the functional behavior of the circuit. However, for given VLSI realizations of the handshake components, such a substitution does affect the circuit's cost and performance. At this point we shall not delve into cost models or metrics. In the examples below the advantage(s) of substitution in one way or the other is hinted at only.

Example 8.0

The following optimizations are the most interesting ones from a practical viewpoint:

0. Removal of connectors as suggested by Examples 4.18.0 and 4.18.1 has only advantages. However, since connectors can be realized by wires only, the expected advantages evaporate during the layout phase.

1. Example 4.18.2 is a useful one. It allows the elimination of most *RUN* components from compiled handshake circuits. Since the proposed compilation function introduces a *RUN* for each internal channel in a Tangram program, this optimization yields interesting savings.

2. Example 4.24 discusses trees of *MIX*, *SEQ*, *PAR*, and *OR* components. Balancing of such trees does not affect the cost of a circuit, but often improves the (average) performance. The same holds for trees of *BAR* components (cf. Example 5.37.18).

3. Read access to a common variable in a Tangram program results in a tree of *MIX* components connected to the read port of the variable. This form of the *MIX* component turns out to be rather expensive. A variable with multiple read ports that can be served in parallel is a cheaper and faster alternative.

This optimization has been applied in order to obtain the handshake circuit of Figure 2.2.

□

Sometimes, a subcircuit may be replaced by a more deterministic circuit. The following optimization has been applied after the translation of the wagging buffer of Section 1.0 in order to obtain the handshake circuit of Figure 1.6.

Example 8.1

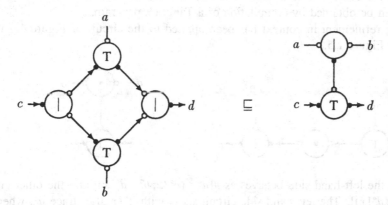

Overlap of handshakes through ports a and b may cause message overtaking via the parallel transfer paths. Such nondeterminism is eliminated by this optimization.

□

In some instances a subcircuit may be replaced by a cheaper subcircuit with an "almost equal" behavior. Such substitutions are allowed if their effect on the external behavior of the circuit cannot be observed by any possible environment. This form of optimization will be called *refinement in context*.

Definition 8.2   (refinement in context)

Let P, Q and R be handshake processes, such that $\mathbf{p}P = \mathbf{p}Q$ and $\mathbf{p}P \bowtie \mathbf{p}R$. Process P *refines to Q in the context of R*, denoted by $P \sqsubseteq_R Q$, if

$$P \parallel R \;\sqsubseteq\; Q \parallel R$$

□

The following properties are given without proof.

Property 8.3

0. $P \sqsubseteq_R P$

1. $P \sqsubseteq_R Q \,\wedge\, Q \sqsubseteq_R T \;\Rightarrow\; P \sqsubseteq_R T$ (Hence, $\sqsubseteq_R$ is a preorder.)

2. $P \sqsubseteq_{CHAOS \cdot \emptyset} Q \;\equiv\; P \sqsubseteq Q$

3. If $\mathbf{p}R = \overline{\mathbf{p}P}$, the defining expression of refinement in context can be rewritten as

$$tP \cap tR \;\supseteq\; tQ \cap tR$$

□

Example 8.4

We assume that the context H is a handshake circuit, such that for refinement $P \sqsubseteq_H Q$ the circuit $P \cup H$ can be obtained by compilation of a Tangram program.

The following refinement in context has been applied to the circuit of Figure 1.4 in order to obtain that of Figure 1.5.

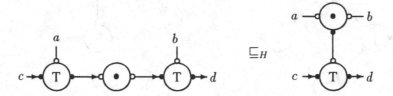

The circuit at the left-hand side behaves as $\#[a^\circ : (c^\bullet?x; b^\circ : d^\bullet!x)]$ and the other circuit as $\#[a^\circ : b^\circ : (c^\bullet?x; d^\bullet!x)]$. The left-hand side circuit starts with $c^\bullet?x$ after trace a_0, whereas the other circuit would then be quiescent.

□

The type of local optimizations presented in this section will be called *peephole optimization* by analogy with optimizations in conventional compilers that generate machine code [McK65]. By scanning over a handshake circuit and looking at a local subcircuit (with a bounded diameter), as if through a peephole, one can find opportunities for improvements by substitution. It is characteristic of peephole optimization that an improvement may spawn opportunities for additional improvements.

8.2   Non-receptive handshake components

By Definition 3.19 handshake processes are required to be receptive. The main advantage of this requirement is the relatively simple definition of parallel composition of handshake processes (Definition 4.14), which guarantees absence of computation interference (Theorem A.12).

Unfortunately, the requirement of receptiveness tends to make the circuit realizations of handshake processes more costly. In particular, the constant readiness for inputs through passive ports requires gates or latches to "shield" or "remember" input transitions for later processing. Moreover, the choice construct requires an arbiter circuit to arbitrate between transitions through the guard inputs. A non-receptive implementation of choice is deterministic and arbitration can therefore be avoided (cf. the *MIX* and *NMIX* components of Example 3.23).

In this section we investigate the conditions under which a (receptive) handshake component may be replaced by a non-receptive component without taking the risk of computation interference. The scope of the following (re-)definition is restricted to the current section.

Definition 8.5

0. A handshake process is a handshake structure that satisfies all conditions of 3.19 except for condition 3.19.4.

1. A *receptive* handshake processes is a handshake process that also satisfies condition 3.19.4. All other handshake processes are *non-receptive*.

□

Let P be a handshake process, and let $t \in tP^{\leq}$ and $a \in iP$, such that $ta \in (\mathbf{a}P)^H$. Receptiveness implies $ta \in tP^{\leq}$. Equivalently, $ta \notin tP^{\leq}$ implies that P is non-receptive. Examples of non-receptive processes are *NMIX* and *NVAR* of Example 3.23.

This generalized form of handshake processes is distinctly more complicated than receptive handshake processes. It is not our intention to develop a theory of (non-receptive) handshake processes. We point out two essential differences in order to prepare ourselves for a particular application of non-receptive handshake processes.

Refinement ordering of handshake processes is rather subtle compared with that of receptive processes. Consider receptive process $CON\cdot(a^\circ, c^\bullet)$. Its trace set is also a valid trace set for a process with port structure A, where $A = a^\circ \cup b^\circ \cup c^\bullet$. Let Q be the handshake process with port structure A and the quiescent trace set of $CON\cdot(a^\circ, c^\bullet)$. Process Q is clearly non-receptive, since trace b_0 is not in its trace set. Interestingly, we have $tQ \subset tMIX\cdot(a^\circ, b^\circ, c^\bullet)$. However, this does not make Q a suitable implementation of the mixer!

Also parallel composition of handshake processes is more complicated when processes are not receptive. Consider the parallel composition of Q and $RUN\cdot\{b^\bullet\}$. In their asynchronous interaction, process $RUN\cdot\{b^\bullet\}$ will output a b_0 despite the fact that Q is not ready to receive it: a clear case of interference.

Note that the trace set of Q **w** $RUN\cdot\{b^\bullet\}$ equals that of Q. Weaving ignores the distinction between input and output, and is therefore not a suitable basis for parallel composition when the danger of interference exists.

The parallel composition of Q and $STOP\cdot\{b^\bullet\}$ is free of interference. (With concealment of b we obtain the receptive process $CON\cdot(a^\circ, c^\bullet)$.) In other words, only if Q operates in an environment that never produces a b_0, may the mixer be replaced by Q. More generally, a process may be refined into a process with fewer possible behaviors when the environment restrains itself appropriately. For the remainder of this section, let P, Q, and R be handshake processes, such that $\mathbf{p}P = \mathbf{p}Q$ and $\mathbf{p}P \bowtie \mathbf{p}R$.

Definition 8.6   (strong refinement in context)

P strongly refines to Q in the context of R, denoted by $P \sqsubseteq_R Q$, if

$$tP \supseteq tQ \quad \wedge \quad (t(P \textbf{ w } R) = t(Q \textbf{ w } R))$$

□

Note that strong refinement does not allow the removal of nondeterminism.

Property 8.7

0. Strong refinement in context is a preorder (cf. 8.3).

1. For receptive handshake processes P, Q and R we have

$$P \sqsubseteq_R Q \;\Rightarrow\; P \sqsubseteq_R Q$$

□

Example 8.8

The relation

$$MIX \cdot (b^\circ, c^\circ, d^\bullet) \sqsubseteq_R NMIX \cdot (b^\circ, c^\circ, d^\bullet)$$

is a strong refinement for

$$R \in \{OR \cdot (a^\circ, b^\bullet, c^\bullet), SEQ \cdot (a^\circ, b^\bullet, c^\bullet), STOP \cdot \{b^\bullet, c^\bullet\}\}$$

but not for

$$R \in \{PAR \cdot (a^\circ, b^\bullet, c^\bullet), RUN \cdot \{b^\bullet, c^\bullet\}\}$$

□

A nice property of strong refinement in context is that it does not introduce interference. The following theorem assumes that the domain of parallel composition (cf. Definition 4.14) is extended to handshake processes.

Theorem 8.9

If $P \parallel R$ is free of interference and $P \sqsubseteq_R Q$, then $Q \parallel R$ is also free of interference.

□

Remember that if P and R are both receptive, absence of interference is guaranteed. In particular, a component in a handshake circuit and its environment are receptive. If this component is, for instance, a *MIX* component it may be replaced by an *NMIX* on account of Example 8.8, provided that the environment avoids overlaps of the handshakes through the mixer's passive ports. The *MIX* components introduced in the compilation function of Chapter 7 are all placed in such a restricted environment. Consequently:

Theorem 8.10

All *MIX* components introduced on the basis of Separation Property 7.23 can be strongly refined into *NMIX* components in their respective contexts.

□

Similar strong refinements in context apply to directed *MIX* components. Also, *VAR* components can be strongly refined into a non-receptive component without overlap in read and write access, because of the required conformance of alphabet structures (cf. Definition 5.12).

8.3   Handshake refinement

Symbols have been introduced as names of events of interest in describing the interaction of a handshake process and its environment. In this section we relate these symbols to wires and to transitions of the states of these wires. In CMOS these state transitions usually correspond to voltage transitions (cf. Section 0.1).

Let p be a port of handshake process P. First we assume that we may use a wire for each symbol of p, the so-called *One-Hot* encoding[0]. With symbol a we associate wire a. The states

---

[0]More economical encodings are discussed in Section 8.4.

of a wire are referred to as *low* and *high*. A transition of wire a from low to high is denoted by $a \uparrow$, and a transition from high to low by $a \downarrow$. If we assume that the initial state of a wire is low, the observed behavior of the state of the wire can be recorded by a sequence in which $a \uparrow$ and $a \downarrow$ alternate, starting with an $a \uparrow$.

The notion of a handshake process can be refined accordingly. We will not develop a formal handshake-process model at the level of transitions. Instead, we simply require port structures to be of the form $A \times \{\uparrow, \downarrow\}$. Also, the projection of a trace of $\mathcal{H} \cdot (A \times \{\uparrow, \downarrow\})$ on a single port must result in the proper alternation of up and down transitions. Without loss of generality we assume that all wires are low initially and that the first event on each wire is therefore an $\uparrow$ transition. A handshake process with these properties is referred to as a *transition handshake process*. Similarly, we speak of transition handshake components and transition handshake circuits.

Useful shorthands for ports $\langle p, \uparrow \rangle$ and $\langle p, \downarrow \rangle$ are $p \uparrow$ and $p \downarrow$. The alphabet structure $A \times \{\uparrow, \downarrow\}$ is abbreviated to A_t. The set of all transition handshake processes with port structure A_t is denoted by $\prod_t \cdot A$.

Handshake action $p \uparrow^\circ$ assumes both wires p_0 and p_1 to be low, and, after successful termination, leaves both wires high. Similarly, action $p \downarrow^\circ$ assumes both wires to be high, and leaves both wires low, provided successful termination. This suggests that we can still use the handshake calculus of Chapter 5, provided that the described process satisfies the rule of alternation of up and down transitions.

In this section we investigate various ways to implement a handshake process by a transition handshake process. The central notion is that of phase reduction.

Definition 8.11 (phase reduction)

A *phase reduction* is a partial function $\phi : \prod_t \cdot A \to \prod \cdot A$ that satisfies:

0. ϕ is surjective

1. $\phi \cdot (P \sqcap Q) = \phi \cdot P \sqcap \phi \cdot Q$

2. $\phi \cdot (P \sqcup Q) = \phi \cdot P \sqcup \phi \cdot Q$

3. $\phi \cdot (P \parallel Q) = \phi \cdot P \parallel \phi \cdot Q$

$\square$

Let $R = \phi \cdot Q$. Then R is said to be the phase reduction of Q. Alternatively, Q will be called a *handshake refinement* of R. A phase reduction is a homomorphism on account of 8.11.1 and 8.11.2.

Transition handshake processes P and Q are *equivalent* if $\phi \cdot P = \phi \cdot Q$. This equivalence is actually a *congruence*, and is the *kernel* of ϕ (cf. [DP90], page 116).

Let P, Q and R be transition handshake processes. On account of 8.11.3 we conclude $P \parallel R$ and $Q \parallel R$ are equivalent if P and Q are equivalent. More generally, the replacement of a transition handshake component by an equivalent one in a transition handshake circuit results in an equivalent handshake circuit.

Two classes of phase reduction are studied in some detail: 2-phase and 4-phase reductions. The associated handshake refinements are called 2-phase and 4-phase refinements respectively.

2-phase refinements

The simplest handshake refinement is based on the phase reduction obtained by ignoring the distinction between up and down transitions.

Definition 8.12 (2-phase reduction)

0. Let t be a handshake trace in A_t^H. The *2-phase reduction* of t, denoted by $\phi_2 t$, is defined by:

$$\phi_2 \cdot t = \begin{array}{ll} \textbf{if} & t = \varepsilon & \rightarrow & \varepsilon \\ {[]} & t = c{\uparrow}\ u & \rightarrow & c\ \phi_2 \cdot u \\ {[]} & t = c{\downarrow}\ u & \rightarrow & c\ \phi_2 \cdot u \\ \textbf{fi} \end{array}$$

1. Let P be a transition-handshake process. $\phi_2 \cdot P$ is the handshake process obtained by applying the 2-phase reduction to all traces of P.

□

The following theorem is hardly a surprise.

Theorem 8.13

ϕ_2 is a phase reduction.

□

ϕ_2 is total and is clearly a bijection. Its inverse will be called the *2-phase handshake refinement* of a handshake process. The 2-phase handshake refinements of a number of handshake components are given next.

Example 8.14

0. $CON \cdot (a^\circ, b^\bullet) = \#[a{\uparrow}^\circ:\ b{\uparrow}^\bullet;\ a{\downarrow}^\circ:\ b{\downarrow}^\bullet]$

1. $SEQ \cdot (a^\circ, b^\bullet, c^\bullet) = \#[a{\uparrow}^\circ:\ (b{\uparrow}^\bullet;\ c{\uparrow}^\bullet);\ a{\downarrow}^\circ:\ (b{\downarrow}^\bullet;\ c{\downarrow}^\bullet)]$

2. $REP \cdot (a^\circ, b^\bullet) = a{\uparrow}^\circ:\ \#[b{\uparrow}^\bullet;\ b{\downarrow}^\bullet]$

3. $MIX \cdot (a^\circ, b^\circ, c^\bullet) = M_{(0,0)},$
   where
   $$\begin{array}{llll} M_{(0,0)} &= [a{\uparrow}^\circ:\ c{\uparrow}^\bullet;\ M_{(1,0)} & |\ b{\uparrow}^\circ:\ c{\uparrow}^\bullet;\ M_{(0,1)}] \\ M_{(1,0)} &= [a{\downarrow}^\circ:\ c{\downarrow}^\bullet;\ M_{(0,0)} & |\ b{\uparrow}^\circ:\ c{\downarrow}^\bullet;\ M_{(1,1)}] \\ M_{(0,1)} &= [a{\uparrow}^\circ:\ c{\downarrow}^\bullet;\ M_{(1,1)} & |\ b{\downarrow}^\circ:\ c{\downarrow}^\bullet;\ M_{(0,0)}] \\ M_{(1,1)} &= [a{\downarrow}^\circ:\ c{\uparrow}^\bullet;\ M_{(0,1)} & |\ b{\downarrow}^\circ:\ c{\uparrow}^\bullet;\ M_{(1,0)}] \end{array}$$
□

The above mixer in particular is considerably more complicated than the *MIX* component of Example 5.3. The 2-phase refinements of directed components such as variables, multiplexers and adders are distinctly more complex than the above mixer.

The handshake protocol that results from 2-phase refinement is also known as 2-cycle signaling or non-return-to-zero signaling [Sei80]. The good news about 2-phase refinement is that it results in handshake circuits in which components interact by the minimum number of transitions possible. Consequently, these circuits are potentially as fast and energy-efficient as possible. The bad news is that circuits sensitive to voltage transitions tend to be significantly larger than circuits sensitive to voltage levels [Sei80]. This overhead in circuit size may reduce the speed and power benefits considerably.

The advantages of 2-phase refinements are likely to dominate in the case of off-chip communication and, to a lesser extent, for long-distance on-chip communication.

4-phase refinements

4-phase refinements form practical alternatives to 2-phase refinements. The resulting handshake protocols are known as Muller signaling, 4-cycle signaling or return-to-zero signaling [Sei80]. The essence of 4-phase refinements is that handshakes are implemented by a signaling sequence of four communications. A first form is based on *complete 4-phase reduction*:

Definition 8.15   (complete 4-phase reduction)

Let $P = \langle A_t, T \rangle$ be a transition handshake process, and let $C = 0A{\uparrow} \cup 1A_t{\downarrow}$ (C consists of the symbols related to the first and fourth phases of a 4-phase handshake). The *complete 4-phase reduction* of P, denoted by $\phi_{4c} \cdot P$, is defined only for P that satisfy

$$(\forall t : t \in T : suc \cdot (t, P) \subseteq iA_t \cup C)$$

and results in the handshake process

$$\langle A, \{t : t \in T \land suc \cdot (t, P) \subseteq C : \phi_2 \cdot (t\lceil C)\} \rangle$$

$\Box$

Complete 4-phase reduction is based on the concealment of symbols in the complement of C, viz. $0A{\downarrow} \cup 1A{\uparrow}$. The restriction on the domain of ϕ_{4c} excludes transition handshake processes that become quiescent while capable of doing an output in the complement of C. The reduction selects only those traces for projection on C that have successors in C. This selection gets rid of those traces that become quiescent while waiting for inputs in the complement of C.

Theorem 8.16

ϕ_{4c} is a phase reduction.

$\Box$

In contrast to ϕ_2, the 4-phase reduction is *not* a bijection. The complete 4-phase handshake refinement of a handshake process is usually not unique. Examples of complete 4-phase expansions of some handshake components are given below.

Example 8.17

0. The two-phase connector is suitable in a four-phase setting as well. Alternatives are

$$\#[a\uparrow°: (b\uparrow•; b\downarrow•); a\downarrow°]$$

and

$$\#[a\uparrow°; a\downarrow°: (b\uparrow•; b\downarrow•)]$$

1. A suitable four-phase version of the sequencer is

$$\#[a\uparrow°: (b\uparrow•; b\downarrow•; c\uparrow•); a\downarrow°: c\downarrow•]$$

An alternative is

$$\#[a\uparrow°: b\uparrow•; a\downarrow°: (b\downarrow•; c\uparrow•; c\downarrow•)]$$

2. A four-phase repeater can be identical to the two-phase version.

3. The four-phase *MIX* is remarkably simple compared to the two-phase version:

$$MIX\cdot(a°, b°, c•) = \#[[a\uparrow°: c\uparrow•; a\downarrow°: c\downarrow• \mid b\uparrow°: c\uparrow•; b\downarrow°: c\downarrow•]]$$

□

An important property of complete 4-phase refinement is that the wires of a port are in their initial states after the completion of each handshake. In most cases the circuits are therefore simpler than their 2-phase counterparts. An obvious disadvantage is the doubling of the number of transitions, with associated penalties in power consumption and computation time. The latter disadvantage can be relaxed somewhat by adopting the following alternative 4-phase reduction:

Definition 8.18   (quick 4-phase reduction)

Let $\langle A_t, T\rangle$ be a transition handshake process, and let $C = 0A\uparrow \cup 1A\uparrow$ (with this choice, C consists of the first and second phases of a 4-phase handshake). The *quick 4-phase reduction* of $\langle A_t, T\rangle$, denoted by $\phi_{4q}\cdot\langle A_t, T\rangle$, is defined in the same way as ϕ_{4c}, taking the difference in symbol set C into account.

□

Theorem 8.19

ϕ_{4q} is a phase reduction.

□

ϕ_{4q} is not a bijection and an associated handshake refinement is therefore not unique. Quick 4-phase refinements tend to be faster than complete 4-phase refinements, because the environment does not need to participate in the return-to-zero transitions. The price for this gain in speed is that the circuits tend to be more complex, because after output transition $a_1\uparrow$ the component must be receptive for $a_0\downarrow$ while possibly engaging in other handshakes.

Mixed forms of complete and quick 4-phase refinements may be considered, with the objective of taking the best of both worlds: quick 4-phase refinement when the speed gain is substantial and the overhead in circuit complexity is acceptable, and complete 4-phase refinement in all other instances. Of course, such mixed refinements must be based on a proper phase reduction. A useful transition handshake component to convert a complete 4-phase refinement into a quick one on a single-port basis is the *quick-return linkage*[1].

Example 8.20   (quick-return linkage)

The transition handshake component $QRL \cdot (a^\circ, b^\bullet)$ is defined as

$$\#[(a\uparrow^\circ : b\uparrow^\bullet); (a\downarrow^\circ \| b\downarrow^\bullet)]$$

□

Component QRL is a quick 4-phase handshake refinement of a connector. Observe that $a\uparrow^\circ$ and $b\uparrow^\bullet$ are coupled as in CON, and that $a\downarrow^\circ$ and $b\downarrow^\bullet$ can occur independently.

Transferrers

Realizations of handshake components using 4-phase handshake refinements lead to reasonably efficient VLSI circuits. The current Tangram compiler (see Chapter 9) uses the complete 4-phase handshake refinement for all handshake components, *except* for the transferrer. Recall that transferrers are introduced abundantly in the compilation of Tangram programs. The behavior of a transferrer with activation port a°, input $b^\bullet$ and output $c^\bullet$ is defined by (assuming appropriate declarations of a, b, c and x):

$$\#[a^\circ : (b^\bullet?x; c^\bullet!x)]$$

A complete 4-phase refinement is:

$$\#[a\uparrow^\circ : (b\uparrow^\bullet?x ; b\downarrow^\bullet?x ; c\uparrow^\bullet!x ; c\downarrow^\bullet!x); a\downarrow^\circ]$$

Other 4-phase refinements have in common that the b and c handshakes are strictly sequential, requiring costly storage of the incoming value between the communications $b\downarrow^\bullet?x$ and $c\uparrow^\bullet!x$.

A transition handshake component with a behavior similar to the transferrer, and with an extremely cheap circuit realization is (cf. Section 8.5):

$$\#[a\uparrow^\circ : (b\uparrow^\bullet?x ; c\uparrow^\bullet!x) ; a\downarrow^\circ : (b\downarrow^\bullet?x ; c\downarrow^\bullet!x)]$$

The reductions in cost and delays have been achieved by creating an overlap between the b and the c handshake. It turns out that, with few exceptions, this handshake refinement of the transferrer is allowed in the compiled handshake circuits. This can be checked for each syntax/compilation rule that introduces transferrers. Exceptions are assignments of the form $x := E$ in which E depends on the value of x. For these so-called *auto assignments* (e.g. $i := i + 1$) we have to accept the more expensive handshake refinement.

---

[1]In [Udd84] attributed to C.L. Seitz.

8.4   Message encoding

In the previous section we assumed a One-Hot encoding of data: to each symbol in the two symbol sets of a port we assigned a wire. A set of 16 symbols then requires 16 wires. On the other hand, 16 wires may encode as many as 2^{16} (= 65536) values. This suggests ample room for improvement over One-Hot encoding. Our prime interest is in encodings that preserve the delay-insensitive nature of the communication among handshake components. [Ver88] presents a definition and an overview of these so-called "delay-insensitive codes". In this section we repeat this definition and link it to the most popular delay-insensitive code: the Double-Rail code, also known as the Dual-Rail code.

A *code* is a pair (I, C), where I is a finite set of indexed wires, and C is a set of subsets of I: the code words. The size of I is called the *length* of the code, and the size of C is called the code's *size*. A One-Hot code of size n has length n.

The implementation of port $\langle 0p, 1p \rangle$ requires a code for both $0p$ and $1p$. In most cases, however, at least one of these two sets is a singleton (code size = 1), and a single wire suffices (code length = 1).

A code word is an element of C and indicates along which wires a transition is to be sent for the transmission of the corresponding message. Not all code words are suitable for delay-insensitive communication. For instance, the empty set is useless, because the receiver would not be able to detect its arrival.

Definition 8.21

A code (I, C) is *delay insensitive* [Ver88] when

$$(\forall x, y : x \in C \land y \in C \land x \subseteq y : x = y)$$

□

That is, when no code word is contained in another code word. This property allows the receiver to detect the arrival of a message. After a transition has arrived on each wire of a code word, the receiver knows that it has received a complete message.

The *concatenation* of codes (I, C) and (J, D) with $I \cap J = \emptyset$ is the code $(I \cup J, CD)$, where CD is defined by

$$\{x, y : x \in C \land y \in D : x \cup y\}$$

The concatenation of two delay-insensitive codes is also delay-insensitive.

The well-known *Double-Rail code* [Sei80] can now be introduced as the concatenation of n (disjoint) One-Hot codes of length 2. Using 16 wires, a Double-Rail code of 8 wire pairs encodes 2^8 (= 256) code words, which is a clear improvement over the 16 code words of the One-Hot code. Arrival detection of Double-Rail encoded messages is simple, so is the conversion from and to (delay-sensitive) Single-Rail codes. These properties make Double-Rail codes fairly popular in the design of delay-insensitive and other self-timed circuits.

However, compared with clocked circuits, in which a transition of the clock announces the arrival of a message, Double-Rail codes are rather wasteful. For a given code size, the overhead in number of wires is 100%, which is considerable in a technology where costs are dominated by wires. Other delay-insensitive codes [Ver88] have considerably less overhead. However, their use in the realization of handshake circuits is constrained by:

- the lack or excessive costs of circuits for arithmetic with such codes,

- the size of encoding and decoding circuits near storage elements, and

- the delays involved in encoding and decoding.

For off-chip and long-distance on-chip communication these overheads of coding and decoding may nevertheless be worthwhile.

When wire delays can be sufficiently controlled, delay-*sensitive* codes become attractive for circuit realization. With n wires, a code of size 2^{n-1} can be implemented, in which one wire is used to signal the arrival of a message. Of course, the delay along that wire must exceed the delay in each of the $n-1$ other wires. This is sometimes called a data-bundling constraint [Sut89]. In practice this requires sufficient control over the spatial layout of handshake components and the connecting wires, introduction of additional delays or a combination of both. Conversion circuits from and to Double-Rail codes are given in [Sei80].

8.5 Handshake components → VLSI circuits

The previous sections show how the specification of a handshake component can be refined by:

0. reducing receptiveness (depending on the component's context),

1. refining handshakes, and

2. encoding messages.

These refinements result in the specification of a circuit in terms of transitions on individual input and output wires. The next step is to decompose such a specification into a circuit of available VLSI primitives such as inverters and *NAND* gates. Methods for these decompositions are emerging [Mar89, Ebe89, MBM90, JU91], with different choices in and emphases on:

0. the handshake protocol chosen,

1. the available VLSI primitives,

2. the degree of delay-insensitivity.

In this section we review decompositions of a few handshake components into circuits of so-called *VLSI operators*.

VLSI operators and (isochronic) forks

The behavior of a VLSI operator is defined by the Boolean values of the output wire(s) in terms of present and past values of the inputs. The behavior of a monadic (single output) operator is specified by a pair of so-called *production rules* [Mar89]

$$F \mapsto z\uparrow$$
$$G \mapsto z\downarrow$$

F and G are Boolean expressions called the *guards* of the operator. The identifiers in F and G are the inputs of the operator. z is the output of the operator. $z\uparrow$ and $z\downarrow$ are shorthand for $z := true$ and $z := false$ respectively. The production rule $F \mapsto z\uparrow$ can be read as "when F holds z becomes *true*".

The guards of an operator are required to be mutually exclusive, i.e. $\neg F \vee \neg G$ must hold at any time. Furthermore, the guards have to be *stable*, i.e. once a guard evaluates to *true*, it has to remain *true* until the completion of the corresponding output transition. Stability of the guards is *not* a property of the operator: it must be satisfied by the environment of the operator. The same holds for the mutual exclusion of the guards of operators for which $\neg F \vee \neg G$ is not a tautology.

An input transition denotes the change of an input variable. An input transition is *productive* if it causes an output transition, and *void* otherwise. The time between a productive input transition and the corresponding output transition may be arbitrary (i.e. positive and finite).

An operator is called "combinational" if $F \vee G$ is a tautology, and "sequential" or "stateholding" otherwise.

Some examples of operators are given below. We will return to them in later examples.

Example 8.22

   0. An inverter is specified by

$$\begin{aligned} \neg a &\mapsto z\uparrow \\ a &\mapsto z\downarrow \end{aligned}$$

$a \;—\!\!\triangleright\!\!\circ— z$

   1. The familiar *AND* operator is specified by

$$\begin{aligned} a \wedge b &\mapsto z\uparrow \\ \neg a \vee \neg b &\mapsto z\downarrow \end{aligned}$$

$\begin{aligned} a \\ b \end{aligned} \;\boxed{\wedge}\; z$

   2. Similarly, the *OR* operator is specified by

$$\begin{aligned} a \vee b &\mapsto z\uparrow \\ \neg a \wedge \neg b &\mapsto z\downarrow \end{aligned}$$

$\begin{aligned} a \\ b \end{aligned} \;\boxed{\vee}\; z$

   3. The previous three operators are combinational operators. A well-known example of a sequential operator is the Muller-C element:

$$\begin{aligned} a \wedge b &\mapsto z\uparrow \\ \neg a \wedge \neg b &\mapsto z\downarrow \end{aligned}$$

$\begin{aligned} a \\ b \end{aligned} \;\boxed{C}\; z$

   Note that this specification allows two successive transitions on one of the inputs, provided the other does not change in the mean time.

□

CMOS implementations of VLSI operators are discussed in [Mar89, vB91]. An example of a CMOS circuit for a Muller-C element is depicted in Figure 8.0. It consists of a Majority

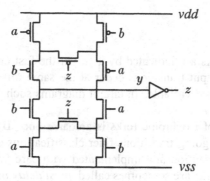

Figure 8.0: A CMOS circuit for a Muller-C element. Wires with the same label are connected. *vdd* and *vss* denote the power and ground rail respectively.

circuit with its output z fed back to one of its inputs. Note that during the (dis-)charging of wire y two paths of transistors pull together.

VLSI operators may be connected by (point-to-point) wires. Wires themselves may be regarded as VLSI operators:

$$a \;\mapsto\; z\uparrow$$
$$\neg a \;\mapsto\; z\downarrow$$

However, since VLSI operators may have arbitrary delays themselves, there is no point in introducing extra variables here. Therefore we treat wires as single variables.

When a value is to be transmitted to the inputs of two operators a *FORK* operator must be used. The *FORK* operator has two outputs, both following the input:

$$a \;\mapsto\; y\uparrow, z\uparrow$$
$$\neg a \;\mapsto\; y\downarrow, z\downarrow$$

The comma between the output transitions expresses concurrency: the two events may occur in either order and no assumption is made about the time duration between these events. (Simultaneous occurrence of both events cannot be expressed in the model.) In implementation technologies where wire delays may dominate other delays (such as CMOS) it turns out to be necessary to represent the outputs of the fork by two distinct variables.

A network of VLSI operators and forks is said to be *delay insensitive* if it functions correctly under arbitrary and possibly varying delays in operators and wires. This rather extreme class of asynchronous circuits has the additional advantage that it simplifies the layout: delays introduced by wires do not affect the behavior of the circuit. Unfortunately, the class of (purely) delay-insensitive circuits constructed from operators and wires only is small and not very interesting from a practical view point (cf. [BE92] and [Mar90]).

The "weakest possible compromise" [Mar90] with respect to delay insensitivity seems to be a forking wire with constraints on the arrival times of transitions at the ends of the fork: the *isochronic fork*. An isochronic fork is a special case of the *FORK* operator. Below we present two types of isochronic fork. An *asymmetric* isochronic fork guarantees that one output transition occurs before the other, as expressed by the semicolon:

$$a \;\mapsto\; y{\uparrow};z{\uparrow}$$
$$\neg a \;\mapsto\; y{\downarrow};z{\downarrow}$$

In circuit diagrams such forks are indicated by a '<' at the fast end. A *symmetric* isochronic fork guarantees that both output transitions occur at the same time: the names of the outputs are simply aliases for the same variable. In circuit diagrams such forks are indicated by a '=' near the fork.

The above classification of isochronic forks is a coarse one. By requiring different timing behaviors for up- and down-going transitions finer classifications can be obtained. Isochronic forks must be applied with caution and implemented with care [vB92a]. Networks of VLSI operators and (isochronic) forks are sometimes called *quasi delay insensitive*. They also belong to the class of *speed independent circuits* [Mil65, Rem91], i.e. they function correctly assuming arbitrary delays in operators and zero wire delays.

Circuit realizations for some handshake components

The circuit realizations of the handshake components below are all based on complete 4-phase refinements (cf. Example 8.14).

Example 8.23

0. A circuit realization of a connector consists of wires only:

1. The repeater consists of a *NOR* and an inverter. Output a_1 is connected to ground: it is not be involved in any transition.

2. A useful auxiliary circuit for the realization of complete 4-phase transition handshake components is the *S-element* [vB92a]. An S-element has as port structure $a^{\circ} \cup b^{\bullet}$, and can be specified by the transition handshake process

$$\#[a{\uparrow}^{\circ} : (b{\uparrow}^{\bullet}; b{\downarrow}^{\bullet}); a{\downarrow}^{\circ}]$$

A possible circuit realization of the S-element is:

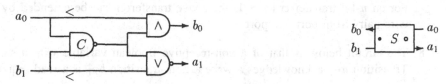

Initially, $a_0 = a_1 = b_0 = b_1 = false$ and $z = true$. The forks connected to a_0 and b_1 are both isochronic. In [Mar89] the circuit is called a Q-element. The D-element of [BM88] behaves similarly, but is not strongly initializable (see Section 8.6), whereas the S-element is.

3. A circuit for the sequencer is based on the S-element.

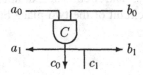

4. The *PAR* component can for instance be realized as:

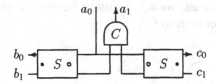

5. A circuit for the non-receptive mixer is:

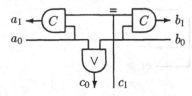

The fork connected to c_1 is isochronic.

6. An undirected *JOIN* can be realized by

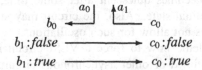

7. A Boolean transferrer can be realized by wires only, provided that the b and c handshakes may overlap (cf. Section 8.3).

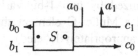

For an n-bit transferrer ($n > 1$) the above transferrer can be extended by adding $n - 1$ wire pairs from port b to port c.

8. The circuit below is that of a non-receptive Boolean variable with a single read port. Transition $a_1 \uparrow$ acknowledges a write action; transition $b_0 \uparrow$ is a read request.

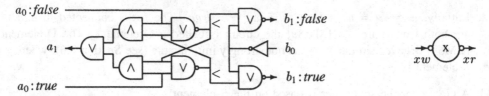

The circuit of a 2-bit variable can be realized by two 1-bit variables, a fork connected to the two read-request inputs, and a Muller-C element that joins the write-acknowledgements (with inputs and outputs appropriately labeled).

9. The selector circuit is the most complex one of this list. The external choice is temporarily stored in a 1-bit *VAR*. The *S*-element sequences the writing and subsequent reading of that choice. The selector below assumes mutual exclusion between communications through $b°$ and $d°$, and is therefore not receptive.

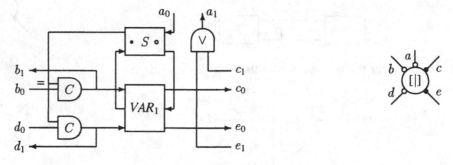

□

The presented circuit solutions are not claimed to be optimal. Clever combinations of operators on the transistor level often yield interesting savings. The circuits of Example 8.23 are sufficient to realize, for example, the optimized handshake circuit of the two-place buffer of Figure 1.5, and the modulo-N counter cells of Figure 2.9.

8.6 Initialization

When a VLSI circuit is connected to a power supply, the circuit generally does not proceed to an initial state by itself. *If* the circuit becomes quiescent after some time, the resulting state may not even be reachable from an initial state. Also, the circuit may start oscillating (diverging), even when its specification does not allow for such oscillations.

So, we have a circuit-initialization problem: how to force a VLSI circuit into its initial state. This problem is not specific to self-timed or other asynchronous circuits. In clocked circuits, this problem is solved by the introduction of additional *reset* circuitry. This circuitry can be used to force a well-chosen subset of all wires into their initial states. This strategy is also applicable to the VLSI circuits studied in this chapter. Nevertheless, we develop a different strategy that avoids the need for additional circuitry and that builds on the properties of compiled handshake circuits.

First we take stock of the properties of handshake components and circuits that will be used:

- The initial state of handshake components is passive: only an input event can cause a handshake component (and hence a handshake circuit) to leave the initial state (cf. 4.19).

- Handshake components and handshake circuits have the initial-when-closed property. Hence, a handshake circuit is in its initial state if and only if all its ports (both internal and external) are also (cf. 4.19).

- The environment of a handshake circuit has control only over the inputs of the external ports of that handshake circuit.

It must be stressed that the behavior of the VLSI circuit after power-on *cannot* be analyzed within the model for handshake circuits, since all kinds of interference may occur. Fortunately, we are not interested in this behavior; we only want a guarantee that the circuit will arrive in an initial state within a finite and predictable amount of time.

The initialization properties of handshake circuits will be analyzed in terms of the binary relation $\rightsquigarrow$ between symbol sets.

Definition 8.24 (initializes)

Let B and C be a symbol sets. $B \rightsquigarrow C$ (pronounced as "B initializes C") is a binary relation with the following properties:

0. $C \subseteq B \Rightarrow B \rightsquigarrow C$

1. $B \rightsquigarrow C \wedge C \rightsquigarrow D \Rightarrow B \rightsquigarrow D$

2. $B \rightsquigarrow C \wedge D \rightsquigarrow E \Rightarrow B \cup D \rightsquigarrow C \cup E$

□

The following properties follow immediately from the definition of $\rightsquigarrow$

Property 8.25

0. From 0 we can see that $\rightsquigarrow$ is reflexive, i.e. $B \rightsquigarrow B$.

1. Together with 1 we conclude that $\rightsquigarrow$ is a preorder.

2. Combining 0 and 1 yields $B \rightsquigarrow C \wedge B \subseteq D \Rightarrow D \rightsquigarrow C$.

3. Alternatively, $B \rightsquigarrow C \wedge D \subseteq C \Rightarrow B \rightsquigarrow D$.

4. Finally, combining 0 and 2 yields $B \rightsquigarrow C \Rightarrow B \rightsquigarrow B \cup C$.

□

Our aim is to develop a $\leadsto$ relation on $(\cup P : P \in H : \mathbf{a}P)$ for handshake circuit H, given such relation for the constituent handshake components.

Definition 8.26 (weak initializability)

0. A handshake component P is weakly initializable if it is passive, initial-when-closed, and $\mathbf{i}P \leadsto \mathbf{o}P$. On the basis of Property 8.25.4 the latter is equivalent to $\mathbf{i}P \leadsto \mathbf{a}P$.

1. A handshake circuit H is weakly initializable if its constituent handshake components are and $\mathbf{i}(\mathbf{e}H) \leadsto \mathbf{o}(\mathbf{e}H)$, where $\mathbf{e}H$ denotes the external port structure of H (cf. Definition 4.8).

□

Clearly, a weakly initializable handshake component can be forced into its initial state by making all inputs initial.

Example 8.27

Without loss of generality we may say that a four-phase handshake port is initial if all its wires are low, as was the case in the circuits of Example 8.23. Relation $\mathbf{i}P \leadsto \mathbf{o}P$ then means that all outputs can be forced low by making all inputs low. Using this encoding of the initial state, it is easy to verify that all circuits of Example 8.23 are weakly initializable.

□

Unfortunately, requiring all handshake components to be weakly initializable (Definition 8.26.0) is not sufficient to make a handshake circuit weakly initializable (Definition 8.26.1). In order to make handshake circuits weakly initializable, additional provisions are required. We first examine a simple strategy that is effectively and efficiently applicable to undirected handshake circuits. A more general, but also more elaborate strategy is sketched next.

Simple initialization strategy

Definition 8.28 (strong initializability)

0. A weakly initializable handshake component P is strongly initializable if $\mathbf{i}P^\circ \leadsto \mathbf{o}P^\bullet$.

1. Accordingly, a weakly initializable handshake circuit H is strongly initializable if its constituent handshake components are and $\mathbf{i}(\mathbf{e}H)^\circ \leadsto \mathbf{o}(\mathbf{e}H)^\bullet$.

□

Example 8.29

All circuits of Example 8.23 *except* the transferrer are strongly initializable, that is, making all passive input wires low forces all active output wires low.

□

The next theorem expresses that strong initializability is preserved under parallel composition, provided that the associated *activity graph* is acyclic.

Definition 8.30   (activity graph)

An activity graph is a directed graph. The activity graph associated with a handshake circuit
has one node for each handshake component and one arc for each channel, directed from the
active port to the passive port of that channel.

□

Theorem 8.31   (initialization)

Let H be a handshake circuit whose associated activity graph is acyclic and whose constituent
handshake components are strongly initializable. Then H is weakly as well as strongly initializable.

Proof   When circuit H is empty or a singleton, the theorem is trivial. In the case H consists
of at least two components, it can be decomposed into two non-empty subcircuits H_0 and H_1
such that $\mathbf{p}^\circ H_0 \cap \mathbf{p}^\bullet H_1 = \emptyset$ (by the acyclicity of H).   We use the following abbreviations
(see picture below):

- $A^\circ = \langle \mathbf{p}^\circ H_0, \emptyset \rangle$

- $B^\bullet = \langle \emptyset, \mathbf{p}^\bullet H_0 \setminus \mathbf{p}^\circ H_1 \rangle$

- $C^\bullet = \langle \emptyset, \mathbf{p}^\bullet H_0 \cap \mathbf{p}^\circ H_1 \rangle$

- $C^\circ = \langle \mathbf{p}^\bullet H_0 \cap \mathbf{p}^\circ H_1, \emptyset \rangle$

- $D^\circ = \langle \mathbf{p}^\circ H_1 \setminus \mathbf{p}^\bullet H_0, \emptyset \rangle$

- $E^\bullet = \langle \emptyset, \mathbf{p}^\bullet H_1 \rangle$

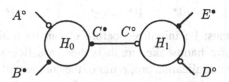

Note that $\mathbf{p} H_0 = \langle A, B \cup C \rangle$ and $\mathbf{p} H_1 = \langle C \cup D, E \rangle$. Also, $\mathbf{i} C^\circ = \mathbf{o} C^\bullet$ and $\mathbf{o} C^\circ = \mathbf{i} C^\bullet$. *Weak*
initializability of H is now proven by (the derivation uses property 8.25.4 implicitly):

$\quad \mathbf{i} A^\circ \cup \mathbf{i} B^\bullet \cup \mathbf{i} D^\circ \cup \mathbf{i} E^\bullet$

$\rightsquigarrow \quad \{ \ H_0 \text{ is strongly initializable } \}$

$\quad \mathbf{o} B^\bullet \cup \mathbf{o} C^\bullet$

$\rightsquigarrow \quad \{ \ H_1 \text{ is weakly initializable; } \mathbf{o} C^\bullet = \mathbf{i} C^\circ \ \}$

$\quad \mathbf{o} C^\circ \cup \mathbf{o} D^\circ \cup \mathbf{o} E^\bullet$

$\rightsquigarrow \quad \{ \ \mathbf{o} C^\circ = \mathbf{i} C^\bullet; \ H_0 \text{ is weakly initializable } \}$

$\quad \mathbf{o} A^\circ$

Clearly, all symbols are initializable from the external inputs. Strong initializability is proven similarly.

□

Theorem 8.32

Let T be a Tangram program. The activity graph associated with $C \cdot T$ is acyclic.

Proof   Can be checked easily from the diagrams that depict the compilation function in Chapter 7.

□

Weak initializability of a handshake circuit is sufficient for practical purposes. Strong initializability allows the environment to postpone the initialization of the active input wires until all passive outputs wires have become low. For the set of undirected handshake components of Example 3.23 four-phase realizations can be designed that are strongly initializable. The simple strategy is then effective. The time needed to initialize a handshake circuit is proportional to the length of the longest directed path in the associated activity graph. In practice this amounts to less than a microsecond for current CMOS realizations.

More general initialization strategy

For the handshake components needed for the implementation of Tangram strongly initializable realizations exist (4-phase). However, for a few components weakly initializable realizations exist, that are significantly cheaper than their strongly initializable counterparts. These cheap variants often have properties that are useful for more elaborate initialization strategies. For example, for $TRF_T \cdot (a^\circ, b^\bullet, c^\bullet)$ a very cheap 4-phase realization exists (cf. Example 8.23) that satisfies

$$ia^\circ \rightsquigarrow ob^\bullet \ \land \ ib^\bullet \rightsquigarrow oc^\bullet \ \land \ ic^\bullet \rightsquigarrow oa^\circ$$

This implies that port $b^\bullet$ must be initialized before $c^\bullet$ can be initialized. Acyclicity of the associated activity graph of a handshake circuit is then insufficient for weak initializability. However, depending on the initialization properties of the components involved, specific classes of weakly initializable handshake circuits may exist. It can, for instance, be proven that with the above transferrer, compiled handshake circuits of full Tangram are still weakly initializable.

8.7   Testing

Introduction

The fabrication processes introduce defects on the surface of an IC. Such defects include spurious blobs of metal, impurities in the oxide layers, silicon-crystal defects, and cracks in wires. These defects cannot be avoided completely and have a density of a few per cm^2 of IC area. Unfortunately, they may cause malfunctioning of the circuit. The fraction of defect-free chips for a given IC technology depends mostly on the size of the chip and ranges from over 90% for chips of a few mm^2 to less than 10% for a large IC of, say, 2 cm^2.

The main purpose of testing is *fault detection*: the discrimination between correctly manu-factured circuits and faulty circuits. Another purpose is that of *fault location* [Fuj85]. This section only addresses the former.

An effective test procedure must make assumptions on how defects affect the circuit behavior. The set of assumptions is commonly referred to as the *fault model*. A popular fault model is the so-called *stuck-at* fault model, which models defects that prevent a wire from being pulled-up from a low state (stuck-at 0) or pulled-down from a high state (stuck-at 1). It must be noted that the stuck-at model only addresses those wires that connect logical gates (cf. VLSI operators, Section 8.5). More elaborate fault models also include, for example, bridging faults (spurious connections between two wires) and crosspoint faults (undesired transistors). Despite its limitations, the stuck-at model is widely used.

Testing of asynchronous circuits has received little attention in the literature. The subject is considered to be difficult ([Fuj85], page 81):

> Test generation is much more difficult for asynchronous circuits than for syn-chronous circuits, because of races, hazards, or oscillations.

This may be true of asynchronous circuits in general, but recent work [DGY90, BM91, MH91] suggests that for asynchronous circuits that are "sufficiently" delay insensitive, the prospects for testability are fairly promising.

The purpose of this section is to show that testing of CMOS realizations of handshake circuits is viable and that the costs of testing can be kept relatively modest. First we address the issue of the generation of test traces: traces that can be used to detect faults. This is based on the stuck-at model, restricted to stuck-at faults on (gate) outputs. For a more general approach that also includes stuck-at faults on inputs see [MH91].

Unfortunately, the length of a test trace or the time to execute a test trace may grow exponentially with the size of the circuit. In order to control the costs of test-trace generation and execution, it is necessary to modify the circuit with the objective of reducing these costs. This so-called *testability enhancement* will be addressed at the handshake-circuit level and forms the second topic of this section.

Both topics are treated informally and rather sketchily. This reflects the immaturity of the discipline of asynchronous-circuit testing and the presence of open problems.

Test traces

Our analysis starts by considering only those wires that connect handshake components. As-sume, without loss of generality, that all these wires are required to be low at an initial state of the circuit. Let a be such a wire, and let Q be the handshake component for which a is an input wire. Stuck-at faults on wire a may have quite different effects on the circuit behavior:

0. A stuck-at 0 on a does not interfere with the initialization of the circuit. (It may even speed up the initialization procedure.) A subsequent up transition $a \uparrow$, however, will never arrive at Q, as if it experiences an infinite delay. Component Q can therefore not participate in any trace that involves $a \uparrow$. In most cases (see below) this can eventually be observed externally by the inhibition of an output transition.

1. A stuck-at 1 on a prevents the correct initialization of Q and hence of the circuit. Unfortunately, this stuck-at may have the same effect on Q as a (premature) up transition on a. In general, not much can be said about the response of Q to such a premature transition. We assume, however, that Q is not able to participate in a subsequent handshake that involves $a\downarrow$.

In either case, the handshake circuit cannot participate in a trace that contains both $a\uparrow$ and $a\downarrow$.

An *internal test trace* is defined as a trace in $\mathbf{W}\cdot H$ that causes each channel wire to make an up transition as well as a down transition. An *external test trace*, or *test trace* for short, is a trace $t \in (\mathbf{e}H)^H$ that satisfies:

$$(\forall u : (u\lceil \mathbf{e}H) = t : u \text{ is an internal test trace})$$

The universal quantification assures that the completion of the internal test trace can be observed externally. The idea is that the behavior of a handshake circuit cannot display a test trace in the presence of a stuck-at fault. Given this definition of test trace, three important questions arise:

0. under which circumstances does a test trace exist?

1. how to compute a test trace?

2. can test traces be executed?

For many handshake circuits no test trace exists, as is reviewed below. Fortunately, for practical circuits escapes are often available.

0. Some wires never make a transition. For instance, wire a_1 of the repeater in Example 8.23. These wires are clearly redundant and should be removed. In the sequel we assume that circuits are not redundant.

1. Sometimes a wire makes at most one transition. For instance, wire a_0 of the repeater of Example 8.23 makes at most one up-transition. There are two ways to deal with this situation. One can either relax the definition of test trace and add circuitry to observe stuck-at faults on these wires, or one can modify the circuit such that it is able to execute a signaling sequence with both transitions (see below under test enhancement).

2. Even if every wire can make both transitions, not all wires need to be covered by a single trace. The way out here is to concatenate several traces, linked with initialization steps into a single test trace.

3. Divergences cause special problems. The occurrence of a divergence can easily be observed in a CMOS realization of a handshake circuit, by measuring the supply current in an (externally) quiescent state. However, since it is not possible in all cases to identify the wires involved in a divergence, a test trace may not exist in a divergent circuit.

4. A more serious problem may be that of internal nondeterminism. Some forms of internal nondeterminism, such as the circuits compiled from Tangram programs with uninitialized variables, are relatively innocent. Other forms of internal nondeterminism involve circuit redundancy. The resulting nondeterminism must then be restricted during test time. Clearly more research is needed for testing internally nondeterministic circuits.

In summary, a test trace does exist, provided that

- the circuit is not redundant, non-diverging, and internally deterministic;

- provisions are made to deal with wires that (would otherwise) make at most one transition;

- re-initializations are allowed.

An undirected handshake channel is tested after the completion of a 4-phase handshake. Testing of a Double-Fail encoded channel requires at least two 4-phase handshakes, so that both wires of each wire pair make both transitions. But how about the wires internal to the handshake components?

It turns out that the handshake components of Example 5.35 can be realized such that the internal wires are covered by a test trace that tests the external wires. This also holds for the handshake components of Example 5.37, except for some of the binary operators, such as adders. For adders an additional handshake is necessary to fully cover the testing of the carry chain.

Given the above testability properties of handshake components, it is in many cases straight-forward to compute a test trace from the handshake circuit and even from the original Tangram program.

Example 8.33

0. Example of a test trace for $BUF_2(a, c)$ (see Figure 1.5):

$$\triangleright^\circ : (a^\bullet?0 \; ; \; c^\bullet!0 \; ; \; a^\bullet?1 \; ; \; c^\bullet!1)$$

This trace tests a ripple buffer of arbitrary capacity! The test time can be reduced by changing the order of $c^\bullet!0$ and $a^\bullet?1$.

1. A test trace of $WAG(a, c)$ (see Figure 1.6) is

$$\triangleright^\circ : (a^\bullet?0 \; ; \; c^\bullet!0 \; ; \; a^\bullet?0 \; ; \; c^\bullet!0 \; ; \; a^\bullet?1 \; ; \; c^\bullet!1 \; ; \; a^\bullet?1 \; ; \; c^\bullet!1)$$

In order to test the two parallel paths in the handshake circuit, twice as many communications are required in comparison with the test trace of $BUF_2(a, c)$.

□

Note that a test trace also detects multiple stuck-at faults on outputs. Masking of one fault by another fault cannot occur.

Test-trace execution

Can a test trace be executed? That is, is it possible to force a correctly manufactured IC to display the behavior specified by the test trace? In a strict sense, this is seldom possible, because of reordering of output transitions. If the question is interpreted "modulo reordering", there still is a problem: that of nondeterminism.

For instance, the first N outputs of an N-place shift register (see Section 1.2) are unknown at test time. The resulting nondeterministic behavior is relatively innocent, because the communication behavior at the port level is not affected. More erratic forms of nondeterminism are hard to handle by existing test equipment.

Given an executable test trace, ICs can be tested. An IC is free of stuck-at faults, if the complete test trace can be executed. The costs of testing are largely determined by the length of the test trace and the time needed to execute it. As a rule, shorter traces require less test time.

Testability enhancement

Testability enhancement of a circuit involves the modification of the circuit with the purposes of

- reducing the length or execution time of a test trace;

- establishing the existence of a test trace.

Consider the duplicator chain of Example 4.24, consisting of N duplicators:

$$a_0 \ —\!\!\circ\!(\textbf{dup})\!\bullet\!—\!\overset{a_1}{}\!\circ\!(\textbf{dup})\!\bullet\!—\overset{a_2}{} \ \cdots \ \overset{a_{N-1}}{}\!\circ\!(\textbf{dup})\!\bullet\!— \ a_N$$

Completion of the handshake through port a_0 requires 2^N handshakes through port a_N. Clearly, the time to execute a test trace of the duplicator chain grows exponentially with the circuit size. The problem is not as artificial as it may seem: a watch is basically a set of counters that can be realized with duplicator chains. The circuitry that counts leap years must then also be tested!

The explosion in test time can be avoided by cutting the chain into two parts, more or less equal in size, and testing them independently. This can be realized by inserting a mixer and a *break* component B.

$$a_i \ —\!\!\circ\!(\textbf{dup})\!\bullet\!—\overset{b}{}\!\circ\!\overset{i}{\diagdown}\!|\!\bullet\!—\overset{c}{}\!\circ\!\overset{t}{\diagup}\!(B)\!\bullet\!—\overset{d}{}\!\circ\!(\textbf{dup})\!\bullet\!— \ a_{i+1}$$

The behavior of component B is defined by (with m a local Boolean variable)

$$m := \textit{false}; \ \#[\ [\ \ t^\circ : m := \neg m$$
$$| \ \ c^\circ : \textbf{if } m \rightarrow \textit{skip } [] \ \neg m \rightarrow d^\bullet \textbf{ fi}$$
$$] \ ]$$

Variable m records whether B is in *test mode*. Initially, B is not in test mode. A handshake through t sets B in test mode (i.e. the front subchain is being tested), and a second handshake through t resets m. If B is in test mode, communications through c° are simply absorbed. If B is not in test mode it acts like a connector, and the back subchain can be tested through i.

The effect of B halfway in the duplicator chain is dramatic. The front subchain of length N **div** 2 can be tested in test mode in $2^{(N \textbf{ div } 2)}$ time units. The back subchain of length $N - (N \textbf{ div } 2)$ can be tested in normal mode roughly in the same amount of time. This results in an overall reduction by a *factor* of $2^{(N \textbf{ div } 2)-1}$.

In general, insertion of mixers and breaks makes it easier to obtain test traces in a systematic way. As illustrated above, it may also reduce the test time significantly.

An example of testability enhancement of the second kind, viz. one that helps to establish the existence of a test trace, is the following. A repeater can be equipped with a passive port that is used to (re-)set the repeater in test mode, similar to the break component in the duplicator chain. By modifying the behavior of the repeater such that in test mode it behaves like a connector, the wires connected to the passive port of the repeater can conveniently be tested. As a bonus, most handshake circuits will then in test mode complete the handshake through port $\triangleright°$.

Chapter 9

In practice

Handshake circuits and the associated compilation method from CSP-based languages were conceived during 1986 at Philips Research Laboratories. A first IC (7000 transistors) was designed using experimental tools to manipulate and analyze handshake circuits (then called "abstract circuits") and to translate them into standard-cell netlists. The IC realized a sub-function of a graphics processor [SvB88] and proved "first-time-right" (September 1987). Extensive measurements hinted at interesting testability and robustness properties of this type of asynchronous circuit [vBS88].

Encouraged by these early results the emphasis of the research shifted from the design of the graphics processor to VLSI programming, compilation methods, and tool design. Generalization and systematization of the translation method resulted in an experimental silicon compiler during spring 1990 [vBKR+91]. Section 9.0 describes these compilation tools and their application to a simple Compact Disc error decoder.

A second test chip was designed and verified during the autumn of 1991 [vBBK+93, RS93]. In addition to some test structures, the IC contains a simple processor, including a four-place buffer, a 100-counter, an incrementer, an adder, a comparator, and a multiplier in the Galois field $GF(2^8)$. The Tangram program was fully automatically compiled into a circuit consisting of over 14 thousand transistors. Section 9.1 discusses this chip and its performance in detail. This chapter concludes with an appraisal of asynchronous circuits in Section 9.2.

9.0   VLSI programming and compilation

Experiences with VLSI programming and compilation will be presented from a programmer's viewpoint. After an overview of the design tools, a benchmark program (that of a Compact Disc error decoder) is used to illustrate various VLSI programming and compilation issues.

Tool overview

An overview of the design tools is depicted in Figure 9.0. Design representations are shown as boxes, tools as arrows. (Arrows labeled with an asterisk denote commercially available tools.)

175

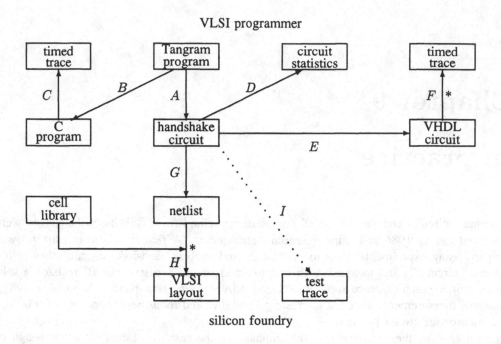

Figure 9.0: Overview of the main Tangram-compilation tools. Boxes denote design representations, arrows denote tools (if labeled with an asterix they denote commercially available tools).

A. translator from Tangram into handshake circuits (text format);

B. translator from Tangram into behaviorally equivalent C programs;

C. fast compiled C-code simulator which produces a trace with coarse timing data;

D. analyzer of handshake circuits which produces statistics at the levels of handshake circuits, CMOS circuits and layout;

E. converter of handshake circuits into VHDL descriptions [LSU89];

F. VHDL simulator which produces a trace with detailed timing data;

G. generator that expands the handshake components into a netlist of standard cells;

H. standard-cell layout package which performs placement of the standard cells and cell-to-cell routing according to the netlist;

I. test-trace generator (under development).

Vehicle

A simple error decoder with application in Compact Disc players (cf. Section 0.0) serves as a benchmark. A precise description of this function can be found in [KvBB+92]. In brief, it receives code words of 32 symbols (of 8 bits), of which four are designated as parity symbols. These parity symbols allow for the correction of two erroneous symbols. The benchmark program can only locate single errors. For each code word the decoder produces an error status (0, 1 or more errors) and, in the case of a single error, an error location and an error value. The actual correction is not performed by the decoder. Code words arrive at a rate of one per 70 microseconds.

VLSI programming

A Tangram program for the decoder can be found in [KvBB+92]. Schematically it can be described by

$$\#[x := input(a);\ \ s := syndrome(x);\ \ e := search(s);\ \ c!e]$$

The incoming code word (through port a) is stored in variable x by function *input*. Function *syndrome* then computes the syndrome of x, which is stored in s (a tuple of four symbols). The syndrome contains the error information in an implicit form. Function *search* makes this information explicit in variable e, using a linear search. The number of steps in this search varies between 0 (for correct words) and 32 (in the case of more than one error). Finally, the error information is output through port c. An important improvement on the above program is obtained by computing the syndrome "on the fly" and thus avoiding the costly storage of the incoming code word.

For the detailed program of the decoder the subset of Tangram of Chapter 6 is insufficient. The applied arithmetic in the Galois field $GF(2^8)$ requires provisions for the definition of the appropriate types and associated operations. These provisions include tuple construction and selection, type casting, and type fitting [SvBB+91]. The structure of the program benefits from function and procedure definitions. Sharing of a number of these procedures (cf. Section 2.7) avoids duplication of circuitry.

The program text consists of 68 lines, divided over three paragraphs that are more or less equal in size. The first paragraph contains type and function definitions for the Galois field arithmetic. The second paragraph consists of declarations of variables, functions and procedures and the third paragraph is the detailed version of the above command.

The transparency of the translation method plays an important role in VLSI programming. As the coarse performance can be read directly from the Tangram text, the selection of the above algorithm may be justified at an early stage. Also, the choice of the amount of parallelism in the syndrome computation and in the error search is guided by the observation that the circuits required for most elementary operations in the Galois field are very cheap.

Simple analysis [KvBB+92] shows that the decoder takes in the worst case about 20 microseconds per codeword, which clearly suffices. In the case of stricter performance requirements, the following program for the decoder may be considered:

$$\#[x := input(a);\ \ s := syndrome(x);\ \ b!s]$$
$$\| \ \#[b?r;\ \ e := search(r);\ \ c!e]$$

It consists of two parallel processes: one for computing syndromes and one for searching errors. The type of the internal channel b is a tuple of four symbols. The resulting form of pipelining is akin to that of the ripple buffer in Section 1.0. The throughput of the above program is approximately twice as large compared with the first decoder program. Highlights of a more detailed comparison of both decoder programs are described below.

Compilation to handshake circuits

The compilation of Tangram programs has been implemented according to an extension of the method of Chapter 7. The compiler translates directly to complete 4-phase handshake circuits, and many of the optimizations of Section 8.1 and 8.2 are included. The compiler generates a handshake circuit in a simple textual format.

The compiler uses the handshake components of Examples 3.23 and 5.37. The extensions of Tangram mentioned above require only a few extra handshake components. The compiled decoder consists of 523 handshake components, including 174 connectors. The pipelined version contains 741 handshake components, of which 244 are connectors.

Simulation

Additional confidence in the correctness of a Tangram program can be obtained by simulation. The compiled-code simulator aims at verifying functional correctness. The Tangram program is translated into a functionally equivalent C program, which is linked to a run-time scheduler. The simulation technique allows very fast simulation of large Tangram programs with large data sets. This often results in a high simulation coverage. However, the produced timing data are not based on the actual handshake-circuit implementations, and are therefore not very accurate.

Accurate timing verification can be obtained by simulation of the compiled handshake circuits. We have based our simulation tools on a commercially available VHDL simulator. A simple program translates the handshake circuit into an equivalent VHDL architecture [LSU89]. Together with a library of VHDL models for the various handshake components, this provides access to simulation tools used in mainstream VLSI design. A major advantage over a specific handshake-circuit simulator is that the above setup also allows interfacing to other circuits, including clocked ones, within the VHDL framework.

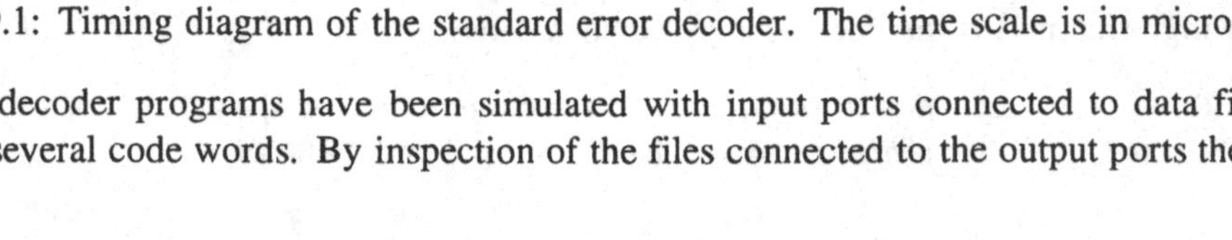

	0 1 2 3 4 5 6 7 8 9 10 11 12 13 14 15 16 17
input	▪▪▪▪▪▪▪▪▪▪▪▪▪▪▪▪▪▪▪▪▪▪▪▪▪▪▪▪▪▪ ▪▪▪▪▪▪▪▪▪▪▪▪▪▪▪▪▪▪▪▪▪▪▪▪▪▪
$s := ..$	▪ ▪
search	▪▪▪▪▪▪▪▪▪▪▪▪▪▪▪▪▪▪▪▪▪▪▪▪▪▪▪▪
output	▪ ▪

Figure 9.1: Timing diagram of the standard error decoder. The time scale is in microseconds.

Both decoder programs have been simulated with input ports connected to data files containing several code words. By inspection of the files connected to the output ports the correct functional behavior was verified. An alternative to file I/O is to model the environment by a Tangram program and to inspect the data transferred along internal channels.

In addition to functional verification, simulation proves useful in analyzing the detailed timing behavior of the compiled circuit. The VHDL models of the handshake circuits have been characterized with regard to timing, based on the timing of their constituent operators and conservative estimations of the average wire capacitances. An interactive post processor of the generated timing data has been used to generate the timing diagrams of Figures 9.1 and 9.2.

Figure 9.1 displays the timing behavior of the standard decoder, obtained by VHDL simulation of the compiled handshake circuit. The square dots are actually short line segments, each indicating a handshake interval, marked from the first phase to the fourth phase. The top line shows the handshakes of the input port, 32 per code word. The second line depicts an intermediate step between the input phase and the search. The third line shows the search: for the first code word (with two errors) the search takes 32 steps, and for the second code word (correct) 0 steps. The output of the error information is on line four. An incorrect code word takes at most 12 microseconds, a correct word about 6 microseconds.

The timing diagram of the pipelined error decoder in Figure 9.2 is markedly different. The same channels have been monitored as in the standard decoder, with the intermediate step replaced by the internal communication along channel b. It is clearly visible that the input of the second code word is in parallel with the error search of the first code word.

The throughput of the pipelined decoder is indeed twice that of the standard decoder, viz. one code word per 6 microseconds. (The simulation interval of 17 microseconds in the timing diagram of Figure 9.2 thus left plenty of room for the decoding of a third code word.) The elapsed time for an incorrectable code word has also improved because less overhead is involved in the sharing of procedures.

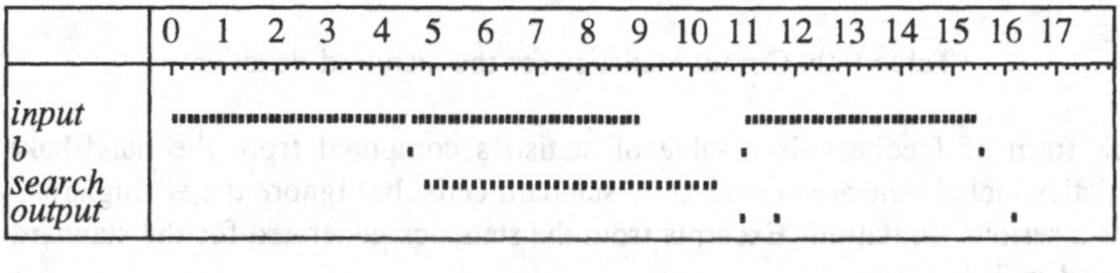

Figure 9.2: Timing diagram of the pipelined error decoder. The time scale is in microseconds.

For critical designs, the timing model may be too conservative. Significant improvements, however, can only be obtained when the handshake circuit is "back annotated" with wiring capacitances from the layout (cf. simulation of power consumption at the end of this section). The VHDL simulator at the handshake-circuit level is several orders of magnitude slower than the compiled C-code simulator at the Tangram level.

Circuit statistics

Comparison of different VLSI programs and optimization of the chosen program with regard to layout area requires feedback about circuit and layout costs. Unfortunately, the automatic generation of relatively small layouts may take several hours. Larger layouts may involve interactive floorplanning and optimization, and their generation may then take a few days or weeks, or even longer.

```
Part                    #MOSTs          cell area [mm2]

Decoder          7292 [100.0 %]   0.931 [100.0 %]
control          1010 [ 13.9 %]   0.121 [ 13.0 %]
communication     938 [ 12.9 %]   0.142 [ 15.3 %]
logic            2772 [ 38.0 %]   0.252 [ 27.0 %]
memory           2568 [ 35.2 %]   0.415 [ 44.5 %]

Cells              #cells            #MOSTs

Decoder           610 [100.0 %]    7292 [100.0 %]
C2                 26 [ 4.3 %]      312 [ 4.3 %]
C3                 37 [ 6.1 %]      444 [ 6.1 %]
EQL               122 [ 20.0 %]    2440 [ 33.5 %]
OR2               130 [ 21.3 %]     780 [ 10.7 %]
S                  34 [ 5.6 %]      612 [ 8.4 %]
VAR1               54 [ 8.9 %]      864 [ 11.8 %]

estimated core area:              1.9    [ mm2 ]
estimated transistor density:     3916   [ mm-2 ]
```

Table 9.0: Circuit statistics for the standard decoder.

A quick form of feedback is a table of statistics computed from the handshake circuit. These statistics include the area covered by standard cells, but ignore the wiring area, which is sometimes a serious limitation. Excerpts from the statistics generated for the standard decoder are displayed in Table 9.0.

The first paragraph reports the MOS transistor count and the area occupied by the standard cells. These quantities are detailed by function, based on the role of the handshake component in the computation (e.g. sequencer: control, mixer: communication, binary operator: logic, and variable: memory). These functional profiles vary considerably from one Tangram program to another.

The second paragraph presents the standard cell counts. It is confined to the six most frequently used cells, accounting for about two thirds of the transistors and cell area.

The third paragraph gives an estimation of the area of the standard-cell part of the layout. Here it is assumed that the routing channels occupy the same area as the standard cells. For this example this is quite accurate, as we shall see later.

The pipelined decoder counts 11376 transistors and 989 cells, occupying a cell area of 1.5 mm^2. The estimated core area is 3.0 mm^2, which will turn out to be rather optimistic.

The problem here is how to take the wiring area into account, without laying out the complete circuit. The ratio core-area/cell-area has been observed to vary between 1.8 and 3. Statistics are helpful with the selection among alternatives and the tuning of a final program, but layout generation is necessary for an accurate assessment of the circuit size of a VLSI program.

Layout generation

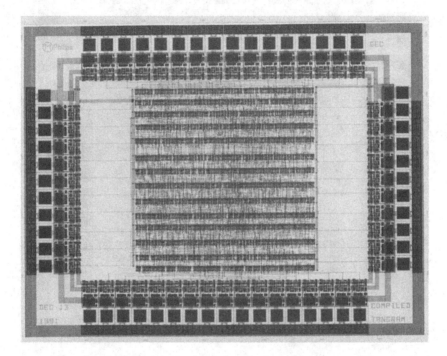

Figure 9.3: Layout of the standard error decoder.

The generation of a layout from a handshake circuit involves two steps. First the handshake circuit is expanded into a netlist of standard cells. These standard cells are then placed and interconnected according to the connectivity information described in the netlist.

We have developed a library of twenty-odd standard cells. Most standard cells implement a single VLSI operator; some implement a combination of a few operators in order to economize on layout area.

The expansion of handshake components also resolves their parameters (e.g. word width, number of read ports). Placement and routing are performed by commercially available layout tools.

Figure 9.3 shows a layout of the standard error decoder, synthesized fully automatically from the Tangram program. The core area (standard cells + inter-cell routing) measures 2.2 mm^2 in a 1.2 μm double-metal CMOS process.

A layout of the pipelined error decoder is shown in Figure 9.4. The difference between the measured core area (4.0 mm^2) and the estimated core area (3.0 mm^2) is visible in the relatively wide routing channels. This is partly a consequence of the 32×2 wires for realizing channel b. Both layouts contain 55 pads: 22 inputs, 31 outputs, 1 power and 1 ground.

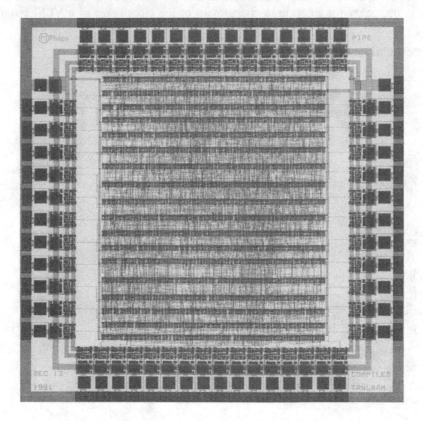

Figure 9.4: Layout of the pipelined error decoder.

Energy consumption

In addition to circuit size and circuit speed, energy consumption is a third cost/performance indicator. The energy consumed and dissipated by the decoder is analyzed next. The number of steps in the error search varies from 0 to 32. The total time to decode a word by the standard decoder varies correspondingly between 6 and 12 microseconds (see Figure 9.1). We may therefore expect to find a variation in energy consumption as well.

A good approximation for the *energy* consumption of a static CMOS circuit can be obtained by summing over all wires the quantity $\frac{N}{2}CV^2$, where N is the number of transitions on that wire, C the capacitance of the wire (including that of the transistor gates connected to it), and V the supply voltage (cf. Section 0.1). Accurate values of all capacitances can be extracted from the layout. The number of transitions can be obtained for given input stimuli by means of switch level simulation. The above summation then yields the energy required for the computation. Division by the specified (or simulated) computation time results in an indication for the power consumption of the circuit.

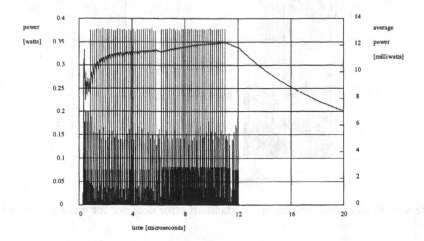

Figure 9.5: Power consumption of the standard error decoder for an incorrectable code word.

Results of such simulations are given in Figures 9.5 and 9.6. The spikiness has no physical meaning, but is characteristic for event-driven simulations, which condense all energy of simultaneously occurring transitions into a single time instant.

Figure 9.5 shows the simulation results for an incorrectable codeword. The two main phases, viz. input with on-the-fly syndrome computation (32 steps) and error search (again 32 steps) are clearly visible. The circuit activity after the search includes output of the error information. Then the circuit is quiescent: *no* power is consumed until a next code word is offered. No energy is dissipated in clock distribution or in a controller that issues "skip" instructions.

The smooth curve represents the average power: the energy consumed so far divided by the elapsed time. After 20 microseconds this quantity reads a little over 7 milliwatts, which is equivalent to stating that the decoder consumes well over 140 nanojoules for decoding an incorrectable code word. As code words in a CD player come at a rate of one per 70 microseconds, this amounts to a power consumption of 2 milliwatts, which we shall round to 2.4 milliwatts to include short-circuit dissipation and leakage.

For correct code words, quiescence is reached soon after the syndrome computation, as shown in Figure 9.6. The power consumption is then only 1.2 milliwatts, assuming the same rate of code words, and including a similar fraction for short-circuit dissipation. This example nicely shows that asynchronous circuits consume energy only when and where needed.

Test trace

A test trace consisting of 3 code words (with 0, 1 and 2 errors) has been verified to test for all stuck-at faults in both decoders. The trace has been generated by hand[0] from the Tangram program text. The transparent compilation rules and some simple properties of the circuit

---

[0]Marly Roncken's

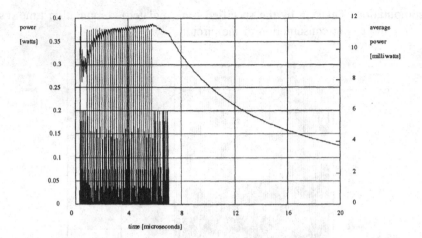

Figure 9.6: Power consumption of the standard error decoder for a correct code word.

realizations of the handshake components made this a feasible task. The fault coverage was checked by switch-level simulation. It may be interesting to note that a single code word already covers 97% of the possible stuck-at faults.

9.1   A compiled Tangram IC[1]

This section presents the characterization and evaluation of an asynchronous IC produced fully automatically by the Tangram compiler. The circuit comprises a 4-place buffer, a 100-counter, an incrementer, an adder, a comparator, and a multiplier. Testing for fabrication faults requires only 135 test handshakes, and the circuit functions correctly with a supply voltage as low as 1.6 volts. This value reduces to 1.2 volts if the pass transistors of a (novel) acknowledge circuit are set aside.

The demonstrator IC consists of the small processor described below and a test structure [RS93]. The processor consists of a four-place buffer *BUF4* and a structure called *MILL*. The latter can execute a variety of instructions with up to two operands. The instruction and operands are input via *BUF4* in order to save input pins. The Tangram program is described in Figure 9.7. The definition of gfmul has been omitted for the sake of brevity.

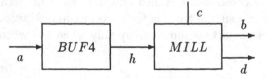

Buffers are popular asynchronous circuits with many practical uses. The 4-place buffer permits accurate and detailed timing measurements. *MILL* has been designed to measure the timing properties for a variety of, mostly arithmetic, operations: count, output, increment, add,

---

[1]This section is adapted from [vBBK+93].

```
word = type (0..255)
|
(a?word & b!word & c~ & d!bool).
begin
  Buf1= proc (a?word & b!word).
      begin x: var word | forever do a?x; b!x od end
& Buf4= proc (a?word & b!word).
      begin
        e, f, g: chan word
      | Buf1(a,e) || Buf1(e,f) || Buf1(f,g) || Buf1(g,b)
      end
& Mill= proc (a?word & b!word & c~ & d!bool).
      begin opcode= type (0..7)
        & tuple = type << opcode, (0..31) >>
        & x,y,z : var word
      |
        forever do
          c~; a?x; y:=x; a?x; z:=x; a?x; c~;
          case (x cast tuple).0
          is 0 then skip
          or 1 then for 100 do skip od
          or 2 then b!y
          or 3 then b!(y+1)
          or 4 then b!(y+z)
          or 5 then d!(y<z)
          or 6 then b!gfmul(y,z)
          or 7 then stop
          si
        od
      end
& h   : chan word
|
  Buf4(a,h)  || Mill(h,b,c,d)
end
```

Figure 9.7: Tangram program of demonstrator chip (definition of gfmul omitted).

compare, and multiply in $GF(2^8)$ [KvBB⁺92]. The ith instruction is specified by input $a[3i+2]$ and the operands are inputs $a[3i]$ and $a[3i+1]$. The gross execution time of this instruction can be measured between signals $c[2i+1]$ and $c[2i+2]$. By appropriately discounting the overheads for output, multiplexing, instruction decoding etc., reasonably accurate timing data can be obtained for the individual operations (see below).

Program segment `for 100 do skip od` translates into the systolic counter of Section 2.4. The `case` command is implemented using a symmetric binary decoding of the least significant three bits of variable x. The four outputs along channel b are multiplexed, using an (unbalanced) tree of binary multiplexers.

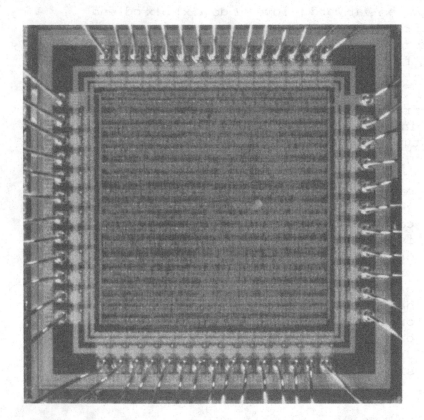

Figure 9.8: Photograph of a bonded version of the demonstrator chip.

Figure 9.8 shows a photograph of a bonded version of the demonstrator chip. The core of the layout measures 2.9 mm² in a 1 μm CMOS process, the die 6.7 mm². The processor subcircuit consists of 11694 transistors (14200), covering a cell area of 0.94 mm² (1.19), and requires 43 out of 52 pins (the bracketed numbers apply to the entire IC).

An estimate of the dynamic energy consumption of the core circuit (ignoring the periphery and off-chip loads) was obtained by switch-level simulation of the circuit, using back-annotation of the parasitic capacitances extracted from the layout. This simulation predicts 30 nanojoules (5 milliwatts × 6 microseconds, see Figure 9.9) for executing each instruction once, involving

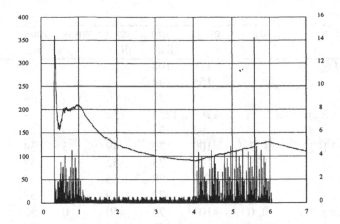

Figure 9.9: Simulated power consumption [milliwatts] versus time [microseconds] (momentary left axis and averaged right axis).

8×3 inputs through b. The low-power interval (from 1 to 4 microseconds) corresponds to the execution of for 100 do skip od.

Testing for stuck-at output faults involves the execution of 23 instructions, resulting in a complete test trace of 135 (4-phase handshake) communications. The GF multiplier accounts for 9 test instructions.

Tests and measurements

The test trace has been used to select the 7 structurally correct chips out of the 11 available chips. These 7 ICs proved correct during all succeeding experiments.

Table 9.1 summarizes the timing measurements [nanoseconds] for the instructions, as well as *ripple_4* (backward propagation of a vacancy through *BUF4*), and *assign* (transfer of three values from *BUF4* to *MILL*). All measurements were performed on a Hewlett Packard 82000 tester at approximately 20 °C, and are accurate to within 1 nanosecond. In column "I/O disc." the overhead of off-chip communication has been discounted. The overhead of the case framework is discounted in the next column, by subtracting the execution time of skip. The overhead of multiplexing is discounted next. Finally, subtraction of the time of reading the operands and outputting the result yields the net evaluation time of the expressions involved. Note the data dependency of some of the operations and the frequency of the systolic counter: 80 megahertz.

In Figure 9.10 the inverse of the skip time is plotted versus the supply voltage (V_{DD}), showing a correct execution for a supply voltage of only 1.2 volts! The solid curve is that of an inverter delay, assuming equal gains (β) and thresholds ($V_t = 1.1$ volts) for NMOS and PMOS transistors [WE85], modified for velocity saturation ([Tsi88], Eqn. 5.3.10):

$$f(V_{DD}) = \frac{1}{\tau(V_{DD})} \times \frac{V_{crit}}{V_{DD} + V_{crit}}$$

Operation	arg .	gross	I/O disc.	skip disc.	#mux	mux disc.	output disc.
ripple_4		119	108	-	-	-	-
assign		155	144	-	-	-	-
skip		34	23	0	-	-	-
100 * skip		1266	1255	1232	-	-	-
b!y		93	65	42	3	27	0
b!(y+1)	127	100	72	49	3	34	7
b!(y+1)	128	103	75	52	3	37	10
b!(y+z)	127, 1	106	78	55	2	45	18
b!(y+z)	128, 1	100	72	49	2	39	12
d!(y<z)	0, 0	101	73	50	0	50	23
d!(y<z)	255, 0	105	77	54	0	54	27
b!gfmul(y,z)		136	108	85	1	80	53

Table 9.1: Measured external timing (gross) and derived internal timings [nanoseconds].

where $\tau(V_{DD})$ is the inverter delay ignoring velocity saturation:

$$\tau(V_{DD}) = \frac{C_L}{\beta(V_{DD} - V_t)} \times \left[\frac{V_t - 0.1V_{DD}}{V_{DD} - V_t} + 0.5 \ln\left(\frac{19V_{DD} - 20V_t}{V_{DD}} \right) \right]$$

Voltage V_{crit} corresponds to the critical field and denotes the voltage where the velocity of electrons is reduced by half due to various electron/hole-velocity saturation effects. Function f was fitted to the measurements by using a critical field of 1.7 volt/micrometer, and a $\frac{C_L}{\beta}$ of 22.5×10^{-9} voltseconds. By discounting off-chip communication and assuming an average β of 200 microamperes/volt^2 one obtains a total capacitive load of 3 picofarads of all the CMOS stages in the critical path of skip, or about 60 femtofarads per stage.

Unfortunately, the chip does not operate fully on a supply voltage 1.2 volts because of the pass transistors used in one of the cells (see next subsection). In Figure 9.11 the ripple frequency is plotted against V_{DD}, showing a minimum supply voltage of approximately 1.6 volts, somewhat above twice the threshold for an NMOS transistor.

The measured energy for executing each instruction once was 55 nanojoules. The difference with the simulated 30 nanojoules for the core can be explained by peripheral energy consumption, short-circuit dissipation and leakage.

The measured temperature dependency can be approximated by the derating factor $1 + 0.0025(T - 20)$, for T ranging from -40 °C to 100 °C.

Write-acknowledge circuit

Figure 9.12 shows the CMOS implementation of the storage section and the write-acknowledge section of a 1-bit variable [vBS90]. The latter is realized using two NMOS transistors as pass transistors. An upward transition on wire ao is produced when $(ai_0 \wedge q_0) \vee (ai_1 \wedge q_1)$, i.e. when the written value agrees with the stored value. Wire ao becomes low after the relevant input

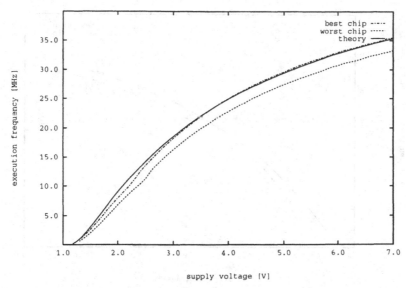

Figure 9.10: `skip` frequency [megahertz] versus supply voltage [volts].

(ai_0 or ai_1) has become low. A clear disadvantage of this circuit is that the voltage of wire *ao* never exceeds $V_{DD} - V_{tn}$, amounting to about 3.6 volts for $V_{DD} = 5$ volts, taking the body effect into account.

The attraction of the above acknowledge circuit is that it requires only two transistors, whereas a full-CMOS circuit would require 10 transistors.

Discussion

We have reported on a fabricated asynchronous circuit compiled fully automatically from a high-level Tangram description. It appeared "almost first time right"[2]. The Tangram program was chosen such that it allowed accurate timing measurements for a variety of basic operations. Although the chosen circuit style was not for maximum speed, a count frequency of 80 megahertz and an 8-bit ripple frequency exceeding 35 megahertz are encouraging.

The delay-insensitive nature of the circuit allows operation over a wide range of supply voltages without worrying about clock-frequencies and varying (ratios of) delays. If pass transistors are omitted by redesigning one of the cells, circuits operate correctly for a supply voltage that exceeds V_{tn} **max** $-V_{tp}$. The dependence of operating frequencies on supply voltage can be modeled accurately by an inverter delay.

---

[2]A bug in the router software resulted in a short circuit between supply and ground, in an input-protection circuit. This was visible as a constant 19 milliampere supply current, but did not affect the operation of the circuit otherwise. The reported energy consumption was measured after laser repair.

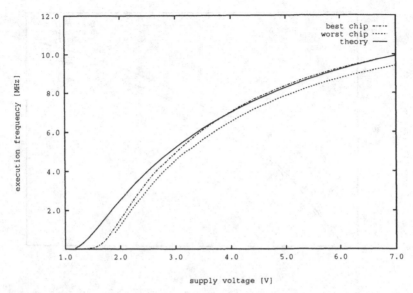

Figure 9.11: *ripple_4* frequency [megahertz] versus supply voltage [volt].

9.2   Appraisal of asynchronous circuits

In Chapter 8 we have seen that handshake circuits are most naturally realized by asynchronous circuits. However, the overwhelming majority of today's VLSI circuits are synchronous. Are there good reasons to educate and train a new generation of designers in asynchronous circuits and VLSI programming? It is hard to tell. The balance of pros and cons is mixed. This section aims at reviewing this balance.

Research on asynchronous circuits is booming. With few exceptions, this research is carried out in academic research institutes. We may expect significant progress in the understanding of these circuits, and we may hope for further improvements in their cost and performance. Synchronous-circuit design has a respectable tradition of several decades, whereas the possibility of asynchronous circuit design has largely been ignored. The appraisal below is therefore

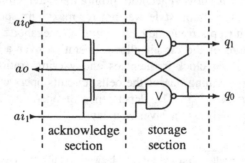

Figure 9.12: Write-acknowledge circuit for a 1-bit variable.

only a 1993 snapshot.

A major problem in comparing asynchronous and synchronous circuits is the large variety in their characteristics and realizations. For both synchronous and asynchronous circuits there exist different architectures, different (detailed) timing disciplines and different building blocks. Quantitative comparisons are therefore hard to make.

The following aspects will be reviewed: ease of design, circuit speed, robustness, testability, circuit size, and energy consumption.

Ease of design

A clock is an artefact. It has been introduced to solve timing problems at the *circuit* level, viz. the controlled usage of latches and the avoidance of critical races. By the evolution of VLSI circuits, the clock gradually became an important *system*-level design issue.

A choice for a single clock frequency in a VLSI system has many repercussions on the modularity of the system, as well as on its performance. In a synchronous circuit there is an excess of synchronization among subcircuits, viz. at the end of each clock period. In an asynchronous circuit synchronization is reduced to its (functional) minimum. This leads to a high degree of modularity, allowing modules to be designed and optimized independently [Sei80, Sut89, MBM90, Men91]. One of the earliest projects in hardware design that addressed the issue of modularity is that of 'Macro modules' [OSC67].

Furthermore, there is no need to design the circuits for the basic functions (shifting, addition, multiplication, etc.) under the restriction that they can be 'evaluated' well within the clock period. In an asynchronous circuit, the delay of a parallel multiplier can be compensated by a fast shift or transfer step in a computation.

Problems with clock distribution and clock skew are of course absent in asynchronous circuits. A gain in design productivity is also expected from VLSI programming and associated compilation techniques.

Circuit speed

Less, and more local synchronization among subcircuits makes circuits faster. Asynchronous circuits also allow one to take advantage of the data-dependence of computation times. A well-known example is that of the n-bit parallel adder in [Sei80]. The average addition time is proportional to the average carry-ripple path ($O(\log n)$), whereas the worst case addition time is proportional to n. In synchronous circuits an $O(\log n)$ response time can only be obtained with additional carry-acceleration circuits. Then the worst-case and average-case performances are equal. A similar advantage has been observed for parallel multiplication [HvBPS93] and division [WH91].

The asynchronous circuits realized from handshake circuits have another speed advantage that stems from the extreme form of control distribution. For instance, a sequencer that activates two transferrers avoids the large timing overheads common to central controllers when sequencing two computation steps.

Circuit speed has been an important motivation for asynchronous circuits in [KTT+88, KTT+89, MBM90]. Although the number of synchronizations is smaller in asynchronous circuits, their explicit nature has its price. Especially in complete four-phase signaling, the associated overheads may easily outweigh the above advantages for regular computations. Quick four-phase refinements and perhaps two-phase refinements may help here.

Robustness and reliability

Insensitivity to delay seems to relate to insensitivity to variations in IC-processing parameters and operating conditions. These issues have hardly been researched, and will only be touched upon by means of a few examples.

A decrease in the width of the polysilicon tracks in a CMOS circuit yields faster transistors (shorter channels) and slower wires (higher resistance). In synchronous circuits this may result in violations of the set-up and hold times of the latches. In speed-independent circuits however, variations in the widths of polysilicon tracks may influence the circuit's performance, but not its correct operation.

Measurements of our test silicon [vBS88] showed a high degree of robustness with respect to variations in power supply voltage. A large self-inductance in the power-supply wires caused the supply voltage to drop below 0 volt for brief periods of time, without affecting the functional correctness of the circuit. Asynchronous circuits operate at low supply voltages, whereas with synchronous circuits there is the worry of having to tune the clock frequencies safely [MBL+89, vBBK+93].

On a related note, it has been reported that fundamental reliability problems that come with the synchronization of independently clocked circuits [Ano73, CM73] can be avoided in delay-insensitive circuits [Sei80]. In clocked circuits synchronization may lead to glitches, caused by arbitrary long durations of metastable states. In asynchronous circuits synchronization does not lead to anomalous behavior, because subsequent computations are simply delayed until metastability has been resolved.

Testability

There are indications that the testing of asynchronous circuits is feasible. It is even expected that speed-independent circuits may be simpler to test, because stuck-at faults can be observed through deadlock [BM91, MH91]. This feature also simplified the generation of tests for our graphics chip [vBS88], the decoder of Section 9.0, and the IC of 9.1. Progress in research towards automatic generation of test traces is nevertheless slow. This presumably reflects that this problem is, "combinatorially speaking", a hard one.

Circuit area

In most cases layout area is dominated by circuits that store, communicate or process data; circuitry for control covers usually less than 15% of the area (cf. the statistics of the decoder in Section 9.0). With Double-Rail encoding, which requires two wires per bit, we may therefore not expect to obtain circuits that can compete in silicon area. What should we think of this roughly 100% area overhead?

Firstly, there are compensations. Availability of two wires per bit simplifies some operations: e.g. the Boolean complement is obtained by simply crossing the two wires. Also, as we have seen with the shift registers in Section 1.2, slave latches can be saved selectively, whenever allowed by the performance requirements. Another compensation is realized by the extreme form of control distribution intrinsic to the form of syntax-directed translation we have applied. This leads to fewer and *shorter* wires. An example of an incidental compensation is the absence of carry acceleration circuitry for applications where the *average* throughput matters.

Secondly, other delay-insensitive codes that require fewer wires may be considered (cf. Section 8.4). Clever encoder and decoder circuits may reduce the costs of (de-)multiplexing, synchronizing and long-distance communications.

Thirdly, and presumably most significantly, compromises with regard to delay insensitivity are required to arrive at competing circuits. Natural candidates for first experiments in this respect are: off-chip communication, Random-Access Memories (RAMs) and Read-Only Memories (ROMs). Existing standards and the availability of well-engineered embedded memories make it impractical to insist on delay-insensitive circuit realizations in these cases. In many ICs the input/output circuitry (including bonding pads) together with the memories account for well over half the circuit area.

Single-rail encoding using "data bundling" for the remaining circuitry has been proposed in [Sut89, PDF+92]. Ultimately this may result in circuits that are even smaller than their synchronous counterparts. Avoidance of interference (cf. Section 0.1), however, requires delay circuitry [KTT+88, KTT+89] or completion detection by using alternative circuit techniques [MBM90]. On a more speculative note, it may be interesting to investigate circuit techniques that encode three states in a single wire. Unfortunately, compromises with regard to delay insensitivity may jeopardize testability and may complicate layout design and circuit verification.

Finally, VLSI programming and automatic silicon compilation allow designers to construct and compare many alternative solutions for the specification at hand. By exploring a large portion of the 'solution space' they may expect to find better designs than they would find with traditional VLSI-design methods.

Energy consumption

Self-timed circuits consume potentially less energy than clocked circuits[3] [PDF+92]. There are several reasons for this. Absence of interference (see Section 0.1) and other transient phenomena such as hazards make each transition productive. This is particularly relevant to deep combinational, XOR-intensive structures, such as multipliers [HvBPS93]. Also, there is no dissipation in clock signals. In high-throughput applications, such as in video-signal processing, the distribution of a high-frequent clock may account for well over 20% of the total power consumption. Furthermore, control distribution leads to a high degree of locality, thus avoiding the power consumption in central controllers and the long wires from and to these controllers.

Viewed differently, one may say that a self-timed circuit only consumes energy where and when needed:

- The circuit compiled from a Tangram procedure or function consumes *no* energy when it is not invoked.

---

[3]Here we assume a circuit technology without static dissipation, such as CMOS.

- The low power consumption of the wagging shift registers of Section 1.2 was realized by having two subregisters doing half the work, operating at half the rate.

- The subcounters of the modulo-Ncounter of Section 2.4 count and dissipate at exponentially lower rates.

- The error decoder of Section 9.0 consumes energy only during the first 12 microseconds of the 70 microseconds available. For correct code words the required energy is only half of that required for incorrect code words.

To what extent these potential advantages can be realized depends on the chosen handshake refinements and data encoding. As a rule, energy savings increase with a decrease in regularity of the computation. Error decoding, where the work load depends on the correctness of the code words, is a nice example of an irregular computation. Circuits that stand-by for most of the time, but that have to respond to exceptional conditions, represent another example (e.g. a processor triggered by keyboard inputs).

This observation concludes both the appraisal of asynchronous circuits and the last chapter of this book.

Appendix A

Delay insensitivity

Introduction

In [Udd84, Udd86, Ebe89, UV88] the notions delay insensitivity, independent alphabet and absence of computation interference have been defined for *directed processes*. In this section we investigate to what extent these notions apply to handshake processes.

Definition A.0 (directed process)

A directed process T is a triple $\langle iT, oT, tT \rangle$, in which iT and oT are disjoint sets of symbols and tT is a non-empty, prefix-closed subset of $(iT \cup oT)^*$.

□

A handshake process is not a directed process: the alphabet of a handshake process has more structure and the trace set is not prefix closed. However, to every handshake process P there *corresponds* a directed process, viz. $\langle iP, oP, tP^{\leq} \rangle$.

All port structures in this appendix have no internal ports.

Composability

Composability of traces captures the notion that symbols communicated between processes arrive no earlier than they were sent. Consider directed processes P and Q such that $iP = oQ$ and $oP = iQ$. Let $s \in tP$ and $t \in tQ$. Composability restricts the way the pair (s, t) *may* evolve from $(\varepsilon, \varepsilon)$. Let $a \in iQ$ (and therefore $a \in oP$). Then ε is composable to a, but the converse is not true, because a must be sent by P before it can be received by Q. Similarly, for $b \in oQ$, we have b composable to ε. Also, trace s is composable to ta if s is composable to t and a is on its way, i.e. $len \cdot (t \lceil a) < len \cdot (s \lceil a)$. With this introduction we have prepared ourselves for the following definition.

Definition A.1 (composability)

0. Let I and O be two disjoint sets of symbols. $\mathbf{C}_{(I,O)}$ is the smallest binary relation on $(I \cup O)^*$ such that for all symbols $a \in I$, symbols $b \in O$, and traces $s, t \in (I \cup O)^*$:

$$
\begin{aligned}
\varepsilon \, \mathbf{C}_{(I,O)} \, \varepsilon &= \textit{true} \\
\varepsilon \, \mathbf{C}_{(I,O)} \, tb &= \varepsilon \, \mathbf{C}_{(I,O)} \, t \\
sa \, \mathbf{C}_{(I,O)} \, \varepsilon &= s \, \mathbf{C}_{(I,O)} \, \varepsilon \\
s \, \mathbf{C}_{(I,O)} \, ta &= s \, \mathbf{C}_{(I,O)} \, t \;\wedge\; len \cdot (t \lceil a) < len \cdot (s \lceil a) \\
sb \, \mathbf{C}_{(I,O)} \, t &= s \, \mathbf{C}_{(I,O)} \, t \;\wedge\; len \cdot (t \lceil b) > len \cdot (s \lceil b) \\
sa \, \mathbf{C}_{(I,O)} \, tb &= sa \, \mathbf{C}_{(I,O)} \, t \vee s \, \mathbf{C}_{(I,O)} \, tb
\end{aligned}
$$

Sets I and O contain the input and output symbols respectively. When (I, O) are clear from the context, $\mathbf{C}_{(I,O)}$ will be shortened to $\mathbf{C}$.

1. Let A be a port structure. $\mathbf{c}_A$ is a relation on A^H and is defined by

$$
s \, \mathbf{c}_A \, t = s \, \mathbf{C}_{(iA, oA)} \, t
$$

   i.e. the restriction of $\mathbf{C}$ to A^H.

□

Relation $\mathbf{C}_{(I,O)}$ is the converse of the composable relation introduced by [Udd84, UV88]. Relation $\mathbf{c}$ is a preorder on A^H. Consequently, we shall write $S^{\mathbf{c}}$ to denote the composability closure of S and $(\mathbf{c}) \cdot S$ to denote the composability closedness of S (cf. Section 3.1). Both operators are lifted to handshake structures in the obvious way. The composability relation plays a central role in much of the theory on delay insensitivity. We shall therefore first analyze a number of its properties.

Property A.2

Let A be a port structure.

   0. $s, t \in A^H \wedge a \in iA \wedge s \, \mathbf{C} \, ta \;\Rightarrow\; ta \in A^H$

   1. $s, t \in A^H \wedge b \in oA \wedge sb \, \mathbf{C} \, t \;\Rightarrow\; sb \in A^H$

□

Relations $\mathbf{r}$ and $\mathbf{c}$ are related by:

Property A.3

For $s, t \in A^H$ we have $s \, \mathbf{r}_A \, t = s \, \mathbf{c}_A \, t \wedge (\#_s = \#_t)$, where $\#_t$ denotes the bag of symbols of trace t.

□

Another way of relating $\mathbf{r}$ and $\mathbf{c}$ is suggested by "welcoming the traveling symbols":

Property A.4

For port structure A and $t, u \in A^H$ we have:

$$
\begin{aligned}
u \, \mathbf{c} \, t = (\;\; &\exists t', u' \\
: \;\; &(\#'_t = \#_{(u \lceil iA)} \setminus \#_{(t \lceil iA)}) \wedge (\#'_u = \#_{(t \lceil oA)} \setminus \#_{(u \lceil oA)}) \\
: \;\; &uu' \, \mathbf{r} \, tt' \\
&)
\end{aligned}
$$

Proof   We derive:

$u \ \mathbf{c} \ t$

$=$ { Property A.2.0; definition of $\mathbf{c}$ }

$(\exists t' : \#_{t'} = \#_{(u \lceil \mathbf{i} A)} \setminus \#_{(t \lceil \mathbf{i} A)} : u \ \mathbf{c} \ tt')$

$=$ { Property A.2.1; definition of $\mathbf{c}$ }

$(\exists t', u' : (\#_{t'} = \#_{(u \lceil \mathbf{i} A)} \setminus \#_{(t \lceil \mathbf{i} A)}) \wedge (\#_{u'} = \#_{(t \lceil \mathbf{o} A)} \setminus \#_{(u \lceil \mathbf{o} A)}) : uu' \ \mathbf{c} \ tt')$

$=$ { Property A.3, using $len \cdot uu' = len \cdot tt'$ }

$(\exists t', u' : (\#_{t'} = \#_{(u \lceil \mathbf{i} A)} \setminus \#_{(t \lceil \mathbf{i} A)}) \wedge (\#_{u'} = \#_{(t \lceil \mathbf{o} A)} \setminus \#_{(u \lceil \mathbf{o} A)}) : uu' \ \mathbf{r} \ tt')$

$\square$

Relations $\mathbf{c}$, $\mathbf{r}$ and $\mathbf{x}$ are related in a remarkable way for prefixed closed handshake structures, as shown in the next theorem.

Theorem A.5

For handshake structure S, such that $(\leq) \cdot S$, we have:

$$(\mathbf{c}) \cdot S = (\mathbf{r}) \cdot S \ \wedge \ (\mathbf{x}) \cdot S$$

Proof   Let $t \in \mathbf{t}S$ and $u \in (\mathbf{p}S)^H$. We derive for $LHS \Leftarrow RHS$:

$t \in \mathbf{t}S \wedge u \ \mathbf{c} \ t$

$=$ { Property A.4 }

$(\exists t', u' : t \in (\mathbf{i} A)^* \ \wedge \ u \in (\mathbf{o} A)^* : uu' \ \mathbf{r} \ tt' \ \wedge \ t \in \mathbf{t}S)$

$\Rightarrow$ { $(\mathbf{x}) \cdot S$ }

$(\exists t', u' : t \in (\mathbf{i} A)^* \ \wedge \ u \in (\mathbf{o} A)^* : uu' \ \mathbf{r} \ tt' \ \wedge \ tt' \in \mathbf{t}S)$

$\Rightarrow$ { $(\mathbf{r}) \cdot S$; calculus }

$(\exists u' : u' \in (\mathbf{o}S)^* : uu' \in \mathbf{t}S)$

$\Rightarrow$ { $(\leq) \cdot S$ }

$(\exists u' : u' \in (\mathbf{o}S)^* : u \in \mathbf{t}S)$

$\Rightarrow$ { calculus }

$u \in \mathbf{t}S$

$LHS \Rightarrow RHS$ follows readily from the definitions of $\mathbf{c}$, $\mathbf{r}$ and $\mathbf{x}$.

$\square$

Corollary A.6

For handshake process P we have $(\mathbf{c}) \cdot P^{\leq}$.

$\square$

Equipped with the above property of handshake processes we are ready to analyze the delay insensitivity of handshake processes.

Delay insensitivity

Delay insensitivity of directed processes has been defined in many ways [Udd84, Udd86, Ebe89, UV88, Sch92]. The cited definitions are all provably equivalent.

Definition A.7 (delay insensitive)

    0. A directed process $\langle I, O, T \rangle$ is delay insensitive if

$$
\begin{aligned}
&(\quad \forall s, t, a \\
&:\ s \in T \wedge t \in T \\
&:\ (a \in I \wedge s\, \mathbf{C}_{(I,O)}\, ta \Rightarrow ta \in T) \wedge (b \in O \wedge sb\, \mathbf{C}_{(I,O)}\, t \Rightarrow sb \in T) \\
&)
\end{aligned}
$$

    (Cf. Definition 23 and Lemma 5 in [UV88]; recall the reversal of the arguments with respect to their definition of $\mathbf{C}$.)

    1. A handshake process is delay insensitive if the corresponding directed process is.

$\square$

Theorem A.8

Handshake processes are delay insensitive.

Proof   Let P be a handshake process and $s, t \in tP^{\le}$.

Case $a \in iP$. We derive:

$a \in iP \wedge s\, \mathbf{C}\, ta$

$\Rightarrow$ { Property A.2 }

$ta \in A^H$

$\Rightarrow$ { $ta \,\mathbf{c}\, t \wedge (\mathbf{c}) \cdot P^{\le}$ }

$ta \in tP^{\le}$

Case $b \in oP$. We derive:

$a \in oP \wedge sb\, \mathbf{C}\, t$

$\Rightarrow$ { Property A.2 ; Definition of $\mathbf{C}$ }

$sb \in A^H \wedge sb\, \mathbf{c}\, t$

$\Rightarrow$ { $(\mathbf{c}) \cdot P^{\le}$ }

$sb \in tP^{\le}$

$\square$

In [Udd84] the notion of independence of a symbol set is introduced. It is nice to view a handshake process as a directed process in which a port forms the 'unit' of independence. Independence of a symbol set C with respect to P embodies the notion that if an input symbol is allowed to occur in $P \lceil C$ it is also allowed to occur in P.

Definition A.9   (independent alphabet)

0. Let P be a delay-insensitive directed process and C a set of symbols such that $C \subseteq (iP \cup oP)$. C is *independent* with respect to P if:

$$(\forall s, a : s \in tP \wedge a \in (C \cap iP) : (sa\lceil C \in tP\lceil C) = (sa \in tP))$$
$$\wedge \quad (\forall s, a : s \in tP \wedge a \in (\overline{C} \cap iP) : (sa\lceil \overline{C} \in tP\lceil \overline{C}) = (sa \in tP))$$

   where the complement of C with respect to $(iP \cup oP)$ is denoted by $\overline{C}$.

1. Let P be a handshake process and A a port structure such that $A \subseteq \mathbf{p}P$. A is independent with respect to P if $\mathbf{a}A$ is independent with respect to the directed process corresponding to P.

□

Not surprisingly, given the receptiveness of handshake processes, we arrive at the following theorem.

Theorem A.10

For handshake process P and port structure A such that $A \subseteq \mathbf{p}P$, we have: A is independent with respect to P.

□

Computation interference

The justification of the definition of parallel composition of handshake processes relies on the absence of interference. Interference may manifest itself in two forms [vdS85]: *transmission* interference and *computation* interference. Transmission interference occurs when more than one transition is on its way along the same link. The restriction to handshake traces excludes this form of interference right from the start. The absence of computation interference in handshake circuits requires some elaboration.

Definition A.11   (computation interference)

0. Directed processes P and Q are connectable if and only if the sets $iP \cap iQ$ and $oP \cap oQ$ are empty.

1. Let H be a finite set of delay-insensitive directed processes, such that elements of H are pairwise connectable. H is *free of computation interference* if [Ebe89]

$$(\forall t, P, a : t \in \mathbf{W} \cdot H \wedge P \in H \wedge a \in oP : ta\lceil \mathbf{p}P \in tP \Rightarrow ta \in \mathbf{W} \cdot H)$$

2. Handshake circuit H is free of computation interference if the set of corresponding directed processes is.

□

Theorem A.12

Handshake circuits are free of computation interference.

□

A similar result has been suggested in Property 4.10 of [vdS85]. Absence of computation interference in handshake circuits follows directly from the receptiveness of handshake processes. If output a may occur for some component P after trace t, trace ta will be in $\mathbf{W} \cdot H$, either because a is external, or because there is another component that is receptive for a.

Appendix B

Failure semantics

Introduction

In Chapter 6 we have developed a handshake semantics for Tangram. An alternative semantics for Tangram can be based on *failure processes* [BHR84]. Failure processes form the underlying model of CSP [Hoa85], and are the basis for a well-established theory for CSP, including a powerful calculus [RH88].

The availability of two distinct semantics for the same program notation suggests several questions, including:

0. Is the handshake-process semantics consistent with the failure semantics? If so, in what sense?

1. Can VLSI programmers use calculi that are based on failure semantics?

The last question is of obvious practical significance.

This appendix starts with a description of failure processes. By means of a simple example it is shown that an embedding of failure processes into all-active handshake processes does not exist. By choosing a more subtle link between handshake semantics and failure semantics, we arrive at positive answers to the above questions.

Failure processes

This subsection describes a process model based on failures. The description below is rather concise; for a more extensive treatment the reader is referred to [BHR84], [BR85] and [Hoa85].

An alphabet structure defines an *alphabet* as a set of communications.

Definition B.0 (alphabet of an alphabet structure)

Let A be an alphabet structure.

0. A *communication* of A is a pair $a{:}v$, such that $a \in \mathbf{c}A$ and $v \in \tau_A \cdot a$.

1. The *alphabet* of A is the set of all communications of A and is denoted by $\mathbf{a}A$.

□

Note that an alphabet is finite, on account of the finite number of ports and the finiteness of types. In CSP a communication is an event in which a process can engage. An alphabet is the set of all communications of interest. The actual occurrence of a communication is regarded as an instantaneous (atomic) event without duration.

Traces on $\mathbf{a}A$ are used to record the communication events in which a process has engaged up to some moment in time. The linear ordering of events in a trace assumes that the simultaneous occurrence of two events can be ignored. When simultaneity of two events is important, as with the synchronization of two processes, it will be represented by a single communication.

Definition B.1 (failure structure)

0. A *failure structure* is a pair $\langle A, F \rangle$, where A is an alphabet structure and F the so-called *failure set*: a relation between $(\mathbf{a}A)^*$ and $\mathcal{P} \cdot (\mathbf{a}A)$.

1. Elements of F are called *failures*. Let $\langle t, X \rangle$ with $t \in (\mathbf{a}A)^*$ and $X \in \mathcal{P} \cdot (\mathbf{a}A)$ be such a failure. Then t is referred to as its *trace* and X as its *refusal set*.

2. Let S be a failure structure. Then $\mathbf{A}S$ denotes its alphabet structure and $\mathbf{f}S$ denotes its failure set. $\mathbf{a}S$ is a shorthand for $\mathbf{a}(\mathbf{A}S)$.

□

Definition B.2   (failure process)

A failure process is a failure structure $\langle A, F \rangle$ that satisfies the following conditions:

0. $\langle \varepsilon, \emptyset \rangle \in F$

1. $\langle st, X \rangle \in F \Rightarrow \langle s, \emptyset \rangle \in F$

2. $\langle s, Y \rangle \in F \wedge X \subseteq Y \Rightarrow \langle s, X \rangle \in F$

3. $\langle s, X \rangle \in F \ \wedge \ x \in \mathbf{a}P \Rightarrow \langle s, X \cup \{x\} \rangle \in F \ \vee \ \langle sx, \emptyset \rangle \in F$

□

This is essentially the definition of [BHR84], restricted to finite alphabets. A quote from [Hoa85] explains the idea behind failures (page 129):

> "If $\langle s, X \rangle$ is a failure of [process] P, this means that P can engage in the sequence of events recorded by s, and then refuse to do anything more, in spite of the fact that its environment is prepared to engage in any of the events of X."

The four conditions have the following implications.

0. A process is a non-empty failure structure; failure $\langle \varepsilon, \emptyset \rangle$ represents its initial state.

1. If trace st can be observed, trace s must be observable as well.

2. If X can be refused then all subsets of X can be refused.

3. After any trace, a particular communication may happen, can be refused, or both.

[BR85] and [Hoa85] present "an improved failures model for communicating processes". The improvement consists of the possibility of distinguishing among various forms of deadlock. The improved model is more powerful and supports a slightly more elegant algebra. For brevity's sake, this improvement is not included in this monograph.

Definition B.3   (maximal failures)

Let F be a failure set. The *maximal failures* of F, denoted by $Max \cdot F$, is defined as

$$\{t, R : \langle t, R \rangle \in F \wedge \neg (\exists R' : \langle t, R' \rangle \in F : R \subset R') : \langle t, R \rangle\}$$

☐

On account of Definition B.2.2 we may conclude that the failure set of a failure process is fully characterized by its maximal failures. The set of all failure processes with alphabet structure A is denoted by $\prod_{\mathcal{F}} \cdot A$.

With each Tangram program a failure process can be associated, by means of a mapping $\mathcal{F}$: from Tangram to $\prod_{\mathcal{F}} \cdot A$. For details of such a mapping we refer to [Hoa85].

The following example provides the failure processes that correspond to a number of elementary Core Tangram programs. They are included as illustration and for later reference. For brevity's sake only the maximal failures are enumerated.

Example B.4

0. Synchronization on a. The failures of $(a\sim) \cdot a$ are:

$$\{\langle \varepsilon, \emptyset \rangle, \langle a, \{a\} \rangle\}$$

1. Extension of a with port b. The failures of $(a\sim, b\sim) \cdot a$ are:

$$\{\langle \varepsilon, \{b\} \rangle, \langle a, \{a, b\} \rangle\}$$

2. Sequential composition of a and b. The failures of $(a\sim, b\sim) \cdot (a; b)$ are:

$$\{\langle \varepsilon, \{b\} \rangle, \langle a, \{a\} \rangle, \langle ab, \{a, b\} \rangle\}$$

3. Parallel composition of a and b. The failures of $(a\sim, b\sim) \cdot (a \parallel b)$ are:

$$\{\langle \varepsilon, \emptyset \rangle, \langle a, \{a\} \rangle, \langle b, \{b\} \rangle, \langle ab, \{a, b\} \rangle, \langle ba, \{a, b\} \rangle\}$$

4. Internal choice between a and b. The failures of $(a\sim, b\sim) \cdot (a \sqcap b)$ are:

$$\{\langle \varepsilon, \{a\} \rangle, \langle \varepsilon, \{b\} \rangle, \langle a, \{a, b\} \rangle, \langle b, \{a, b\} \rangle\}$$

5. External choice between a and b. This does not correspond to any Core Tangram. A possible syntax is $(a\sim, b\sim) \cdot [a \mid b]$, with failures:

$$\{\langle \varepsilon, \emptyset \rangle, \langle a, \{a, b\} \rangle, \langle b, \{a, b\} \rangle\}$$

6. Internal choice between $a; b$ and $b; a$. The failures of $(a\sim, b\sim) \cdot (a; b \sqcap b; a)$ are:

$$\{\langle \varepsilon, \{a\}\rangle, \langle \varepsilon, \{b\}\rangle, \langle a, \{a\}\rangle, \langle b, \{b\}\rangle, \langle ab, \{a, b\}\rangle, \langle ba, \{a, b\}\rangle\}$$

7. External choice between $a; b$ and $b; a$. The failures of $(a\sim, b\sim) \cdot [a; b \mid b; a]$ are:

$$\{\langle \varepsilon, \emptyset\rangle, \langle a, \{a\}\rangle, \langle b, \{b\}\rangle, \langle ab, \{a, b\}\rangle, \langle ba, \{a, b\}\rangle\}$$

□

The remainder of this section is used to discuss the structure of $\prod_{\mathcal{F}} \cdot A$. For more background, appreciation and proofs, the reader is referred to material cited earlier.

Failure processes with the same alphabet structure can be ordered.

Definition B.5   (refinement order)

Let P and Q be failure processes with alphabet structure A.

0. P refines to Q, denoted by $P \sqsubseteq Q$, if $\mathbf{f}P \supseteq \mathbf{f}Q$. Process Q has fewer failures than P and is therefore better.

1. Process $CHAOS \cdot A$ is defined as $\langle A, (\mathbf{a}A)^* \times \mathcal{P} \cdot (\mathbf{a}A)\rangle$.

2. An (ascending) chain is an infinite sequence $(i : 0 \leq i : P_i)$ of processes such that $P_i \sqsubseteq P_{i+1}$.

□

Clearly, $\langle \prod_{\mathcal{F}} \cdot A, \sqsubseteq\rangle$ is a partial order. According to [BR85], $(\prod_{\mathcal{F}} \cdot A, \sqsubseteq)$ is also a CPO, with $CHAOS \cdot A$ as least element and $(\sqcup i : 0 \leq i : P_i)$ as limit of chain $(i : 0 \leq i : P_i)$.

Example B.6

In the following refinements $S \sqsubseteq T$ is a shorthand for $\mathcal{F} \cdot S \sqsubseteq \mathcal{F} \cdot T$, where S and T are Core Tangram programs.

0. $(a\sim, b\sim) \cdot (a \sqcap b) \ \sqsubseteq \ (a\sim, b\sim) \cdot a$

1. $(a\sim, b\sim) \cdot (a; b \sqcap b; a) \ \sqsubseteq \ (a\sim, b\sim) \cdot (a; b)$

2. $(a\sim, b\sim) \cdot (a; b \sqcap b; a) \ \sqsubseteq \ (a\sim, b\sim) \cdot (a \parallel b)$

3. $(a\sim, b\sim) \cdot [a; b \mid b; a] \ = \ (a\sim, b\sim) \cdot (a \parallel b)$

□

Embedding of Failure Processes into Handshake Processes

We are looking for a mapping from failure processes to handshake processes that preserves the 'essential' properties of the original processes. By this we mean that the mapping must respect ordering and that the image of all failure processes must be equally rich in structure. Such a mapping is called an *embedding*:

Definition B.7   (embedding)

Let $\mathcal{E}$ be a function from CPO X to CPO Y. Function $\mathcal{E}$ is an embedding [DP90] of X into Y if:

0. $\mathcal{E} \cdot P \sqcap \mathcal{E} \cdot P \;=\; \mathcal{E} \cdot (P \sqcap Q)$

1. $\mathcal{E} \cdot P \sqcup \mathcal{E} \cdot P \;=\; \mathcal{E} \cdot (P \sqcup Q)$

2. $P = Q \;\equiv\; \mathcal{E} \cdot P = \mathcal{E} \cdot Q$

☐

The following property of an embedding follows immediately.

Property B.8

An embedding is order preserving, i.e. $P \sqsubseteq Q \;\Rightarrow\; \mathcal{E} \cdot P \sqsubseteq \mathcal{E} \cdot Q$.

☐

Our search for such an embedding starts with comparing a few refinements in the two process models. In the domain of failure processes we have (cf. Example B.6.2):

$$a; b \sqcap b; a \;\sqsubseteq\; a \parallel b$$

A similar refinement in the domain of handshake processes, however, does not hold:

$$a^\bullet; b^\bullet \sqcap b^\bullet; a^\bullet \;\not\sqsubseteq\; a^\bullet \parallel b^\bullet$$

The left-hand side requires the handshakes through $a^\bullet$ and $b^\bullet$ to exclude each other in time. The parallel composition at the right hand side, however, has e.g. $a_0 b_0 a_1 b_1$ as quiescent trace.

The above example shows that a mapping based on $\mathcal{H}$ (see Section 6.3) is not order preserving, and hence not an embedding. It also suggests that there does not exist an embedding from failure processes to all-active handshake processes.

However, in the space of *all-passive* processes we do have (cf. B.6.2)

$$a^\circ; b^\circ \sqcap b^\circ; a^\circ \;\sqsubseteq\; a^\circ \parallel b^\circ$$

Moreover, as with failure processes we have (cf. B.6.3):

$$[a^\circ; b^\circ \mid b^\circ; a^\circ] \;=\; a^\circ \parallel b^\circ$$

Both examples show that order of passive handshakes is masked by reordering. Because of this masking effect there is less distinction in the space of all-passive processes than in the space of all-active processes. This insight will be elaborated along two different lines that will meet at the end of this appendix:

- *handshake expansion*: an embedding of failure processes into the set of all-passive handshake processes, and

- *passivation*: a transformation of an all-active process into an all-passive process.

Handshake expansion

Handshake expansion is a mapping from failure structures to handshake structures. Handshake expansion is also defined for alphabet structures, traces, refusal sets and failures.

Definition B.9 (handshake expansion)

0. The *handshake expansion* of alphabet structure A, denoted by $\mathcal{E} \cdot A$, is the port structure defined by

$$(\mathcal{E} \cdot A)^\circ = \{a : a \in \mathbf{p}?A : a^\circ?\tau_A \cdot a\} \cup \{a : a \in \mathbf{p}!A : a^\circ!\tau_A \cdot a\}$$
$$(\mathcal{E} \cdot A)^\bullet = \emptyset$$

Note that all ports are chosen to be passive.

1. The *handshake expansion* of trace t with respect to alphabet structure A, denoted by $\mathcal{E} \cdot (t, A)$, is defined by

$$
\begin{aligned}
\mathcal{E} \cdot (\varepsilon, A) \quad &= \varepsilon \\
\mathcal{E} \cdot (a{:}v\,t, A) \quad &= \textbf{if} \quad a \in \mathbf{p}!A \;\rightarrow\; a_0\;a_1{:}v\;\mathcal{E} \cdot (t, A) \\
&\quad\;\; [\!] \quad a \in \mathbf{p}?A \;\rightarrow\; a_0{:}v\;a_1\;\mathcal{E} \cdot (t, A) \\
&\quad\;\, \textbf{fi}
\end{aligned}
$$

2. The *handshake expansion* of refusal set X with respect to alphabet structure A, denoted by $\mathcal{E} \cdot (X, A)$, is defined as the symbol set

$$\{a, v : a \in \mathbf{p}?A \land a{:}v \in X : a_0{:}v\} \cup \{a : a \in \mathbf{p}!A \land a \in X : a_0\}$$

These symbols are received, but refused in the sense that they are not acknowledged.

3. The *handshake expansion* of a failure $\langle t, X \rangle$, with respect to alphabet structure A, denoted by $\mathcal{E} \cdot (\langle t, X \rangle, A)$, is defined as the handshake-trace set

$$\{u : \#_u = \mathcal{E} \cdot (X, A) : \mathcal{E} \cdot (t, A)u\}^{\mathbf{r}}$$

where $\#_u$ denotes the bag of symbols of trace u. Actually, u is a permutation of $\mathcal{E}\langle X, A \rangle$.

4. The *handshake expansion* of failure structure $\langle A, F \rangle$, denoted by $\mathcal{E} \cdot \langle A, F \rangle$, is defined as the handshake structure

$$\langle \mathcal{E} \cdot A, \{f : f \in F : \mathcal{E} \cdot (f, A)\} \rangle$$

□

The crux of the above definition is in the handshake expansion of a failure $\langle t, X \rangle$ (see Definition B.9.3). The postfix u corresponds with refusal set X. If the environment continues with handshakes through all ports in X (by sending the corresponding ~-symbols) the state resulting after tu is quiescent.

The following property is helpful in understanding function $\mathcal{E}$.

Property B.10

Let f and g be failures defined on alphabet structure A. Then

$$f \neq g \;\Rightarrow\; \mathcal{E} \cdot (f, A) \cap \mathcal{E} \cdot (g, A) = \emptyset$$

$\square$

Theorem B.11

Let A be an alphabet structure and let $P \in \prod_{\mathcal{F}} \cdot A$. Then:

   0. $\mathcal{E}$ is an embedding;

   1. $\mathcal{E} \cdot P$ is a handshake process;

   2. $\mathcal{E} \cdot CHAOS \cdot A = CHAOS \cdot \mathcal{E} \cdot A$;

   3. $\mathcal{E}$ is continuous;

   4. hence, $\mathcal{E} \cdot (\prod_{\mathcal{F}} \cdot A)$ is a CPO.

$\square$

The definition of $\mathcal{E}$ ignores the issue of successful termination. Extending $\mathcal{E}$ to such a more comprehensive process model is relatively straightforward. Given such an extended embedding, equalities such as

$$\begin{aligned}
\mathcal{E} \cdot (P; Q) &= \mathcal{E} \cdot P; \mathcal{E} \cdot Q \\
\mathcal{E} \cdot (P \parallel Q) &= \mathcal{E} \cdot P \parallel \mathcal{E} \cdot Q \\
\mathcal{E} \cdot \#[P] &= \#[\mathcal{E} \cdot P]
\end{aligned}$$

can easily be verified.

Passivation

Another way to obtain an all-passive process is to connect passivators to the active ports of a handshake process. The following definition is restricted to all-active processes with undirected ports only. Extension to general handshake processes is straightforward.

Definition B.12   (passivation)

The passivation of an all-active handshake process P, denoted by $\pi \cdot P$, is defined as

$$\underline{l} \cdot P \;\parallel\; (\parallel a : a \in \mathbf{p}^{\bullet} P : PAS \cdot (la^{\circ}, a^{\circ}))$$

where $\underline{l} \cdot P$ denotes the l-renaming of P defined in Definition 7.0.

□

The effect of passivation is illustrated by the following example.

Example B.13

$$(la^\bullet; lb^\bullet \ \sqcap \ lb^\bullet; la^\bullet) \ \| \ \#[la^\circ : a^\circ] \ \| \ \#[lb^\circ : b^\circ] \ = \ (a^\circ; b^\circ \ \sqcap \ b^\circ; a^\circ)$$

□

Let T be a Tangram program. The following theorem expresses that the passivation of $\mathcal{H} \cdot T$ equals the handshake expansion of $\mathcal{F} \cdot T$.

Theorem B.14

$$\pi \circ \mathcal{H} \ = \ \mathcal{E} \circ \mathcal{F}$$

□

An important corollary is obtained when this theorem is combined with the compilation theorem. Graphically this corollary is illustrated in Figure B.0.

Corollary B.15

$$\pi \circ \| \circ \mathcal{C} \ = \ \triangleright^* \circ \mathcal{E} \circ \mathcal{F}$$

□

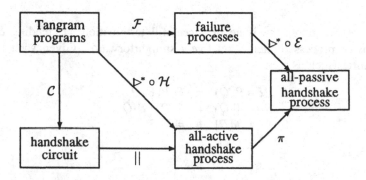

Figure B.0: Failure processes related to handshake circuits.

Corollary B.15 may be applied as follows. We call two all-active processes P and Q π-*equivalent* if their passivations are identical. Let the behaviors of two compiled handshake circuits G and H be π-equivalent. Then there does not exist any third compiled handshake circuit that can distinguish G from H when it is connected to them by passivators. Under such circumstances, the designer may use the all-passive semantics of Tangram, as obtained by $\pi \circ \mathcal{H}$. The existence of the embedding $\mathcal{E}$ then demonstrates that the VLSI programmer can then apply programming laws that are based on a failure semantics of Tangram (cf. [RH88]).

Bibliography

[Ano73]   Anonymous. Science and the citizen. *Scientific American*, 228:43--44, 1973.

[BE92]   Janusz A. Brzozowski and Jo C. Ebergen. On the delay-sensitivity of gate networks. *IEEE Transactions on Computers*, 41(11):1349--1360, November 1992.

[BHR84]   S.D. Brookes, C.A.R. Hoare, and A.W. Roscoe. A Theory of Communicating Sequential Processes. *Journal of the ACM*, 31(3):560--599, 1984.

[BM88]   Steven M. Burns and Alain J. Martin. Synthesis of Self-Timed Circuits by Program Transformation. In G.J. Milne, editor, *The Fusion of Hardware Design and Verification*, pages 99--116. Elsevier Science Publishers B.V., 1988.

[BM91]   Peter Beerel and Teresa Meng. Semi-Modularity and Self-Diagnostic Asynchronous Control Circuits. In Carlo H. Sequin, editor, *Proceedings of the 1991 University of California/Santa Cruz Conference*, pages 103--117. The MIT Press, 1991.

[BR85]   S.D. Brookes and A.W. Roscoe. An Improved Failures Model for Communicating Sequential Processes. In *Proceedings NSF-SERC Seminar of Concurrency*, pages 281--305. Springer-Verlag, 1985.

[Bro89]   R.W. Brockett. Smooth Dynamical Systems which Realize Arithmetical and Logical Operations. In Hendrik Nijmeijer and Johannes M. Schumacher, editors, *Three Decades of Mathematical Systems Theory: A Collection of Surveys at the Occasion of the 50th Birthday of J.C. Willems*, pages 19--30. Springer-Verlag, 1989.

[Bro90]   Geoffrey M. Brown. Towards Truly Delay-Insensitive Circuit Realizations of Process Algebras. In Geraint Jones and Mary Sheeran, editors, *Designing Correct Circuits*, Workshops in Computing, pages 120--131. Springer-Verlag, 1990.

[Bru91]   Erik Brunvand. *Translating Concurrent Communicating Programs into Asynchronous Circuits*. PhD thesis, Carnegie Mellon University, 1991.

[BS89]   Erik Brunvand and Robert Sproull. Translating Concurrent Programs into Delay-Insensitive Circuits. In *IEEE International Conference on Computer*

Aided Design; Digest of Technical Papers, pages 262--265. IEEE Computer Society Press, 1989.

[CM73]   T.J. Chaney and C.E. Molnar. Anomalous Behavoir of Synchronizer and Arbiter Circuits. *IEEE Transactions on Computers*, C-22(4):421--422, 1973.

[Cro90]   T.R. Crompton. *Battery Reference Book*. Butterworths, 1990.

[DGY90]   Ilana David, Ran Ginosar, and Michael Yoeli. Self-Timed is Self-Diagnostic. Technical report, University of Utah, 1990.

[Dij75]   E.W. Dijkstra. Guarded commands, nondeterminacy and the formal derivation of programs. *Communications of the ACM*, 18:453--457, 1975.

[Dij76]   E.W. Dijkstra. *A Discipline of Programming*. Prentice Hall, 1976.

[Dil89]   David L. Dill. *Trace Theory for Automatic Hierarchical Verification of Speed-Independent Circuits*. An ACM Distinguished Dissertation. MIT Press, 1989.

[DNS92]   David L. Dill, Steven M. Nowick, and Robert F. Sproull. Specification and automatic verification of self-timed queues. *Formal Methods in System Design*, 1(1):29--60, July 1992.

[DP90]   B.A. Davey and H.A. Priestley. *Introduction to Lattices and Order*. Cambridge Mathematical Textbooks. Cambridge University Press, 1990.

[DS90]   Edsger W. Dijkstra and Carel S. Scholten. *Predicate Calculus and Program Semantics*. Springer-Verlag, 1990.

[Ebe89]   Jo C. Ebergen. *Translating Programs into Delay-Insensitive Circuits*. CWI Tract 56 (Centre for Mathematics and Computing Science, Amsterdam), 1989.

[Elf76]   Joost Elfers. *Tangram; the Ancient Chinese Shapes Game*. Penguin Books, 1976.

[EP92]   Jo C. Ebergen and Ad M. G. Peeters. Modulo-N counters: Design and analysis of delay-insensitive circuits. In J. Staunstrup and R. Sharp, editors, *2nd Workshop on Designing Correct Circuits, Lyngby*, pages 27--46. Elsevier, North Holland, 1992.

[Fuj85]   Hideo Fujiwara. *Logic Testing and Design for Testability*. The MIT Press, 1985.

[Haa92]   Jaco Haans. VLSI Programming of Multipliers. M.Sc. Thesis at the Eindhoven University of Technology, 1992.

[H.B90]   H.B.Bakoglu. *Circuits, Interconnections, and Packaging for VLSI*. Addison-Wesley Publishing Company, 1990.

[Hoa78]   C.A.R. Hoare. Communicating Sequential Processes. *Communications of the ACM*, 21(8):666--677, 1978.

[Hoa85]   C.A.R. Hoare. *Communicating Sequential Processes*. Series in Computer Science. Prentice-Hall International, 1985.

[HvBPS93]   Jaco Haans, Kees van Berkel, Ad Peeters, and Frits Schalij. Asynchronous Multipliers as Combinational Handshake Circuits. In S. Furber and M. Edwards, editors, *Proceedings of the IFIP WG 10.5 Working Conference on Asynchronous Design Methodologies, Manchester*, pages 149--163. Elsevier Science Publishers B.V., 1993.

[INM89]   INMOS Limited, editor. *Occam 2 Programming Manual*. Series in Computer Science. Prentice-Hall International, 1989.

[JHJ89]   Mark B. Josephs, C.A.R. Hoare, and He Jifeng. A Theory of Asynchronous Processes. Technical Report PRG-TR-6-89, Oxford University, Computing Laboratory, 1989.

[Jon85]   B. Jonsson. A model and proof system for asynchronous networks. In *Proc. 4th ACM Symposium on Principles of Distributed Computing*, pages 49--58. ACM, 1985.

[Jos92]   Mark B. Josephs. Receptive process theory. *Acta Informatica*, 29(1):17--31, 1992.

[JU90a]   M.B. Josephs and J.T. Udding. Delay-insensitive circuits: an algebraic approach to their design. In J.C.M. Baeten and J.W. Klop, editors, *ConCur '90: Theories of Concurrency: Unification and Extension*, volume 458 of *Lecture Notes in Computer Science*, pages 342--366. Springer-Verlag, 1990.

[JU90b]   M.B. Josephs and J.T. Udding. The Design of a Delay-Insensitive Stack. In Geraint Jones and Mary Sheeran, editors, *Designing Correct Circuits*, Workshops in Computing, pages 132--152. Springer-Verlag, 1990.

[JU91]   Mark B. Josephs and Jan Tijmen Udding. An Algebra for Delay-Insensitive Circuits. In *DIMACS Series in Discrete Mathematics and Theoretical Computer Science*, volume 3, pages 147--175. AMS-ACM, 1991.

[Kal86]   Anne Kaldewaij. *A Formalism for Concurrent Processes*. PhD thesis, Eindhoven University of Technology, 1986.

[Kes91a]   J.L.W. Kessels. Designing Counters with Bounded Response Time. In W.H.J. Feijen and A.J.M van Gasteren, editors, *C.S. Scholten dedicata: van oude machines en nieuwe rekenwijzen*, pages 127--140. Academic Service, Schoonhoven, The Netherlands, 1991.

[Kes91b]   J.L.W. Kessels. The Systematic Design of a Systolic RSA Converter. In *Proc. Workshop on Correct Hardware Design Methodologies*, pages 235--251. Elsevier Science Publishers B.V., 1991.

[KR90]   Joep L.W. Kessels and Martin Rem. Designing systolic, distributed buffers
             with bounded response time. *Distributed Computing*, 4:37--43, 1990.

[KS90]   J.L.W. Kessels and F.D. Schalij. VLSI Programming for the Compact Disc
             Player. *Science of Computer Programming*, 15:235--248, 1990.

[KTT+88]   Shinji Komori, Hidehiro Takata, Toshiyuki Tamura, Fumiyasu Asai, Takio
             Ohno, Osamu Tomisawa, Tetsuo Yamasaki, Kenji Shima, Katsuhiko Asada,
             and Hiroaki Terada. An Elastic Pipeline Mechanism by Self-Timed Circuits.
             IEEE Journal of Solid-State Circuits, 23(1):111--117, 1988.

[KTT+89]   Shinji Komori, Hidehiro Takata, Toshiyuki Tamura, Fumiyasu Asai, Takio
             Ohno, Osamu Tomisawa, Tetsuo Yamasaki, Kenji Shima, Hiroaki Nishikawa,
             and Hiroaki Terada. A 40-MFLOPS 32-bit Floating-Point Processor with Elas-
             tic Pipeline Scheme. *IEEE Journal of Solid-State Circuits*, 24(5):1341--1347,
             1989.

[KU92]   Anne Kaldewaij and Jan Tijmen Udding. Rank order filters and priority queues.
             Distributed Computing, 6(2):99--106, 1992.

[KvBB+92]   Joep Kessels, Kees van Berkel, Ronan Burgess, Marly Roncken, and Frits
             Schalij. An Error Decoder for the Compact Disc Player as an Example of
             VLSI Programming. In *Proceedings of the European Conference on Design
             Automation*, pages 69--74, 1992.

[KZ90]   Anne Kaldewaij and Gerard Zwaan. A systolic design for acceptors of regular
             languages. *Science of Computer Programming*, 15:171--184, 1990.

[LSU89]   Roger Lipsett, Carl Schaefer, and Cary Ussery. *VHDL: Hardware Description
             and Design*. Kluwer Academic publishers, 1989.

[LvMvdW+91] P.E.R. Lippens, J.L. van Meerbergen, A. van der Werf, W.F.J. Verhaegh, B.T.
             McSeeney, J.O. Huisken, and O.P. McArdle. PHIDEO: A Silicon Compiler for
             High Speed Algorithms. In *Proceedings of the European Design Automation
             Conference*, pages 436--441, 1991.

[Mar85a]   Alain J. Martin. Compiling Communicating Processes into Delay-Insensitive
             VLSI Circuits. Technical report, California Institute of Technology, Depart-
             ment of Computer Science, Pasadena CA 91125, USA, 1985.

[Mar85b]   Alain J. Martin. The Design of a Self-Timed Circuit for Distributed Mutual
             Exclusion. In Henry Fuchs, editor, *Chapel Hill Conference on VLSI*, pages
             245--260, 1985.

[Mar89]   Alain J. Martin. Programming in VLSI: From Communicating Processes to
             Delay-Insensitive Circuits. In C.A.R. Hoare, editor, *UT Year of Programming;
             Institute on Concurrent Programming*. Addison-Wesley, 1989.

[Mar90]   Alain J. Martin. The Limitations to Delay-Insensitivity in Asynchronous Circuits. In William J. Dally, editor, *Sixth MIT Conference on Advanced Research in VLSI*, pages 263--278. MIT Press, 1990.

[MBL⁺89]   Alain J. Martin, Steven M. Burns, T.K. Lee, Drazen Borkovic, and Pieter J. Hazewindus. The First Asynchronous Microprocessor: The Test Results. In *Computer Architecture News*, volume 17, pages 95--110. MIT Press, 1989.

[MBM90]   Teresa H.-Y. Meng, Robert W. Broderson, and David G. Messerschmitt. A Clock-Free Chip Set for High-Sampling Rate Adaptive Filters. *Journal of VLSI Signal Processing*, 1(4):345--365, 1990.

[MC80]   C. Mead and L. Conway. *Introduction to VLSI Systems*. Addison-Wesley, 1980.

[McK65]   W.M. McKeeman. Peephole Optimization. *Communications of the ACM*, 8:443--444, 1965.

[Men91]   Teresa H.-Y. Meng. *Synchronization Design for Digital Systems*. Kluwer Academic Publishers, 1991. Contributions by David Messerschmitt, Steven Nowick, and David Dill.

[MH91]   Alain J. Martin and Pieter J. Hazewindus. Testing Delay-Insensitive Circuits. In Carlo H. Sequin, editor, *Proceedings of the 1991 University of California/Santa Cruz Conference*, pages 118--132. The MIT Press, 1991.

[Mil65]   Raymond E. Miller. *Switching Theory Volume II: Sequential Circuits and Machines*. John Wiley & Sons Inc., 1965.

[Mis84]   J. Misra. Reasoning about networks of communicating processes. Presented at INRIA Advanced Nato Study Institute on Logics and Models for Verification and Specification of Concurrent Systems, La Colle-sur-Loupe, France., 1984.

[Mis87]   F.C. Mish et al. *Webster's Ninth New Collegiate Dictionary*. Merriam-Webster Inc., 1987.

[ND91]   Steve M. Nowick and David L. Dill. Automatic verification. In Teresa H.-Y. Meng, editor, *Synchronization Design for Digital Systems*, chapter 7. Kluwer Academic Publishers, 1991.

[NvBRS88]   Cees Niessen, C.H. (Kees) van Berkel, Martin Rem, and Ronald W.J.J. Saeijs. VLSI Programming and Silicon Compilation; A Novel Approach from Philips Research. In *Proceedings of the 1988 IEEE Int. Conf. on Computer Design: VLSI in Computers & Processors*, pages 150--151, 1988.

[OSC67]   S.M. Ornstein, M.J. Stucki, and W.A. Clark. A Functional Description of Macromodules. In *Sprint Joint Computer Conference*, pages 337--355. AFIPS, 1967.

[PDF⁺92]   N. C. Paver, P. Day, S. B. Furber, J. D. Garside, and J. V. Woods. Register locking in an asynchronous microprocessor. In *Proc. Int'l. Conf. Computer Design*. IEEE Computer Society Press, October 1992.

[Phi90]   Philips Components. *Integrated Circuits Data Handbook; Radio, audio and associated systems; Bipolar, Mos; CA3089 to TDA1510A*. Philips Components, 1990.

[Rem81]   Martin Rem. The VLSI Challenge: Complexity Bridling. In John P. Gray, editor, *VLSI 81*, pages 65--74. Academic Press, 1981.

[Rem87]   Martin Rem. Trace Theory and Systolic Computations. In J.W. de Bakker et al., editor, *PARLE Parallel Architectures and Languages in Europe*, volume 258 of *Lecture Notes in Computer Science*, pages 14--33. Springer-Verlag, 1987.

[Rem91]   Martin Rem. The Nature of Delay-Insensitive Computing. In Graham Birtwistle, editor, *IV Higher Order Workshop, Banff 1990*, pages 105--122. Springer-Verlag, 1991.

[RH88]   A.W. Roscoe and C.A.R. Hoare. The Laws of OCCAM Programming. *Theoretical Computer Science*, 60:177--229, 1988.

[RS93]   Marly Roncken and Ronald Saeijs. Linear Test Times for Delay-Insensitive Circuits: a Compilation Strategy. In S. Furber and M. Edwards, editors, *Proceedings of the IFIP WG 10.5 Working Conference on Asynchronous Design Methodologies, Manchester*, pages 13--27. Elsevier Science Publishers B.V., 1993.

[Sch92]   Huub Schols. *Delay-insensitive Communication*. PhD thesis, Eindhoven University of Technology, 1992.

[Sch93]   Frits Schalij. Tangram manual. Technical Report UR 008/93, Philips Research Laboratories Eindhoven, P.O. Box 80.000, 5600 JA Eindhoven, The Netherlands, 1993.

[Sei80]   Charles L. Seitz. System Timing. In C.A. Mead and L.A. Conway, editors, *Introduction to VLSI Systems*, chapter 7. Addison-Wesley, 1980.

[Sei84]   Charles L. Seitz. Concurrent VLSI Architectures. *IEEE Transactions on Computers*, C-33(12):1247--1265, 1984.

[SM77]   Ivan E. Sutherland and Carver A. Mead. Microelectronics and Computer Science. *Scientific American*, 237(9):210--228, 1977.

[Str92]   Pieter Struik. *Designing Parallel Programs of Parameterized Granularity*. PhD thesis, Eindhoven University of Technology, 1992.

[Sut89]   Ivan Sutherland. Micropipelines. *Communications of the ACM*, 32(6):720--738, 1989.

[SvB88]   Ronald W.J.J. Saeijs and C.H. (Kees) van Berkel. The Design of the VLSI Image-Generator ZaP. In *Proceedings of the 1988 IEEE Int. Conf. on Computer Design: VLSI in Computers & Processors*, pages 163--166, 1988.

[SvBB+91]   Frits Schalij, Kees van Berkel, Ronan Burgess, Joep Kessels, Marly Roncken, and Ronald Saeijs. What makes Tangram a general-purpose VLSI-programming language? Manuscript, 1991.

[Tsi88]   Yannis P. Tsividis. *Operation and Modeling of the MOS Transistor*. McGraw-Hill International Editions, 1988.

[Udd84]   Jan Tijmen Udding. *Classification and Composition of Delay-Insensitive Circuits*. PhD thesis, Eindhoven University of Technology, 1984.

[Udd86]   Jan Tijmen Udding. A formal model for defining and classifying delay-insensitive circuits and systems. *Distributed Computing*, 1(4):197--204, 1986.

[UV88]   Jan Tijmen Udding and Tom Verhoeff. The Mathematics of Directed Specifications. Technical Report WUCS-88-20, Dept. of Computer Science, Washington Univ., St. Louis, MO, 1988.

[vB91]   C.H. van Berkel. Beware the isochronic fork. Technical Report UR 003/91, Philips Research Laboratories Eindhoven, P.O. Box 80.000, 5600 JA Eindhoven, The Netherlands, 1991.

[vB92a]   Kees van Berkel. Beware the isochronic fork. *Integration, the VLSI journal*, 13(2):103--128, 1992.

[vB92b]   Kees van Berkel. *Handshake circuits: an intermediary between communicating processes and VLSI*. PhD thesis, Eindhoven University of Technology, 1992.

[vB93]   Kees van Berkel. VLSI programming of a modulo-N counter with constant response time and constant power. In S. Furber and M. Edwards, editors, *Proceedings of the IFIP WG 10.5 Working Conference on Asynchronous Design Methodologies, Manchester*, pages 1--11. Elsevier Science Publishers B.V., 1993.

[vBBK+93]   Kees van Berkel, Ronan Burgess, Joep Kessels, Marly Roncken, and Frits Schalij. Characterization and evaluation of a compiled asynchronous IC. In S. Furber and M. Edwards, editors, *Proceedings of the IFIP WG 10.5 Working Conference on Asynchronous Design Methodologies, Manchester*, pages 209--221. Elsevier Science Publishers B.V., 1993.

[vBKR+91]   Kees van Berkel, Joep Kessels, Marly Roncken, Ronald W.J.J. Saeijs, and Frits Schalij. The VLSI-programming language Tangram and its translation into handshake circuits. In *Proceedings of the European Design Automation Conference*, pages 384--389, 1991.

[vBRS88]   C.H. (Kees) van Berkel, Martin Rem, and Ronald W.J.J. Saeijs. VLSI Programming. In *Proceedings of the 1988 IEEE Int. Conf. on Computer Design: VLSI in Computers & Processors*, pages 152--156, 1988.

[vBS88]   C.H. (Kees) van Berkel and Ronald W.J.J. Saeijs. Compilation of Communicating Processes into Delay-Insensitive Circuits. In *Proceedings of the 1988 IEEE Int. Conf. on Computer Design: VLSI in Computers & Processors*, pages 157--162, 1988.

[vBS90]   C.H. van Berkel and R.W.J.J. Saeijs. Latch with write acknowledge. NL. Patent Application 9000544, 1990.

[vdS85]   Jan L.A. van de Snepscheut. *Trace Theory and VLSI Design*, volume 200 of *Lecture Notes in Computer Science*. Springer-Verlag, 1985.

[Vee84]   Harry J.M. Veendrick. Short-Circuit Dissipation of Static CMOS Circuitry and Its Impact on the Design of Buffer Circuits. *IEEE Journal of Solid-State Circuits*, SC-19(4):468--473, 1984.

[Ver88]   Tom Verhoeff. Delay-insensitive codes -- an overview. *Distributed Computing*, 3:1--8, 1988.

[Ver89]   Tom Verhoeff. Personal communications, 1989. Eindhoven University of Technology.

[WBB91]   Sam Weber, Bard Bloom, and Geoffrey Brown. Compiling Joy to Silicon. Extended Abstract for the Brown/MIT VLSI Conference, 1991.

[WD89]   R. Woudsma and A. Delaruelle. The Design of DSP Components for the CD Digital Audio System using Silicon Compilation Techniques. In *Proceedings of IEEE Custom Integrated Circuits Conference*, pages 20.4.1--20.4.5, 1989.

[WE85]   Neil H.E. Weste and Kamran Eshraghian. *Principles of CMOS VLSI Design; A System Perspective*. Addison-Wesley Publ. Company, 1985.

[WH91]   Ted E. Williams and Mark A. Horowitz. A 160ns 54bit CMOS Division Implementation Using Self-Timing and Symmetrically Overlapped SRT Stages. In Peter Kornerup and David W. Matula, editors, *Proceedings of 10th IEEE Symposium on Computer Arithmetic*, pages 210--217, 1991.

Glossary of symbols

Sets

Notation	Meaning	Definition
$B^{\leq}$	$\leq$-closure of set B	3.0
$(\leq)\cdot B$	B is $\leq$-closed	3.0
$B \rightsquigarrow C$	B initializes set C	8.24

Traces

Notation	Meaning	Definition
ε	empty trace	3.7
$len\cdot t$	length of trace t	3.7
$s \leq t$	s is a prefix of t	3.7
st	concatenation of traces s and t	3.7
B^*	set of all traces over alphabet B	3.7
$t\lceil B$	projection of t on B	3.7
$\#_t$	bag of symbols in t	A.3

Ports, port structures and port definitions

Notation	Meaning	Definition
$\mathbf{a}p$	symbol set of port p	3.3
$\mathbf{0}p$	$\mathbf{0}$ symbols of p	3.3
$\mathbf{1}p$	$\mathbf{1}$ symbols of p	3.3
A°	passive ports of port structure A	3.3
$A^{\bullet}$	active ports of A	3.3
$\mathbf{i}A$	input symbols of A	3.4
$\mathbf{o}A$	output symbols of A	3.4
a°	passive nonput port (structure) a	3.5
$a^{\circ}?T$	passive input port (structure) a of type T	3.5
$a^{\circ}!T$	passive output port (structure) a of type T	3.5
$a^{\bullet}$	active nonput port (structure) a	3.5
$a^{\bullet}?T$	active input port (structure) a of type T	3.5
$a^{\bullet}!T$	active output port (structure) a of type T	3.5

$\overline{A}$	reflection of A	4.0
$\mathbf{e}A$	external port structure of A	4.8
$A \bowtie B$	A and B are connectable	4.0
$A \bowtie\!\!\!\!\!\bowtie B$	A and B are conformant	5.12
$A \cup B$	pairwise union of A and B	3.3
$A \setminus B$	pairwise set difference of A and B	3.3
$\triangleright^{\circ}$	passive port 'go'	6.7

Handshake traces and handshake-trace sets

Notation	Meaning	Definition
$closed \cdot t$	all handshakes in handshake trace t are closed	3.26
A^H	set of handshake traces over port structure A	3.8
$u \, \mathbf{R}_A \, v$	u reorders v w.r.t. A, and $u, v \in (\mathbf{i}A \cup \mathbf{o}A)^*$	3.14
$s \, \mathbf{r}_A \, t$	s reorders t w.r.t. A, and $s, t \in A^H$	3.14
$s \, \mathbf{r} \, t$	$s \, \mathbf{r}_A \, t$ with A obvious from context	3.14
$B^{\mathbf{r}}$	r-closure of handshake trace set B	3.0
$(\mathbf{r}) \cdot B$	B is r-closed	3.0
$s \, \mathbf{x}_A \, t$	s is an input extension of t w.r.t. A	3.17
$s \, \mathbf{x} \, t$	$s \, \mathbf{x}_A \, t$ with A obvious from context	3.17
$B^{\mathbf{x}}$	x-closure of B	3.0
$(\mathbf{x}) \cdot B$	B is x-closed	3.0
$s \, \mathbf{c}_A \, t$	s is composable with t w.r.t. A	A.1
$s \, \mathbf{c} \, t$	$s \, \mathbf{c}_A \, t$ with A obvious from context	A.1
$B^{\mathbf{c}}$	c-closure of B	3.0
$(\mathbf{c}) \cdot B$	B is c-closed	3.0

Handshake structures

Notation	Meaning	Definition
$\mathbf{p}S$	port structure of handshake structure S	3.10
$\mathbf{t}S$	handshake-trace set of S	3.10
$suc \cdot (t, S)$	successor set of trace t in S	3.11
$pas \cdot (t, S)$	t is passive in S	3.11
$Pas \cdot S$	passive restriction of S	3.11
$after \cdot (t, S)$	handshake structure after t	3.25
$div \cdot S$	divergences of S	4.10
$S \sqsubseteq T$	S refines to T	3.29
$S \sqcap T$	union of S and T	3.34
$S \sqcup T$	intersection of S and T	3.36
$(\sqcup i : 0 \leq i : S)$	limit of chain $(i : 0 \leq i : S)$	3.37
$S \, \mathbf{w} \, T$	weave of S and T	4.3
$S \, \mathbf{b} \, T$	blend of S and T	4.8

| $S \parallel T$ | parallel composition of S and T | 4.14 |

Handshake processes

Notation	Meaning	Definition
$P \sqsubseteq_R Q$	P refines to Q in the context of R	8.2
$P \preceq_R Q$	P strongly refines to Q in the context of R	8.6
$\phi \cdot P$	phase reduction of P	8.11
$\phi_2 \cdot P$	2-phase reduction of P	8.12
$\phi_{4c} \cdot P$	complete 4-phase reduction of P	8.15
$\phi_{4q} \cdot P$	quick 4-phase reduction of P	8.18
$\pi \cdot P$	passivation of P	B.12

Handshake circuits

Notation	Meaning	Definition
$\bowtie H$	handshake circuit H is connectable	4.20
$\mathbf{e}H$	external port structure of H	4.21
$\mathbf{W} \cdot H$	weave of H	4.21
$\mathbf{B} \cdot H$	blend of H	4.21
$\parallel \cdot H$	parallel composition of the components of H	4.21

Sequential handshake processes

Notation	Meaning	Definition
skip, stop		5.9
a°	passive handshake through port a	5.9
$a^\bullet$	active handshake through a	5.9
$P \sqsubseteq Q$	sequential handshake process P refines to Q	5.4
$P \sqcup Q$	intersection of P and Q	5.6
$P \parallel Q$	P in parallel with connectable Q	5.10
$P \overset{\bullet\bullet}{\parallel} Q$	all-active P in parallel with all-active Q	6.5
$(A) \cdot P$	P extended with port structure A	5.15
$[\![A \mid P]\!]$	P with A concealed	5.18
$P \sqcap Q$	nondeterministic choice between P and Q	5.5, 5.21
$P; Q$	P followed by Q	5.23
$\#N[P]$	N-fold repetition of P	5.26
$\#[P]$	infinite repetition of P	5.28
$a^\circ : P$	P enclosed by a°	5.30
$[P \mid Q]$	choice between guarded processes P and Q	5.33
$\triangleright^* \cdot P$	repeatable go of P	6.7
σ	σ-function	7.22

Alphabet structures

Notation	Meaning	Definition
$\mathbf{p}A$	ports of alphabet structure A	6.0
$\mathbf{p}?A$	input ports of A	6.0
$\mathbf{p}!A$	output ports of A	6.0
$\mathbf{v}A$	variables of A	6.0
$\mathbf{v}?A$	read ports of A	6.0
$\mathbf{v}!A$	write ports of A	6.0
τ_A	type function of A	6.0
$A \bowtie_{\Delta} B$	A and B are conformant	6.2
$A \cup_{\Delta} B$	conformant union of A and B	6.2
$A \setminus_{\Delta} B$	conformant difference of A and B	6.2
$A \bowtie B$	A and B are connectable	6.2
$A \cup_{\bowtie} B$	connectable union of A and B	6.2
$\mathcal{H} \cdot A$	port structure of A	6.3
$\underline{l} \cdot A$	l-renaming of A	7.0
$\underline{r} \cdot A$	r-renaming of A	7.0
$\mathcal{E} \cdot A$	handshake expansion of A	B.9

Core Tangram

Notation	Meaning	Definition
$a\sim$	synchronization port	6.1
skip		6.4
stop		6.4
a	synchronization on a	6.4
$(A) \cdot S$	S extended with alphabet structure A	6.4
$S \sqcap T$	nondeterministic choice between S and T	6.4
$S; T$	S followed by T	6.4
$\#N[S]$	N-fold repetition of S	6.4
$\#[S]$	infinite repetition of S	6.4
$S \parallel T$	S in parallel with T	6.4
$[\![A \mid S]\!]$	S with A concealed	6.4
$\underline{l} \cdot S$	l-renaming of S	7.0
$\underline{r} \cdot S$	r-renaming of S	7.0
$\mathcal{C} \cdot S$	handshake circuit of S	7.20
$\mathcal{F} \cdot S$	failure process of S	in B

Failure structures

Notation	Meaning	Definition
AS	alphabet structure of failure structure S	B.1
fS	failure set of S	B.1
$S \sqsubseteq T$	S refines to T	B.5
$\mathcal{E} \cdot S$	handshake expansion of S	B.9

Index

A

active port 49
activity graph 167
ADAPT 107
adapter 107
ADD 27, 28
adder 27
after 65
alphabet 49
alphabet structure 112
    conformant 113
    connectable 113
    type compatible 113
asymmetric fork 161
asynchronous circuits 8
auto assignment 157

B

BAR 109
BIN 107
binary operator 107
biput port 50
blend 78
block sorter 31
broadcast 15, 28, 44
BUF 14
buffer
    1-place 14
    2-place 14
    handshake circuit 16, 17, 19
    wagging 15

C

chain 68, 204
CHAOS 58, 91, 204
choice 36, 37, 102
circuit area 9, 192

circuit speed 8, 191
closed trace 65
code 158
    delay insensitive 158
    Double-Rail 158
code concatenation 158
combinational operator 160
command separation 142
comparator 32
compatible 49
complete 4-phase reduction 155
complete partial order 70
composability 195, 196
composability closed 196
composability closure 196
computation interference 199
Con separation 142
Con term 129
concealment 97
connectable 74, 85
connection diagram 83
connector 61, 103, 106, 162
constant 106
constant power 35, 38, 39
continuous 69
Core Tangram
    command 119
    program 121
COUNT 35
COUT 104
CPO 70
CSP 12
CST 106

D

delay insensitive 8, 161, 198
demultiplexer 19
directed process 195

distributivity 72
divergences 78
DO 109
DUPN 87
DUP 62, 84, 103
duplicator 62, 84, 87, 103
duplicator chain 87, 172
dynamic nondeterminism 71

E

embedding 205
enclosure 101
energy consumption 9, 182, 193
extension 96
external port 49
external port structure 78

F

failure process 202
failure structure 202
FIR filter 27
FORK operator 161

G

go 121
greatest common divisor 33
guard component 40
guarded command 29, 34
guarded selection 29, 31
guarded selections 46

H

handshake circuit 13, 85
handshake components 85
handshake expansion 206
handshake process 57
handshake refinement 153, 154
handshake structure 52
    after 65
    intersection 68
    union 67
handshake trace 52
HEAD 35

I

IF 108
if component 29
independent alphabet 199
infinite repetition 101
initial-when-closed 67
initialization 164
initializes 165
input 50
input extension 56
input port 50
interference 6
internal port 49
intersection 92
isochronic fork 7, 161

J

JOIN 63, 103, 108, 163
Join separation 142
Join term 131

L

layout 181
limit 68

M

maximal failures 203
median filter 29
MIX 63, 103, 107
Mix separation 142
Mix term 129, 130
mixer 19, 62, 63, 103, 107
    non-receptive 163
modulo-N counters 35
Muller-C element 160
multiplexer 19
mutual exclusion of guards 160

N

N-fold repetition 100
nacking arbiter 42
NMIX 62, 163
nondeterministic composition 92, 98
nonput port 50
NVAR 64, 164
N-fold repeater 32

O

OCCAM 12
OR 61, 103
order preserving 67
output 50
output port 50

P

PAR 62, 103, 163
parallel composer 17, 62, 103, 163
parallel composition 80, 94
PAS 63, 103
passivation 207
passivator 63, 103
passive 53
passive in 53
passive port 49
passive restriction 53
peephole optimization 150
permanent sequential process 90
phase diagram 7
phase reduction 153
    2-phase 154
port 49
    active 49
    biput 50
    definition 112
    input 50
    nonput 50
    output 50
    passive 49
port definition 50
port name 51
port set 49
port structure 49, 119
    compatible 49
    conformance 95
    connectability 74
    difference 50
    reflection 74
    union 49
power consumption 182
prefix 51
    closed 52
    closure 52

prefix closed 52
prefix closure 52
preorder 48
preorder closed 48
preorder closure 48
priority queue 41
production rule 159
productive transition 160
proper port set 49
proper transition 7

Q

quantified expression 47
quick-return linkage 157
quick 4-phase reduction 156

R

receptive 57
refinement 66, 92, 204
reflection 74
reliability 192
renaming 126
reorder 55
reorder closed 55
reorder closure 55
REP 62, 103, 162
repeatable go 121
repeater 16, 62, 103, 162
ripple buffer 14
robustness 192
run 17
RUN 58, 61, 91, 103, 105, 106
Run term 128

S

S-element 162
selector 37
self-timed 8
separation 142
SEQ 61, 103, 163
sequencer 16, 61, 103, 163
sequential composition 98
sequential handshake process 90
sequential operator 160
sequential process 90

set construction 47
shift register 20
    ripple 23
    wagging 23
sigma function 141
silicon compilation 2
simulation 178
SKIP 91
SRA 21
SRB 22
SRC 22
SRD 23
SRE 23
SR 20, 28
stability of guards 160
stacks 39
state graph 59
static nondeterminism 71
statistics 179
STOP 58, 61, 91, 103, 105
Stop term 127
strong initializability 166
strong refinement in context 151
successor set 53
symmetric fork 162
synchronizer 17
systems on silicon 1

T

Tangram 13
    command 14
    composite command 115
    expression 27, 116
    guarded command 29, 31, 34, 116
    guarded selection 29
    primitive command 114
    program 114
testability 10, 183, 192
testing 168
transferrer 17, 108, 157, 163
transition 5, 160
transition handshake process 153
TRF 108, 163

U

UN 106
unary operator 106

V

VAR 64, 108
variable 17, 64, 108, 164
VLSI operator 159
void transition 160

W

WAG 15, 19
wagging buffer 15
weak initializability 166
weave 75
wire 161

Printed in the United States
By Bookmasters